ORNAMENTAL WALL PAINTING

CUNEIFORM MONOGRAPHS 28

Managing Editor Geerd Haayer

Edited by

T. Abusch, M.J. Geller, M.P. Maidman
S.M. Maul and F.A.M. Wiggermann

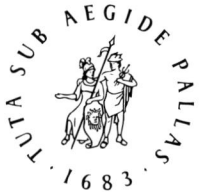

BRILL · STYX

LEIDEN · BOSTON

2005

CUNEIFORM MONOGRAPHS 28

ORNAMENTAL WALL PAINTING
IN THE ART OF THE ASSYRIAN EMPIRE

by

Pauline Albenda

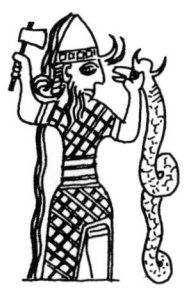

BRILL · STYX
LEIDEN · BOSTON
2005

This book is printed on acid-free paper.

Library of Congress Cataloging-in-Publication Data

Albenda, Pauline
    Ornamental wall painting in the art of the Assyrian Empire / by Pauline Albenda.
        p.   cm. — (Cuneiform Monographs; ISSN 0929–0052 ; 28)
    Includes bibliographical references and indexes.
    ISBN 90–04–14154–5
    1. Mural painting and decoration, Assyro-Babylonian–Themes, motives. 2. Mural
painting and decoration, Ancient–Iraq–Themes, motives. I. Title. II. Series.

    ND2819.17A23 2004
    751.7'3'0935–dc22

                                                                                2004057556

ISSN 0929–0052
ISBN 90 04 14154 5

PRINTED IN THE NETHERLANDS

Dedicated to

David, Anne, Rose, and Stella

TABLE OF CONTENTS

List of Illustrations ix
Acknowledgements xiii

Chapter I. Introduction 1

Chapter II. Discoveries of the Wall Paintings 9
    Ninth Century B.C. 10
        Nimrud 10
        Fort Shalmaneser 14
    Ninth to Eighth Centuries B.C. 14
        Nimrud, upper chambers 14
        Nimrud, outer town 20
        Al Rimah 21
    Late Eighth Century B.C. 21
        Khorsabad 21
    Late Eighth and Seventh Centuries B.C. 25
        Arslan Tash 25
        Til Barsip, building E 27
        Tell Sheikh Hamad 27
        Fort Shalmaneser 29
    Overview of the Discoveries 30

Chapter III. Til Barsip 33
    Room 26 36
    Rooms 25 and 27 38
    Room 46 40
    Room 1 43
    Room 21 44
    Room 24 47
    Room 47 50
    Room 22 51
    Discussion 52
    Til Barsip Textile Patterns 55
    Discussion of Textile Designs 66
    Dating the Til Barsip Wall Paintings 69

Table of Contents

Chapter IV. The Ornamental Painted Designs 75
    The Ornamental Compositions 76
    Symmetries of the Ornaments 82
    The Ornamental Motifs 84
        Single Motif 84
        Guilloche 101
        Arcaded Garlands 106
    Symmetrical Grouping 118
        Animal Group 118
        Figural Group 127

Chapter V. Concluding Commentary 129

Bibliography 137

Indices 145
    Index of Akkadian words 145
    Index of Proper names 145
    Subject Index 148

LIST OF ILLUSTRATIONS

Figures

Figure 1a   Reconstructed wall painting from Northwest Palace, Nimrud. Redrawn. Layard 1849b, pl. 84.

Figure 1b   Painted guilloche design from Northwest Palace, Nimrud. Redrawn. Tomabechi 1986, fig. 6.

Figure 2   Top left: painted fragment of hexagon and alternating rows of circles and rosettes. Redrawn and expanded. Loud 1936, pl. I: 5.

Top right: painted fragments of hexagon designs from room 12, Khorsabad. Redrawn and expanded. Loud 1936, pl. I: 2.

Bottom left: painted fragment of circle design from room 12, Khorsabad. Redrawn and expanded. Loud 1936, pl. I: 3.

Bottom right: painted fragment of grid design from the throne room, Khorsabad. Redrawn and expanded. Loud 1936, pl. III: 8.

Figure 3   Painted fragments of pattern motifs from the throne room, Khorsabad. Loud 1936, pl. III: 7, 10.

Figure 4a   Wall painting from royal apartments, Arslan Tash. Redrawn. Thureau-Dangin *et al.* 1931, pl. XLVIII:1.

Figure 4b   Wall painting from small apartment, Arslan Tash. Thureau-Dangin *et al* 1931, pl. XLVIII: 2.

Figure 4c   Painted fragments and reconstruction of wall painting from building E, Til Barsip. Abbate 1997, fig. 3.

Figure 5a   Wall painting with design of circles and stripes, from building G at Dur-Katlimmu. Nunn 1988, fig. 101.

Figure 5b   Wall painting with garden scene, from room B, building G. at Dur-Katlimmu. Kühne 1989, Abb. 138.

Figure 5c   Wall painting with ostriches and band of concentric circles, Dur-Katlimmu. Kühne 1993, fig. 6.

Figure 6   Wall Painting from throne room S5, Fort Shalmaneser. Mallowan 1966, pl. 308.

Figure 7   Plan of royal residence at Til Barsip. Redrawn. Thureau-Dangin and Dunand 1936, plan B.

Plates

Plate 1   Layard, drawing of ornamental wall painting from the Northwest Palace. *Original Drawings*. III, 86c. British Museum.

Plate 2   Fragments of painted bricks from the Northwest Palace. Layard 1849b, pl. 84. British Museum.

Plate 3   Layard, drawings of (left) upper chamber A, (right) upper chamber B. *Original Drawings* III, 80. British Museum.

Plate 4   Layard, drawing of upper chamber A. *Original Drawings* III, 79. British Museum.

Plate 5   Layard, drawings of (left) upper chamber C, (right) upper chamber B. *Original Drawings* III, 85. British Museum.

Plate 6   Layard, drawing of painted ornament (unfinished). *Original Drawings* III, 82. British Museum.

Plate 7   Boutcher, drawings of painted bricks and wall designs. *Original Drawings* I, 30. British Museum.

Plate 8   Boutcher, detail of painted design, no. 2. *Original Drawings* I, 30. British Museum.

Plate 9   Cavro, ornamental wall painting with goats. Room 26 in the Assyrian palace at Til Barsip. Thureau-Dangin and Dunand 1936, pl. XLVI.

Plate 10   Painted goat. Fragment of wall painting from room 26 at Til Barsip. Musée du Louvre AO 23010. Photo RMN, Chuzeville.

Plate 11   Cavro, ornamental wall painting with winged female genies. Room 25 in the Assyrian palace at Til Barsip. Musée du Louvre AO 25067 K.

Plate 12   Winged genie. Fragment of wall painting from room 27 at Til Barsip. Musée du Louvre AO 23009. Photo RMN, Chuzeville.

Plate 13   Cavro, ornamental wall painting with winged female genies. Room 46 in the Assyrian palace at Til Barsip. Musée du Louvre AO 25067 M.

Plate 14   Cavro, wall painting of winged bird-headed genie and bull.
             Passage 24/28 in the Assyrian palace at Til Barsip. Museé du
             Louvre AO 25067 S.

Plate 15   Cavro, wall painting of winged bull and male genie. Passage
             24/25 in the Assyrian palace at Til Barsip. Musée du Louvre
             AO 25067 B.

Plate 16   Cavro, wall painting of winged genie. Passage 24/26 in the
             Assyrian palace at Til Barsip. Thureau-Dangin and Dunand
             1936, pl. XLVII, 2. Musée du Louvre AO 25067 F.

Plate 17   Cavro, ornamental wall painting with bulls. Room 21 in the
             Assyrian palace at Til Barsip. Musée du Louvre AO 25068 A.

Plate 18   Cavro, ornamental wall paintings from the Assyrian palace
             at Til Barsip: (left) room 22, Musée du Louvre AO 25068 F;
             (right) room 24, Musée du Louvre AO 25068 E.

Plate 19   Cavro, wall painting from room 47 in the Assyrian palace at Til
             Barsip. Musée du Louvre AO 25068 D.

Plate 20   Cavro, wall painting of an Assyrian king. Room 24, panel d, in
             the Assyrian palace at Til Barsip. Musée du Louvre AO 25067 C.

Plate 21   Assyrian attendants standing behind the throne covered with
             patterned cloth. Fragment of wall painting from room 47 at Til
             Barsip. Musée du Louvre AO 23011. Photo RMN, Chuzeville.

Plate 22   Bell, threshold slab from Kuyunjik (Nineveh), 'between winged
             bulls and chamber C.' *Original Drawings* IV, 10. British
             Museum.

Plate 23   Cavro, detail: wall painting of an enthroned Assyrian king.
             Room 47, panels a, b, c, in the Assyrian palace at Til Barsip.
             Musée du Louvre AO 25067 T.

Plate 24   Cavro, detail: wall painting of an Assyrian court official. Room
             24, panel i, in the Assyrian palace at Til Barsip. Musée du
             Louvre AO 25067 D.

Plate 25   Cavro, detail: wall painting of an enthroned Assyrian king. Wall
             painting from room 24, panels a, b, c, in the Assyrian palace at
             Til Barsip. Musée du Louvre AO 25067 N.

Plate 26   Carved threshold slab discovered between room 116 and the
             central court of residence L at Khorsabad. Inscription identifies
             Sinahusur as Sargon's brother and grand vizier. Oriental
             Institute, University of Chicago A 17597.

Plate 27   Reconstructed wall painting from the north side of palace
            terrace at Kar-Tukulti-Ninurta. 13th century B.C. Andrae 1925,
            pl. 1.

Plate 28   Reconstructed wall painting from the south side of palace
            terrace at Kar-Tukulti-Ninurta. 13th century B.C. Andrae 1925,
            pl. 2.

Plate 29   Reconstructed wall painting from the south side of palace
            terrace at Kar-Tukulti-Ninurta. 13th century B.C. Andrae 1925,
            pl. 3.

Plate 30   Small fragments of wall paintings from the palace terrace at
            Kar-Tukulti-Ninurta. 13th century B.C. Andrae 1925, pl. 4.

Plate 31   Fragments of painted plaster from citadel buildings at Khorsa-
            bad. Loud and Altman 1938, pl. 91. Oriental Institute, Univer-
            sity of Chicago.

Plate 32   Restored wall paintings in residence K at Khorsabad. Loud and
            Altman 1938, pl. 89. Oriental Institute, University of Chicago.

Plate 33   Detail: restored wall painting in residence K at Khorsabad.
            Loud and Altman 1938, pl. 89. Oriental Institute, University of
            Chicago.

Plate 34   Glazed brick fragment with guilloche design. Nimrud, 9th
            century B.C. Metropolitan Museum of Art, Roger Fund 1958,
            58.31.58.

Plate 35   Glazed brick with painted narrative scene and guilloche border.
            9th century B.C. British Museum WA 90859.

Plate 36   Glazed brick fragment with guilloche design. Nimrud, 9th
            century B.C. Metropolitan Museum of Art, Roger Fund 1958,
            58.31.59.

Plate 37   Layard, threshold slab from 'centre palace' (central palace) at
            Nimrud. Period of Tiglath-pileser III. *Original Drawings* VI,
            37. British Museum.

ACKNOWLEDGEMENTS

The original intent of my study of the ornamental wall paintings of Assyrian art was to survey their decorative aspects, by only singling out the motifs, patterns, and overall organizations found in those works. Informal discussion with Ann Guinan encouraged me to expand upon this research. Thus I have ventured into comparative analyses with other art forms originating from different sources and historical periods, and tried to examine through text and art the probable significance behind the selection of specific motifs and designs. Central to this study have been the wall paintings discovered at Til Barsip. I am grateful to Annie Caubet, Conservateur Général du Département des Antiquités Orientales, Musée du Louvre, who generously made available to me the color slides of Cavro's renderings of the Til Barsip paintings. During the time I spent at the museum in 1997, I also benefited from the kind cooperation of Elisabeth Fontan, Conservateur en Chef du Département des Antiquités Orientales, with whom I discussed and examined several of the original works by Cavro, once they were rolled out on the floor of the storeroom. I must add a special mention of gratitude to Lydie Shufro, who volunteered to read a late draft of my manuscript and suggested many improvements on the phrasing of the text.

Additional research and access to volumes not readily obtainable required the use of the facilities of the Humanities and Social Sciences Library at the New York Public Library, with the assistance of the staff of the Asian and Middle Eastern Division, and of the Wilbour Library at the Brooklyn Museum of Art, New York. Permissions to reproduce the photographs and line drawings of the Assyrian wall paintings and other art works illustrated in this volume were given by the following institutions and individuals: Musée du Louvre, Paris; Courtesy of the Trustees of the British Museum, British Museum, London; The Oriental Institute of the University of Chicago, Chicago; Metropolitan Museum of Art, New York; Guy Bunnens (excavations at Til Barsip); Hartmut Kühne (excavations at Tell Sheikh Hamad).

CHAPTER ONE.   INTRODUCTION

The present study of ornamental wall painting produced during the Assyrian empire, from the ninth to seventh centuries B.C., aims at providing insights into Assyrian taste in the decorative arts. It identifies the specific motifs and patterns and describes their arrangements on wall surfaces, as indicated by the archaeological record. The extent to which certain motifs persisted through a period of time may reflect traditional preferences, either for their visual appeal or possibly for their symbolic significance. New motifs, sometimes combined with the traditional ones to produce groupings that were repeated on the wall surface, furnish the degree of innovative tendencies that prevailed in the designing of the decorative wall paintings. An important aspect of the wall paintings is in the use of color, and in most instances when in addition to black and white two or more color pigments are applied to the designs. An overview of the application of the different hues within a given design shows that the procedure was not random, rather that it followed one or more formulas so as to maintain clarity in the presentation. Identification of the particular formulas used for the respective ornamental paintings may provide further insight into the processes undertaken by the Assyrian artisans in planning and finalizing the design.

Glazed wares

Painted ornamental designs also occur on glazed ceramic wares such as plaques, knobbed cones or nails (*sikkatu*), knobbed wall plates, bricks, and vessels. Although the glazed decorative material is not the focus of the present study, it is of interest to point out that the ceramic objects sometimes display designs that are similar to those found in wall paintings, albeit abbreviated and modified to suit the particular shape of the clay surface. On the glazed wares the use of select decorative motifs, generally in ordered and symmetrical arrangements, makes it likely that the designers of wall paintings and of glazed ceramic objects were taught in the same workshops, or that those artisans relied on pattern books available to all of them.[1]

Scholarly studies have been undertaken with regard to the ceramic assemblages; several of these published works are singled out. An early volume, authored by Walter Andrae, remains an important resource among the studies on glazed wares.[2] In this volume Andrae assembles and discusses the deco-

---

[1] On this subject, see: Moorey 1985, pp. 184–185.
[2] Andrae 1925, pp. 63–76.

1

rated ceramic wares from Ashur, the royal city of Assyria, excavated by the German archaeological team during the years preceding World War I. Among the wares included are knobbed wall plates and cones. Knobbed plates and fragmentary cones were also discovered at Nimrud, (ancient Kalhu), and cuneiform inscriptions on several examples date the assemblage to the reign of the Assyrian king Ashurnasirpal II (883–859). The ornamental designs belonging to this group of ceramic wares are the subject of an article by Pauline Albenda.[3]

Early European excavators sometimes described the designs on the glazed bricks as paintings; therefore it is not always clear in those instances whether the decorations are merely painted or glazed. Nonetheless decorated glazed bricks have been excavated in a number of ancient Near Eastern sites. At Fort Shalmaneser (ancient Ekal Masharti) the British excavation team unearthed a mass of fallen bricks belonging to a polychrome glazed brick panel above the portal of a courtyard doorway.[4] Julian Reade undertook the reconstruction of the panel. He showed that originally the panel was a semi-elliptical gate-arch, about 4.07 meters in height.[5] The main central field consists of two groups of representations: the Assyrian king facing each other and two bulls flanking a tree, which are separated by an inscription identifying the king as Shalmaneser III (858–824). Surrounding the central field are five borders that contain repeats of small rosette, guilloche, rosette, palmette and bud, goat and palmette, from inside out. Another group of almost 80 complete or fragmentary polychrome glazed bricks was discovered in a room at Fort Shalmaneser.[6] These bricks display floral (palmette and rosette) and geometric motifs (stripe, chevron, four concentric circles in a row). The cuneiform inscription found on the front of six bricks gives the genealogy of Shalmaneser III. Fragments of polychrome decorated bricks have been discovered at Nineveh, and they probably date to the reign of Sennacherib (704–681) or later.[7] It is difficult to identify the designs on the bricks, but several may show details of garment patterns. During the mid-nineteenth century Paul Emile Botta and Victor Place several years later, excavated polychrome glazed bricks at Khorsabad (ancient Dur-Sharrukin). The assemblage of glazed bricks from that site is firmly dated to the reign of Sargon II (721–705). The polychrome bricks published by the French excavators and the extant ones presently housed in the Musée du Louvre are

---

[3] Albenda 1991, pp. 43–53. For the technical analysis of the ceramic material, see Freestone 1991, pp. 53–58.

[4] Mallowan 1966, pp. 454–456.

[5] Reade 1963, pp. 38–47.

[6] J. Curtis *et al* 1993, pp. 21–30.

[7] Russell 1999, p. 96. Over 100 fragments of glazed bricks were recovered, but the decorated surface was poorly preserved. Color photographs and watercolor versions of twenty-two fragments are reproduced; see pls. 1–5.

the subjects of an informative article written by Reade.[8] At the same site, the American archaeological team uncovered additional assemblages of glazed brick decorations forming 'tableaus', during the years 1929–1935.[9]

Wall painting

The early use of wall painting for the decoration of Assyrian buildings is demonstrated by several fragments of paintings on plaster from Kar-Tukulti-Ninurta, dated to the Middle Assyrian period (thirteenth century B.C.).[10] The residential city was founded by Tukulti-Ninurta I (1244–1208) and is situated on the east bank of the Tigris River, a short distance north of the capital city of Ashur.[11] The painted fragments were found alongside the palace terrace. Four colors were used – red, blue, white and black. The pictorial compositions of goats and winged griffin-headed human figures flanking trees, floral motifs, and garlands were reconstructed into a series of panels framed by ornamental bands. Anton Moortgat observed that the Middle Assyrian compositions resemble the earlier Mitannian wall paintings from the governor's palace at Nuzi near Kirkurk. He assigned the Nuzi wall paintings to the mid-fifteenth century B.C.[12]

The Iraqi excavations of Aqar Kuf (ancient Dur-Kurigalzu) near Baghdad revealed indications of walls and ceilings ornamented with paintings in the palace of the Kassite kings.[13] Evidence points to Kurigalzu I (c. 1375) as the founder of the palace, which remained occupied by Kassite rulers for several centuries.[14] Among the recognized motifs were geometric designs (parallel bands, guilloches, chevrons, rosettes, clusters of fruits) and representational scenes. The colors in these paintings were red, cobalt blue, dark blue, yellow, white, and black. The most extensively preserved remains of wall paintings came from a group of rooms labeled Unit H, dated somewhere between 1232 and 1159 B.C. Several rooms were decorated with conventional designs of red, yellow and blue rosettes outlined in black. Processional scenes of human figures, framed by red and blue horizontal bands, were painted on the opposite walls of four excavated doorways leading to an open court. The painted figures ranging from eight to ten per wall, measured about 62 cm in

---

[8] See: Albenda 1986, pls. 150–151; Pottier 1924, pp. 148–149; Reade 1995, pp. 227–251.
[9] Loud 1936, pp. 92–98, figs. 99, 101,105,106,115. For the decipherment of the five or seven designs (symbols) on the glazed brick panels, see Finkel and Reade 1996, pp. 248–250.
[10] Frankfort 1954, pp. 135–137, figs. 152–153.
[11] Grayson 1972, nos. 779–780, 785.
[12] Moortgat 1969, p. 109, fig. 77; Moortgat 1959, pp. 13–14, 46, Tf. 15.
[13] Tomabechi 1983, pp. 123–131, studied and published several of the extant fragments housed in the Iraq Museum, together with references to the excavation reports.
[14] Clayden 1996, pp. 112–117.

height, and were outlined in black on a yellowish ground. The clothes were white with red details. The spaces between the figures appear to have been painted blue.

In a text of Tiglath-pileser I (1114–1076), the Assyrian king mentions that he conquered Dur Kurigalzu, one of the great cult centers of Karduniash (Babylonia).[15] Presumably, at that time the Assyrian king would have seen or else would have been made aware of the impressive array of paintings that ornamented the walls of the Kassite palace. Tiglath-pileser I himself gives brief descriptions of ornamentation applied to several buildings erected during his reign. The palace at Kuyunjik (ancient Nineveh) which the king completed was decorated with 'brick glazed the color of obsidian, lapis-lazuli, *pappardilû*-stone and *parûtu*-alabaster,' (black, blue, banded, white).[16] In the same text the Assyrian king mentions the building of a pleasure palace on a terrace within a planted garden, portrayed therein 'the victory and *might* which the gods Ashur and Ninurta ... had granted me.' This description suggests a painted scene of some kind. Another text states that the rebuilt shrine of the gods An and Adad had its interior decorated like the 'interior of heaven,' and its walls were decorated 'as splendidly as the brilliance of rising stars.'[17] From this description we may surmise that, against a blue ground color, a painted pattern of six or eight pointed stars and/or other geometric shape enriched the walls and ceilings. As late as the seventh century B.C. brief descriptions of wall decoration are cited in royal Assyrian texts. Esarhaddon (680–669) decorated his palace at Nineveh with a glazed or painted frieze – like a garland – with pigments of obsidian and lapis-lazuli (black, blue).[18]

Wall painting designed for the embellishment of royal buildings was established by the start of the Neo-Assyrian Empire in the ninth century B.C. The Northwest Palace of Ashurnasirpal II at Nimrud had painted decorations on the ceilings and on the walls above the carved stone blocks that lined the lower walls of the royal residence.[19] Ornamental wall paintings were also discovered in other buildings on the Nimrud mound, but from the archaeological evidence those structures are datable to different periods of the Assyrian empire. Evidence for Assyrian wall painting also derives from other sites in Assyria proper and include Fort Shalmaneser and the outer town, both located near Nimrud, and Khorsabad. In northern Syria, wall

---

[15] Grayson 1976, no. 100.
[16] Ibid, nos. 124–126. *Pappardilu*-stone may be identified with a banded agate or an onyx, or an artificially stained chalcedony that looks like one of the stones. On this subject, see: Galter 1987, pp. 15–17; Sollberger 1987, pp. 379–381.
[17] Grayson 1976, no. 55.
[18] Turner 1970, pp. 80–84.
[19] For the list of rooms in which paintings have been located, and line drawings of fragments of wall paintings housed in the Iraq Museum, see: Tomabachi 1986, pp. 43–54.

paintings decorated the walls of Assyrian royal and elite private residences which have been excavated at Arslan Tash (ancient Hadatu), Tell ʿAhmar (ancient Til Barsip/ Kar-Shalmaneser), and Tell Sheikh Hamad (ancient Dur-Katlimmu).[20] The excavated finds of Assyrian wall paintings at the various sites range from small plaster fragments to large *in situ* murals which, unfortunately, had extensive surface damage when first exposed. Only a few painted examples could be saved; however, the excavated material was described in the published reports and in a number of instances recorded in line drawings and in photographs taken at the time of discovery.

Early discoveries

Botta was the first European to mention the finding of a block of color, and in a letter dated May 2, 1843, describing his initial exploration at Khorsabad, he writes (English version), 'I must yet remark that, as well as copper plugs, numerous pieces of thick stucco are found in the earth, of a beautiful azure blue color, similar to that which adorns the bas-reliefs.'[21] In his letter dated October 31, 1843, Botta writes:

> 'Very probably, the gypsum slabs ... were surmounted by some layers of bricks. In fact, an immense number of them are found in the earth filling up the chambers and passages. These bricks have not the hardness of those used in making the platform, and are without inscriptions; but the chief difference consists of their being enameled, or rather, I imagine, painted. Generally, one side is white or yellow, or presents portions of ornamental patterns, which, when all was in place, must have been completed by other bricks adjoining. Some of them even offer the remains of fine cuneiform characters painted in yellow upon a dark green ground, the brick itself displaying a white border.'[22]

Eugene Flandin, the artist assigned to record the discoveries at Khorsabad, illustrated in color some of the bricks described by Botta; however, no examples of wall painting are discernible among the collection of original drawings. Henry Austen Layard, who first excavated the site of Nimrud between the years 1845–1847, mentions that in one area of the Northwest Palace:

> 'I discovered that I was now digging into chambers formed by walls of sun-dried bricks, over which a thin coating of plaster had been laid. They had been painted

---

[20] A survey of Assyrian wall paintings listed by sites, appears in Nunn 1988, pp. 102–134.
[21] Botta 1850, p. 26. Fragments of blue material and pieces of bricks in blue, recovered from Khorsabad by the French excavators, are in the Louvre; see Pottier 1924, p. 151.
[22] Botta 1850, p. 69.

with figures and ornaments; but the colors had faded so completely, that scarcely any of the subjects or designs could be traced … I was able to draw a few of the ornaments, in which the colors chiefly distinguishable were red, blue, black and white. The subjects of the paintings appeared to be generally processions, in which the king is represented followed by his eunuchs and attendant warriors. The figures were merely in outline, in black upon a blue ground, and I was unable to distinguish any other color.'[23]

In their published account of the 1929–1930 discovery of the small palace of Ashurnasirpal II at Nineveh, R. Campbell Thompson and R.W. Hutchinson observed that the building was 'decorated with beautiful paintings, rosettes, pattern figures, and scenes of the king himself, often in relief.'[24] The illustrated line drawings of the 'painted bricks' from the palace may include examples of painted ornaments, such as the guilloche and hexagon.

A British expedition undertaken in the 1830s was the first to record two large lion sculptures at Arslan Tash in northern Syria, after which the site was named.[25] A century later, during two brief campaigns in 1928, F. Thureau-Dangin and his team discovered decorative wall paintings still adhering to the walls in the royal apartments of the palace.[26] The painted friezes were composed of the same design, which consisted of geometric motifs. To date, the most extensive assemblage of painted decoration is that which covered the walls of an Assyrian royal residence discovered at the site of Tell 'Ahmar near the Euphrates River. The site is identified with ancient Til Barsip, which was conquered by the Assyrian king Shalmaneser III and re-named Kar-Shalmaneser. During three campaigns of excavations between the years 1929 and 1931, F. Thureau-Dangin and Maurice Dunand exposed the royal residence. The excavators noted that they did not have the means of either lifting the paintings from the walls or conserving them in place, and the paintings were too faint to be recorded in photographs. Instead, Lucien Cavro made color renderings of the polychrome wall paintings; later published in black and white.[27] Cavro's original color renderings of the wall paintings are presently housed in the Musée du Louvre.

The Til Barsip wall paintings consist of ornamental designs and representational scenes, which originally covered the walls of the corridors and rooms in the residential area of the palace. The ornamental designs appeared on the walls above the mural scenes and were composed of decorative bands made of geometric, floral and animal motifs. Problematic is the dating of the painted narrative murals, as well as the ornamented decorations. Various

---

[23] Layard 1849, vol. 2, p. 17.
[24] Thompson and Hutchinson 1931, pp. 82–83, pl. XXIX.
[25] Chesney 1850, p. 114. The published sketch of one lion was made in 1836.
[26] Thureau-Dangin *et al* 1931, p. 28.
[27] Thureau-Dangin and Dunand 1936, pp. 6–7, 42–43.

dates have been attributed to the Til Barsip paintings which, interestingly, do not belong to one period of production.[28] In the present study the Til Barsip wall paintings are examined primarily for their decorative appeal, as well as with an intent to determine their chronological sequence. A general assumption is that the ornamental designs and the narrative murals from a particular chamber are contemporary in date. However, this assumption needs to be verified, since it is evident that the Til Barsip wall paintings were produced at different times. One means of establishing firm dates for the wall paintings is through the study of the textile patterns found on the costumes worn by the various persons represented in the narrative scenes. The textile patterns from Til Barsip are therefore studied in a separate section.

Visual data

Central to the study of ornamentation in Assyrian wall painting is the visual documentation. The primary sources that are discussed must of necessity derive from those excavation reports which provide one or more of the following: written descriptions, polychrome or black and white drawings, photographs of *in situ* views, and the relatively few fragments of original wall paintings. The selection of the illustrated material in the present work includes some of the original drawings made at the time of the discovery of the wall paintings and line drawings showing details of specific motifs that occur within the respective wall paintings. The length of time in the Neo-Assyrian period during which specific motifs comprising the respective decorative units continued to be used, may determine their importance either as a purely decorative feature or as having a religious or symbolic meaning. In this regard comparison with other art forms, such as ceramic wares, carved ivories, stone reliefs, and glyptic art, should furnish additional information.

---

[28] The various opinions on the dating of the Til Barsip wall paintings are assembled in Nunn 1988, pp. 118–123.

CHAPTER TWO. DISCOVERIES
OF THE ORNAMENTAL WALL PAINTINGS

In the course of their explorations and excavations of Assyrian sites in the Near East, European and American archaeologists recovered examples of wall paintings that include both figurative and ornamental decorations. The wall paintings were discovered either adhering to the walls or on plaster and brick fragments fallen to the ground when first exposed. The types of architectural structures that were originally decorated with paintings on the walls and, on occasion, on the ceilings have been identified. They include royal palaces, private residential buildings belonging to Assyrian officials of high rank and, less frequently, temples. Several of those structures can be firmly dated to the reign of a particular Assyrian king, based upon the textual information found in conjunction with the respective building, and it is therefore likely that the painted wall decorations are contemporary to these buildings. Other structures continued in use over a period of time, as demonstrated by the archaeological evidence and, therefore it is not always ascertainable under whose king's reign the wall paintings associated with the particular building were produced.

The ninth century B.C. Northwest Palace of Ashurnasirpal II provides the earliest examples of Assyrian wall paintings dated to the Neo-Assyrian period. The paintings discovered in the royal residence at Nimrud have been dated to that king's reign. The royal residence excavated in the outer town, a short distance from Nimrud, can be dated to the reign of Adad-nirari III (810–783), based upon the finding of floor slabs with the king's name inscribed upon them. The wall paintings discovered *in situ* and described in the excavation reports also belong to that period. Other wall paintings datable to the reign of a specific Assyrian king are those that were found in the palace built by Sargon II (721–705) in his new royal city at Khorsabad. This royal residence was abandoned shortly after the death of the Assyrian king. At this same site, residence K contained elaborate wall paintings, of which the excavators made a photographic record and a reconstruction in drawings.

The Assyrian royal palaces mentioned above provide the framework for assigning the wall paintings from the various different sites to a reasonable time period within a given century, during the Neo-Assyrian period. The ability to place the architectural structures containing the wall paintings in a general chronological order is important for the study of ornamentation. The examination of those Assyrian wall paintings should demonstrate not only how certain standard motifs were modified over time, but also when the introduction of other motifs that formed new decorative groupings may have first occurred. Such occurrences would indicate the changing trends

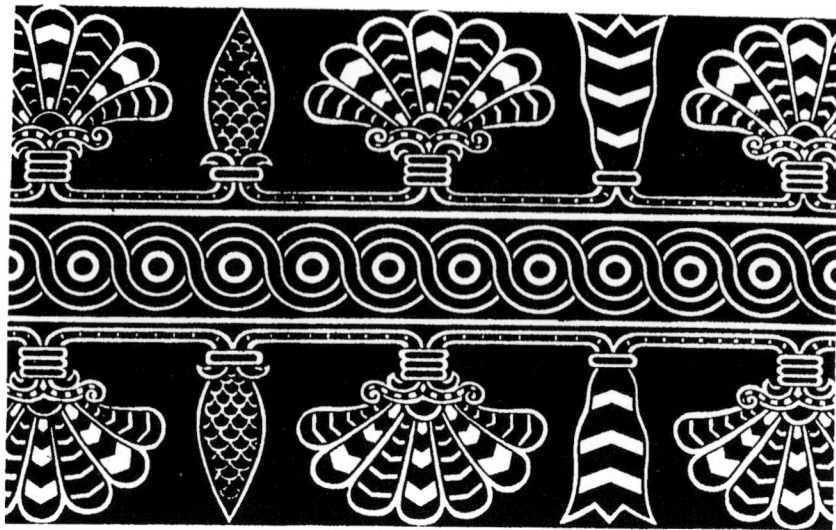

Fig. 1a. Reconstructed wall painting from Northwest
Palace, Nimrud. Redrawn. Layard 1849b, pl. 84.

pertaining to one major medium of the decorative arts – large-scale painted
ornamentation – assuredly originating from the royal sphere of the Assyrian
Empire.

Ninth Century B.C.

Nimrud

Layard excavated the site of Nimrud in the mid-nineteenth century. He reported on the discovery of decorative wall paintings in two areas: the Northwest Palace of Ashurnasirpal II, the text of which was quoted previously, and
the so-called upper chambers (see below). He remarked that in the Northwest
Palace the walls of chambers were made of sun-dried bricks, coated over with
plaster on which were added figures and ornaments. Later excavation teams
also discovered fragments of wall paintings in the Northwest Palace. Yoko
Tomabechi has published the list of rooms where the paintings have been
located.[1] She also discusses and illustrates the extant fragments originating
from rooms B and F.

---

[1] Tomabechi 1986, pp. 44–54.

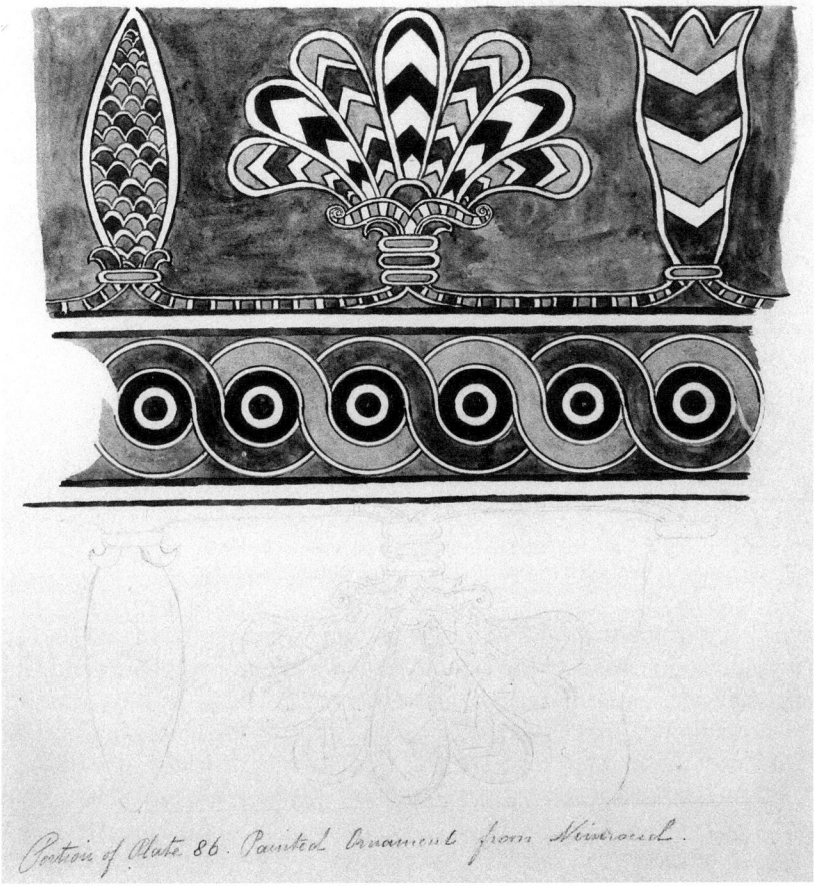

Pl. 1. Layard, drawing of ornamental wall painting from the
Northwest Palace. *Original Drawings*. III, 86c. British Museum.

Layard was able to draw a few of the ornaments, including those represented on glazed bricks, in which the distinguishable colors were red, blue,
white and black. The drawing of one ornamental decoration, which was later
published in color as a complete design, illustrates part of a frieze divided
into three wide bands, all showing a blue background (pl. 1, fig. 1a).[2] The
two outer bands have a mirror-image design consisting of a cone, a palmette
and a tulip, the three motifs connected at the base by stems to form a garland.
The cone is filled with a scale pattern, while a repeat of chevrons is found

---

[2] Layard 1849b, pl. 84.

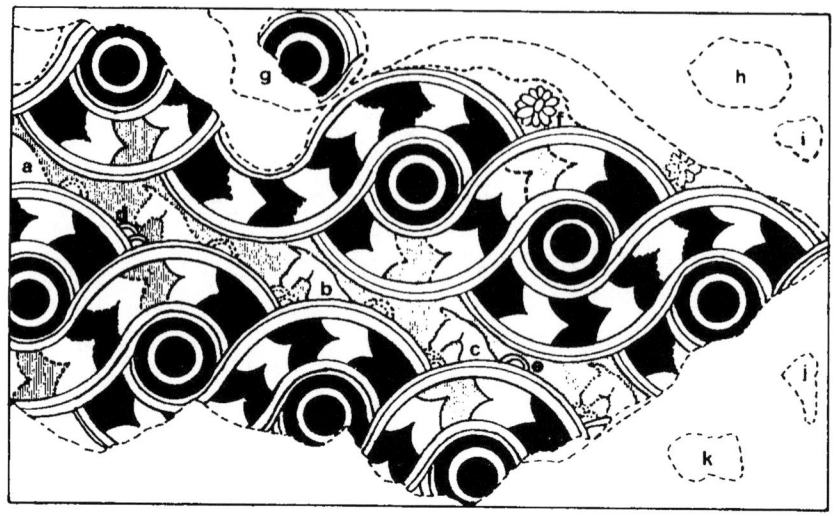

Fig. 1b. Painted guilloche design from Northwest
Palace, Nimrud. Redrawn. Tomabechi 1986, fig. 6.

inside each of the two flowers. In the band between the two floral garlands
is a guilloche or interlocking ribbons of red and blue with black and white
target centers.

The guilloche motif recurred elsewhere in the Northwest Palace. The
British excavation team reported that frescoes were found in the center of
room F in the palace, some came from the wall and some probably from the
ceiling or second floor. The motif was a geometric design of interlocking
circles in blue, red and black; no details of the decoration were mentioned.
The mounted remains of the wall paintings were exhibited in the Mosul
Museum. The Iraqi expedition team excavated other painted fragments, and
these paintings were mounted and exhibited on the southern end of room F
of the Northwest Palace.[3]

Tomabechi studied the two remains of ornamental wall paintings discovered by the British and Iraqi teams. The designs on the fragments are
described as essentially identical and consist of rows of about 55 cm thick
guilloche set apart about 3.6 cm against a bright cobalt blue background. The
guilloche consists of black and white target centers with interlocking ribbons,
each of which has chevron stripes. The color pattern of the chevron stripes alternates between black/white and blue/white/red combinations. The border of
the guilloche is framed with yellow-ochre and white lines. Tomabechi noted

---

[3] Tomabechi 1986, 49–54. The author also gives an alternate restoration of the existing
fragments showing a chariot scene.

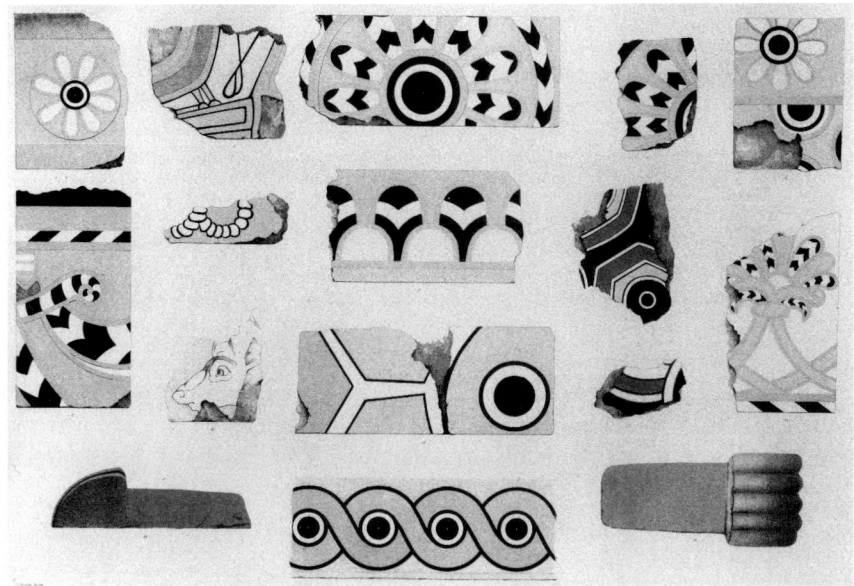

Pl. 2. Fragments of painted bricks from the Northwest
Palace. Layard 1849b, pl. 84. British Museum.

that one exhibited piece has unusual additional elements. Heads of horses
and mountain motifs are discernible above every juncture of the rising bands
of guilloche, and flower motifs in the spaces between (fig. 1b).[4]

In the course of re-exposing the throne room of the Northwest Palace
(room B), the British excavation team discovered fallen frescoes done directly
on to a prepared mud plaster. One painting showed part of a blue, red and
white geometric design which depicted a coffered ceiling to which were
attached traces of roof beams.[5] The polygonal design – probably a pattern of
hexagons – was not illustrated. However, a pattern of hexagons was included
among Layard's published drawings of glazed bricks from the Northwest
Palace. It is in white, black and red, and the last color indicates that the
fragment is a painted plaster (pl. 2).[6] In the center of room B the Iraqi
team found numerous pieces of painted plaster with rosette motifs, and the

---

[4] Ibid. The guilloche pattern is mounted obliquely, thus the suggestion is made that the painting
with the horse-heads originated from the second floor.

[5] Mallowan 1966, pp. 105–106.

[6] The drawing has been published previously in Reade 1995, fig. 4, top left. It may be noted
that in the photograph are included three painted sketches on bricks presently housed in the
British Museum, two of which show the head of a goat and the third a head of an Assyrian.
The bricks may be among those that Layard discovered, showing designs in black of men and
animals on the back sides and sides not colored; Layard 1849a (vol. 2), p. 18.

upper part of the beardless figure of an Assyrian official. Horizontal bands of rosettes in blue, red, white, and black were found on a wall in the southern room of a building complex to the west of throne room B. The frescoes with rosettes were not illustrated.[7]

Fort Shalmaneser

Evidence for painted hexagons produced during the reign of Shalmaneser III comes from the traces of painted murals discovered underneath the throne base in room T-1 at Fort Shalmaneser.[8] The published photograph shows one complete and two partially preserved hexagons. To judge from the photograph the geometric motif, outlined in black, is composed of three concentric red and blue hexagons separated by narrow white stripes outlined in black, and with a target center consisting of two concentric black circles and dot. Between each hexagon measured space may have formed part of the patterned frieze.

Late Ninth/Eighth Centuries B.C.

Nimrud, upper chambers

In the so-called upper chambers at Nimrud, situated on a high elevation immediately south of the Northwest Palace, Layard exposed a suite of three connecting rooms aligned side by side, which he labeled B, A, C, and part of a fourth that led into room A.[9] Threshold slabs in two entrances were inscribed with texts of Adad-nirari III and provide evidence that the wall paintings uncovered in the three connecting rooms were probably completed during the same period. Layard was able to make careful sketches of the paintings, which showed them to be ornamental decorations. His description of the wall paintings is precise:

> 'The painted ornaments were elaborate and graceful in design. The Assyrian bull was frequently portrayed, sometimes with wings, sometimes without. Above the animals were painted battlements, similar to those of castles, as represented in the sculptures. Below them, forming a kind of cornice, were squares and circles tastefully arranged; and more elaborate combinations were not wanting.'[10]

---

[7] Tomabechi 1986, p. 54. Reade 1995, pp. 227–228, notes that rosettes also decorated glazed bricks, which might be regarded as simple architectural decoration.
[8] Oates 1963, p. 28. The faint outline of a cushion frieze was also noted. Illustrated in Reade 1979, pp. 45, 47, Tf. 11 b.
[9] Layard 1849a (vol. 2), pp. 18–20.
[10] Ibid, p. 20.

Layard observed further that these rooms had been painted twice. The outer coating, when carefully detached, revealed the undercoat on which painted designs differing from those over them were exposed. Unfortunately, Layard did not describe this second group of paintings. The four original drawings have been published (pls. 3–6), in detail they differ from the nineteenth century published versions.[11]

In one sketch Layard added detailed measurements of the individual ornamental motifs. This information indicates that the total height of the wall decoration was about 1.20 m. Moreover, the color rendering in three of Layard's drawings (pls. 3–5) shows that the wall paintings were blue on a white background, with occasional accents of red. Layard observed that the ground of the wall paintings revealed a pale yellow color, but he thought that the original white had changed to this color.

Layard's three sketches make it clear that the decorative wall designs in Adad-nirari III's palace derive from the same master pattern; however, as Layard noted, specific motifs varied from chamber to chamber. The individual wall paintings are composed of three wide horizontal registers with narrow bands and stripes between them. Each register contains one or more motifs repeated at regular intervals. The top register is ornamented with a three-stepped battlement parapet. Centered within the middle register is a circle enclosing a rosette – a flower showing twelve chevron-decorated petals arranged around a central disk. This motif is repeated at a widely spaced interval (see pls. 3–5). A winged bull is drawn in one sketch (chamber A; pl. 3) and a wingless bull is drawn in another sketch (chamber C; pl. 5). Each bovine animal stands with the far foreleg bent under. There probably would have been a winged bull or a wingless bull between each rosette, assuming the use of an alternate repeat. In the bottom register patterned squares with incurving sides are drawn to the full height and alternate with rosette-centered circles (chamber A); in chambers B and C, however, other motifs decorate the bottom register. A row of small rosettes above an arcaded garland of disk-shaped flowers occurs in chamber B, and an arcaded garland of target-shaped flowers fills the bottom register of chamber C (pls. 3, 5).

One sketch (pl. 5) shows, centered between two chevron-decorated bands, a row of rosettes that are different from those in chamber A. This sketch is labeled 'recess ch. B.' However, the correct location may be chamber C since Layard observed that there were two recesses in that room. Thus the painted decoration was probably applied to the narrow wall(s) framing one or both recesses. As Layard remarked, no remains of plaster or color could be found on the sun-dried bricks forming the back of the recesses.

---

[11] Albenda 1994, pp. 2–8.

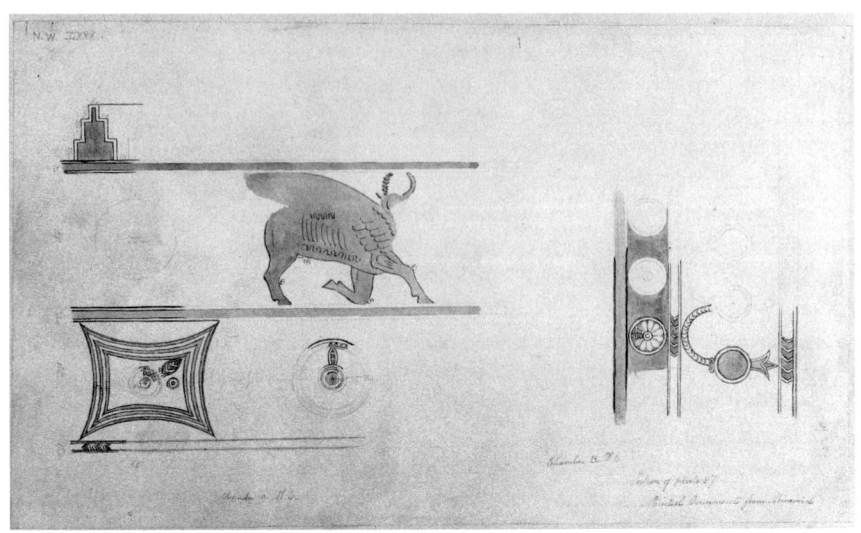

Pl. 3. Layard, drawings of (left) upper chamber A, (right)
upper chamber B. *Original Drawings* III, 80. British Museum.

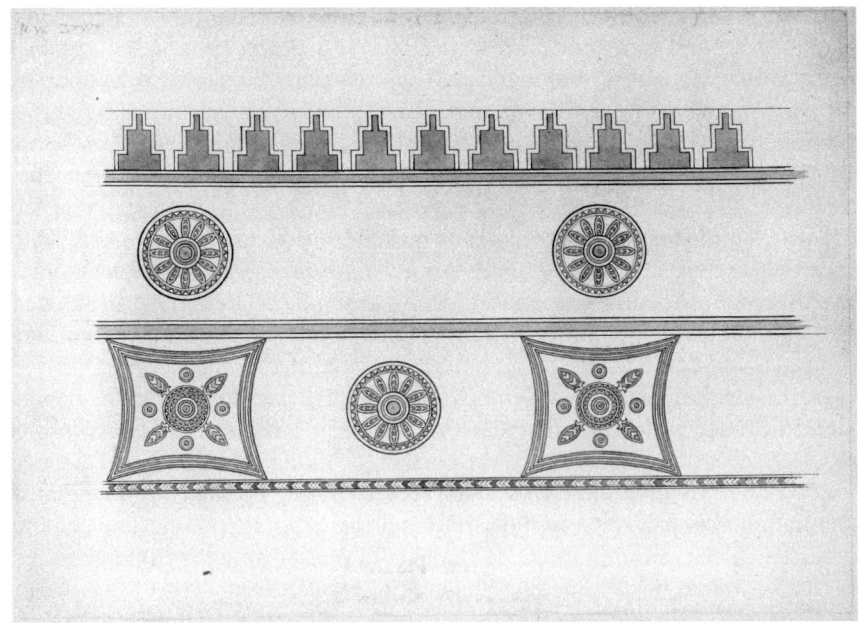

Pl. 4. Layard, drawing of upper chamber A. *Original Drawings* III, 79. British Museum.

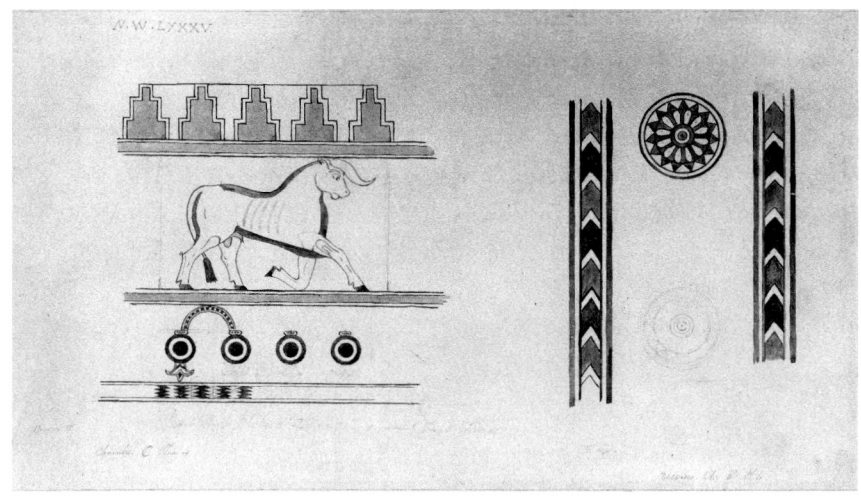

Pl. 5. Layard, drawings of (left) upper chamber C, (right)
upper chamber B. *Original Drawings* III, 85. British Museum.

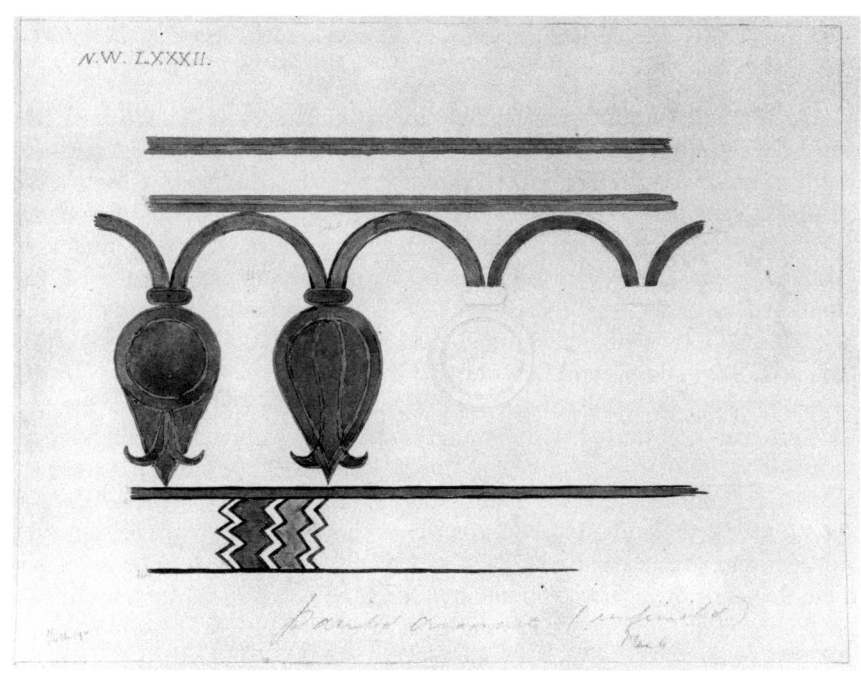

Pl. 6. Layard, drawing of painted ornament
(unfinished). *Original Drawings* III, 82. British Museum.

17

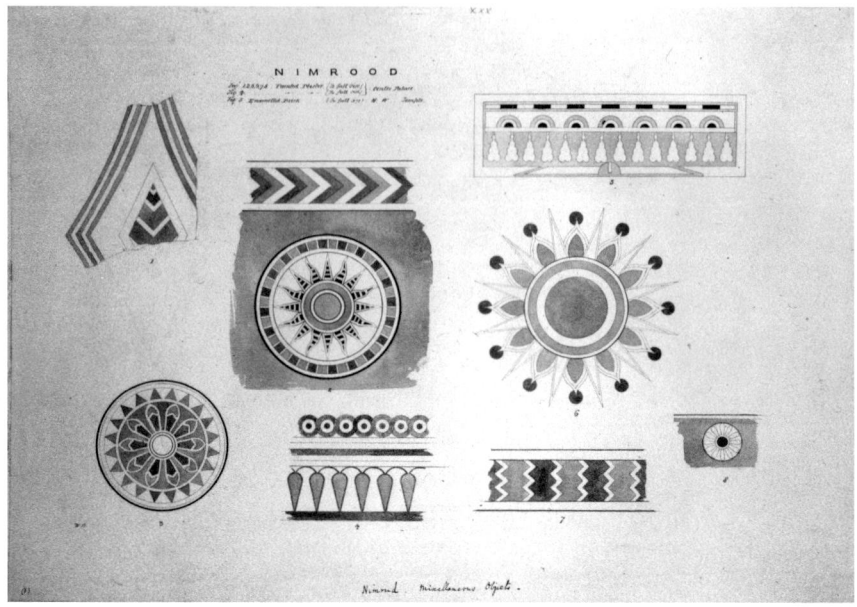

Pl. 7. Boutcher, drawings of painted bricks and wall
designs. *Original Drawings* III, 82. British Museum.

On the wall paintings from the suite of chambers in Adad-nirari III's
palace at Nimrud, the inclusion of battlements in the top register suggests
that the façade of a lofty structure was the intended image of the overall
design. The square and circle depicted in the bottom register of chamber A
are painted versions of terracotta knobbed plates and knob-pegs that were
originally fixed to the wall surfaces of Assyrian temples and palaces. The
combined circle and bull motifs may derive from contemporary architectural
decoration. Decorated glazed bricks may have inspired the depictions of the
painted floral garlands and figural motifs.

Underneath the wall paintings in chambers A, B, C, Layard exposed a
second coating of plaster with painted ornaments. Although he did not provide a description, Layard may have made a sketch of one small fragmentary
section, reproduced in Plate 6 and labeled '(unfinished) Plan 4.' If this assumption is correct, then the floral garland shown in the sketch predates the
wall paintings from chambers A, B, C, described previously. The two complete flowers shown in the sketch are closed buds with slightly out-curving
petal tips. Both flowers are red outlined in gray, with two-gray-black concentric circles in the center of one and a double ovoid-shaped line in the
other. Each flower rests on a plain base from which an arched stem extends
to connect them. The rendering of these flowers is to some extent naturalistic
and represents a departure from the more abstract floral types that appear in

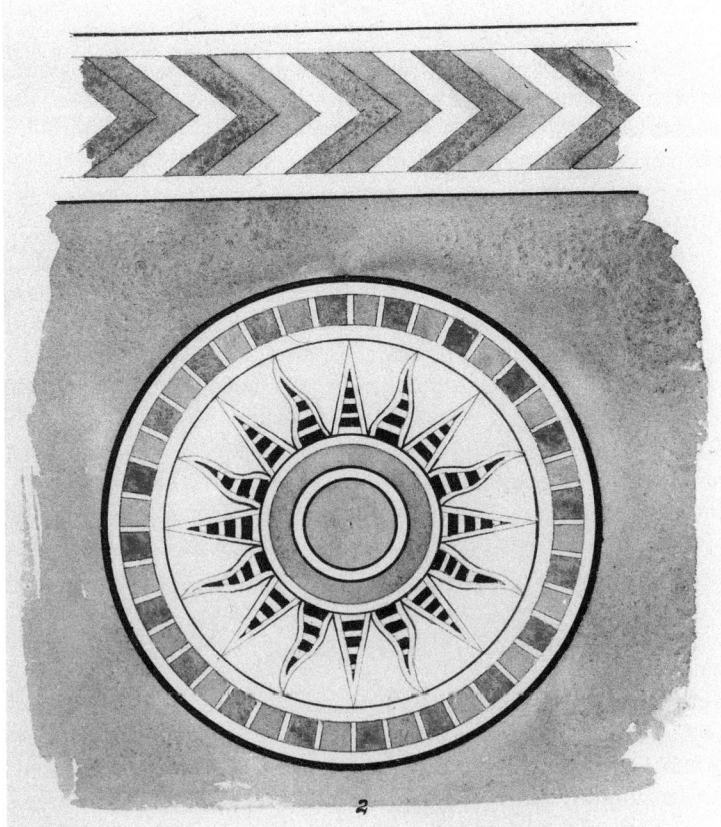

Pl. 8. Boutcher, detail of painted design, no. 2. *Original Drawings* I, 30. British Museum.

chambers B and C. If, indeed, the arcaded red bud precedes the other painted decorations in chambers A, B, C, it must have been executed early in the reign of Adad-nirari III.[12] Of further interest, below the garland is a narrow band, a section of which contains a pattern of zigzags. A similar pattern appears in one of Layard's other sketches of the wall paintings (pl. 5), and also in a polychrome drawing of William Boutcher made about 1854, depicting isolated painted motifs labeled as originating from the Centre Palace at Nimrud (pls. 7–8).[13] The zigzag motif in the drawings of Layard and Boutcher suggests that the painted designs are contemporary and therefore both groups of wall decorations derive from the Centre Palace of Adad-nirari III.

---

[12] See the brief comments of Albenda 1994, n. 16.
[13] First published in color in Reade 1983, fig. 23. It is of interest to observe that a purplish

Nimrud, outer town

The British excavators discovered part of a large Assyrian palace at the northwest end of the outer town at Nimrud.[14] In many chambers the walls were decorated with paintings rendered on carefully prepared mud-plaster. The best surviving paintings were discovered in room 9 (royal bathroom) where the burnt-brick pavement was stamped with the name of Adad-nirari III. In that chamber the wall paintings, 0.85 m wide, were 1.40 m above floor level. The motifs, unfortunately not drawn, are described as mainly geometric and include stylized plant designs, pomegranates, and young bulls running rampant on either side of a solid circle.[15] On the east wall, within the framing lines of the painting, the center panel consists of a design of bulls, heads turned back, on either side of a circle. The bodies of the bulls are red; the geometric designs are cobalt blue and white, all with a black outline. On either side of the central panel, a cushion-shaped square completes the painted decoration that extended across the length of the east wall.

In room 11, a spacious hall, some strips of the painted mural survived and the main design on one wall seems to have represented a series of striding bulls, the bodies rendered in cobalt blue, alternating with the cushion-shaped square and stylized flowers which were used as a filling at the corners.[16] The background of the square motif was blue and the flowers were red outlined in black.

In one corner of room 11 was a stylized tree – the so-called sacred tree – that consisted of an interlaced network of branches terminating in alternate pomegranate and lotus buds. The pigments used were red, blue and black. In his description of the tree, Mallowan noted that the treatment was similar to that of some of the sacred trees on the bas-reliefs of Ashurnasirpal II.[17] However, the carved representations of the sacred trees from the Northwest Palace have branches that terminate in palmettes only. The stylized tree in room 11 may therefore be an early version of a type found among the relief fragments re-excavated in a trench at Nimrud, which certainly derived from the so-called Central Palace of Tiglath-pileser III (745–727).[18]

---

color was applied to the blue areas, and one small design consists of a row of attached green circles with a red dot in each center.

[14] Mallowan 1953, pp. 70, 153–154, pl. XII.

[15] Ibid, p. 158, n. 9, pl. XXXVI. The photograph of the bathroom shows the murals *in situ*; however the designs are indistinct. Color renderings of the painted murals were made, with the hope of future publication. Unfortunately the copies were less than accurate, which accounts for their not being published.

[16] Ibid, pp. 153–155, 158.

[17] Ibid, pp. 160–162.

[18] For the study of the stylized (sacred) trees in the Northwest Palace of Ashurnasirpal II, see Albenda 1994. For the rendering of the stylized tree carved on a relief dated to the reign of Tiglath-pileser III, see Bleibtreu 1980, pp. 90–93, Tf. 5 b, 7.

Al Rimah

In the late Assyrian temple excavated at Tell al Rimah, a limestone stela of Adad-nirari III was discovered *in situ* in the cella of the building.[19] Probably contemporary in date are the paintings that decorated the interior walls of the structure. They are described as simple cushion and target friezes placed at shoulder level. A reconstructed line drawing of the inside of the temple shows, on one wall, a frieze of alternate cushion-shaped squares and circles, between a bitumen dado and a bitumen relief representing a composite winged creature.[20]

Late Eighth Century B.C.

Khorsabad

The American expedition team of the Oriental Institute uncovered fragments of plaster painted with various designs in the palace of Sargon II at Khorsabad. In addition, large sections of wall paintings and painted plaster fragments were discovered in several rooms of residences K, L and M, situated on the lower terrace of the citadel mound. Since the frescoes could not be removed, they were copied in color and in several instances also photographed.

In room 12 of the palace, identified as a royal bathroom, remains of painted plaster were found scattered in five areas [21] The patterned designs on the plaster originally decorated the upper walls, above the stone blocks that lined the lower walls and on which were carved greater-than-life size attendants advancing to the figure of the Assyrian king.[22] The published copies of the painted fragments (in color) illustrate two independent motifs, each repeated at regular intervals to form an all-over pattern: hexagons and plain and decorated circles. In three of the published fragments hexagons and circles occur together, but a narrow white strip separates the two motifs. This separation may indicate that each pattern was restricted to a particular section of wall surface, although it may be noted that the designs on the three plaster fragments are not entirely identical. Probably, the hexagons filled the uppermost surfaces, including the ceiling, and below were the circle motifs arranged in horizontal bands. In the publication the scale of the painted

[19] Oates 1968, pp. 122–125, pl. XXXII.
[20] Dalley 1984, pp. 193–199, figs. 64, 66, 67.
[21] Loud 1936, pp. 20–21, figs. 22–27, pl. I.
[22] Albenda 1986, pp. 62–63, pl. 64. General views of the re-excavated room appear in Loud 1936, figs. 24–26.

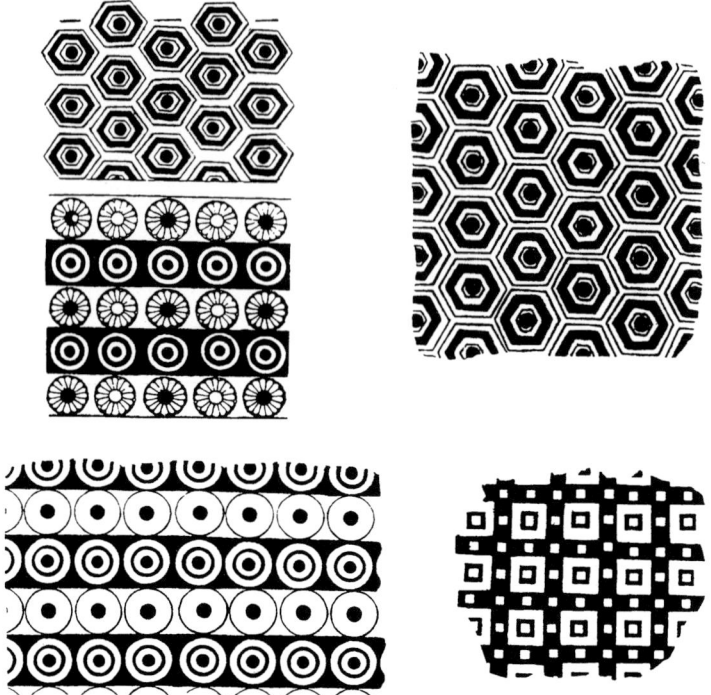

Fig. 2. Top left: painted fragment of hexagon and alternating rows of circles and rosettes. Redrawn and expanded. Loud 1936, pl. I: 5. Top right: painted fragments of hexagon designs from room 12, Khorsabad. Redrawn and expanded. Loud 1936, pl. I: 2. Bottom left: painted fragment of circle design from room 12, Khorsabad. Redrawn and expanded. Loud 1936, pl. I: 3. Bottom right: painted fragment of grid design from the throne room, Khorsabad. Redrawn and expanded. Loud 1936, pl. III: 8.

fragments is given as 1:10; therefore, the width of each hexagon is 10 to 15 cm and the diameter of each circle is 10 cm. These measurements make it likely that, despite the density of repeats, the two types of polychrome patterns adorning the ceiling and upper walls were intended to be distinguishable from below, within the chamber.

The closely spaced hexagons exhibit some variation in the sequence of the alternating red, blue and white colors (fig. 2, top). For example, one group of hexagons shows a blue dot center and another group shows a white dot center. Greater variation is observable among the patterned circles that are arranged and repeated within alternate bands of blue and red (fig. 2, bottom left). From the fragments that were published, the blue color marks the first band below the white strip that separates the two geometric patterns. All the circles have a white ground, and where a target or rosette fills the circular shape, it is always outlined in black. To the otherwise monochrome rosette

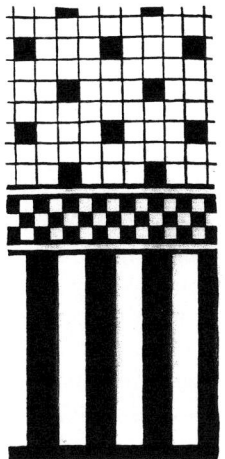 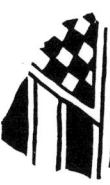

Fig. 3. Painted fragments of pattern motifs from
the throne room, Khorsabad. Loud 1936, pl. III: 7, 10.

is added an alternating red and blue dot center. Thus the organization of the patterned circles within the individual bands was designed according to a simple yet varied set of repeats. One can readily imagine the sparkling visual effect that must have resulted from the polychrome patterns of hexagons and circles, when they originally adorned the ceiling and upper walls of room 12. It should be noted, however, that one published pattern of plain circles, unlike in the other examples, does not include a black outline, and this suggests that the painted decorations in room 12 were never completed.

In the throne room of Sargon's palace were many fragments of painted plaster from the ceiling and upper part of the walls that had fallen to the ground.[23] Many blue plaster fragments were distributed throughout the entire chamber, suggesting that the ceiling was painted a plain blue. There were also many fragmentary geometrical designs on painted plaster. Bands of white circles, blue centered on a red background or red centered on blue background, and white rosettes may have been used as decorations for the exposed faces of the ceiling beams. A design of repeats of palmettes, possibly with connecting stems but without the commonly used buds alternating with the blossoms may have been set up high upon the walls, or else formed part of the arcaded palmettes of a stylized tree.[24]

---

[23] The find spots of the fragments of painted plaster are indicated in the plan of the throne room; Loud 1936, fig. 82.

[24] Ibid, pp. 67–69, pls. II, III. For the arcade of palmettes framing the tree, see Albenda 1986, pl. 76.

23

Throughout the throne room the excavators could distinguish portions of human figures on several fragments of painted plaster, and this observation indicates that life-size human figures adorned the walls. Other fragments contained several types of designs made up of squares that may be patterns of the decorated garments worn by ranked officials. One pattern of white squares with a single concentric square, formed by a grid of intersecting red bands decorated with open squares at regular intervals (fig. 2, bottom right), is almost identical with that on a garment of an Assyrian official on the glazed bricks from the same site.[25] Of related interest are the glazed bricks discovered by Botta in the nineteenth century and illustrated by Flandin, showing similar stripe-and-box patterns in combinations of white, yellow and green.[26]

Two additional painted plaster fragments from the throne room are note-worthy, since several patterns appear on those individual pieces (fig. 3). One fragment shows a wide band filled with three rows of a red and blue check-ered design set between a plain grid and alternating blue and red vertical bands. The other fragment is divided into two sections: a triangular section filled with a checkered motif and a section showing vertical stripes in alter-nating red and blue. The painted patterns on the fragments discovered in the throne room and the glazed brick designs noted earlier indicate that, during the reign of Sargon II, single and elaborate checks and multi-colored stripes were favored cloth patterns.

Many fragments of wall paintings that were discovered in residences K, L, and M, which belonged to high-ranked officials, show figural and ornamental subjects (pl. 31). Among those residences, the most elaborate ornamental painted mural was discovered in room 12 (great hall) of residence K (pl. 32). The frieze reached a height of some forty feet, about 12 meters, and as reconstructed it is divided into six wide registers. Three registers are each subdivided into narrow rosette-decorated bands and alternate with three registers ornamented with figural, animal and geometric motifs. Above the decorated frieze a semi-circular arch, bordered with additional decorative elements, contains a figural grouping of the Assyrian king followed by an attendant worshipping a male deity who stands on a pedestal.[27]

The upper and lower ornamented registers of the painted mural show identical features: two half-kneeling bearded and winged genies confront a large circle filled with decorative elements including an encircling lotus and bud garland (pl. 33). Behind each genie is a large circle filled with concentric circles. Thus the symmetrical grouping of the two genies on either side of a circle forms the unit for the pattern of repeats, separated by

[25] See the frieze (tableau) of glazed bricks as found by Place in Loud 1936, fig. 101.
[26] Albenda 1986, pp. 112, 153, pls. 150–151.
[27] Loud and Altman 1938, pp. 83–86, pls. 31, 43, 87–90.

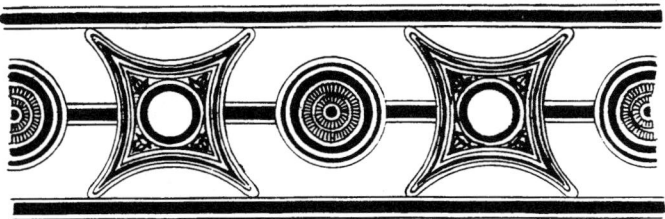

Fig. 4a. Wall painting from royal apartments, Arslan Tash.
Redrawn. Thureau-Dangin *et al.* 1931, pl. XLVIII:1.

a single circle. The central ornamented register likewise shows a three-part symmetrical grouping, but between each unit of repeat is a cushion-shaped square. Each unit consists of two bulls confronting a large square. The animals are animated. They stand upright and their downward-turned heads press against the edge of the respective curved side of the square, while at the same time their tails arch upward over their bodies. All the large squares show an identical decoration that consists of decorated concentric circles and a bud at the corners. As reconstructed in color, the background of each of the three ornamented registers with figural motifs is blue, and the colors used for the details are red, blue, black and white.

Late Eighth and Seventh Centuries B.C.

Arslan Tash

Thureau-Dangin excavated an impressive royal palace at Arslan Tash, where in some places the remaining walls of the structure reached a height of about three meters. In the north wing the walls of the rooms were generally covered with a white plaster. On the walls of the public and private rooms of the royal apartments (rooms 17 to 28) was the same decoration that consisted of a continuous polychrome frieze. The frieze, 0.78 m wide, was at a height of 1.60 to 2 m above the level of the floor. The colors employed on the white plaster ground were cobalt blue and an Indian red; the contours were outlined in black. Unfortunately, the placement of the color pigments in the frieze was not described; however, Thureau-Dangin did observe that in places under the black lines there appeared red lines.[28]

A drawing of the frieze was published (fig. 4a). The frieze is composed of alternating cushion-shaped squares and circles. Upper and lower border

---

[28] Thureau-Dangin *et al*, 1931, pp. 28–29, pl. XLVIII 1.

25

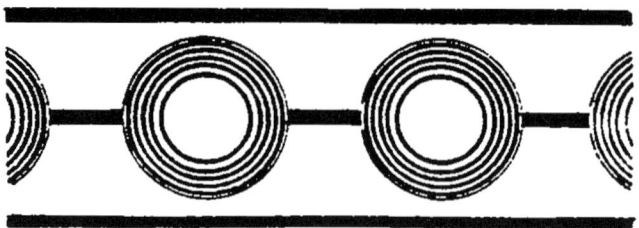

Fig. 4b. Wall painting from small apartment, Arslan
Tash. Thureau-Dangin *et al* 1931, pl. XLVIII: 2.

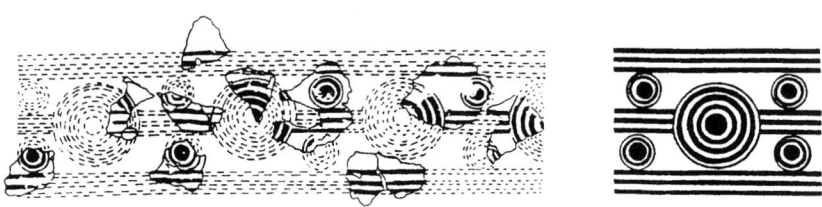

Fig. 4c. Painted fragments and reconstruction of wall
painting from building E, Til Barsip. Abbate 1997, fig. 3.

bands set between thin lines frame the frieze, and a third band centered in the
frieze connects the individual geometric shapes. Within each large square are
concentric squares that, in turn, surround concentric circles. At each corner
between the innermost concentric square and outermost concentric circle is
a bud. Each large circle contains concentric circles and a dot center, and
continuous bars radiate around two of the inner circles.

Near the royal apartments was a small apartment consisting of a chamber
and bathroom.[29] At a height of 1.30 m above the floor level the walls of the
chamber were decorated with a modest frieze that was 36 cm in width and
outlined entirely in black (fig. 4b). The monochrome decoration is framed
by a plain upper and lower band and shows large circles repeated at regular
intervals. A central band connects the geometric shapes. Each large circle
shows five concentric circles and plain center.

---

[29] Ibid, p. 30, pl. XLVIII 2.

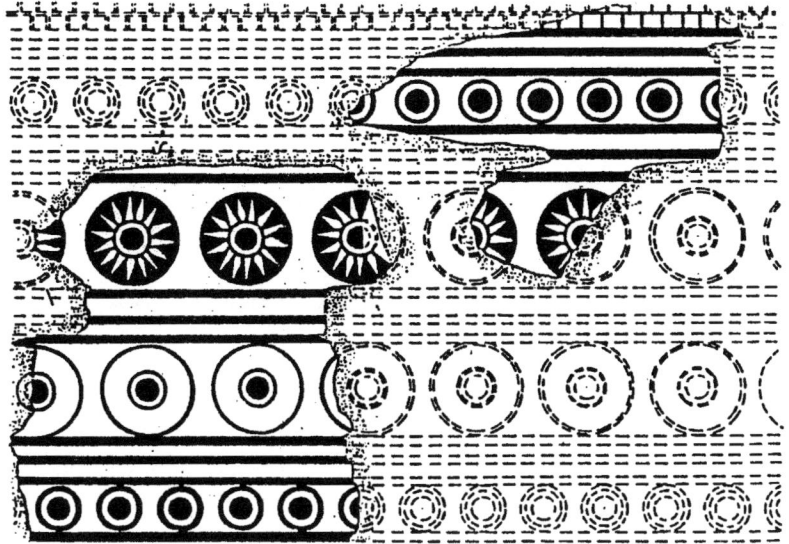

Fig. 5a. Wall painting with design of circles and stripes,
from building G at Dur-Katlimmu. Nunn 1988, fig. 101.

Til Barsip, building E

Extensive painted murals were discovered in the royal palace at Til Barsip;
a description and discussion of the ornamental paintings are given in the
next chapter. In building E at Til Barsip, the Australian excavation team
discovered fragments of wall painting fallen to the ground.[30] Two phases of
a painted frieze were noted and as reconstructed the later phase was the more
elaborate (fig. 4c). Painted in black on a white ground, the frieze consists of an
upper and lower border, each formed by three narrow horizontal stripes, and
in the center three similar stripes connect large target-like circles repeated at
regular intervals. Simplified targets, one above the other, occupy the narrow
spaces formed by the three groups of horizontal stripes and alternate with
the large circles.

Tell Sheikh Hamad

The German excavation team discovered impressive black-on-white ornamental wall paintings at the north Syrian site of Tell Sheikh Hamad, the
Assyrian provincial city of Dur-Katlimmu. Monochrome painted decora-

---

[30] Abbate 1994, pp. 7–16, pls. 1–3.

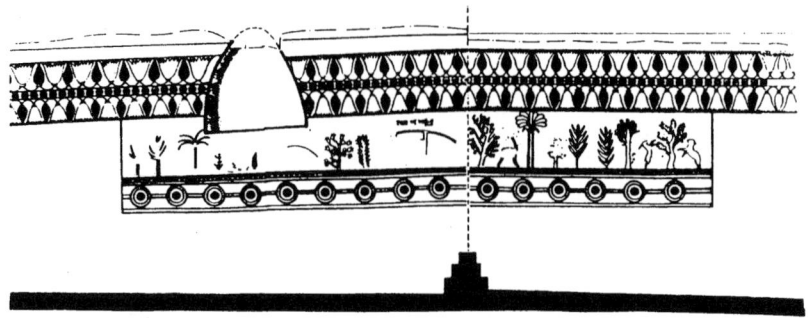

Fig. 5b. Wall painting with garden scene, from room
B, building G. at Dur-Katlimmu. Kühne 1989, Abb. 138.

tions dated to the end of the eighth century and into the seventh century were
found on long sections of walls in the Lower Town (Unterstadt II), building
G.[31] On the north side of wall 1 in that building, two phases of painting
were revealed. The later one was painted directly over the earlier one (fig.
5). The published photograph of the later decoration shows that the design
consists of a continuous frieze about 1.50 m above floor level and reaching
to the top of the preserved wall, at an average height of 2 m. The frieze is
composed of four decorated registers, one above the other, with three closely
spaced stripes between each register and five stripes below the bottom register. Within each of the two inner registers is a row of black circles containing
white rosette flowers with a black dot in the center. Each of the two outer,
narrower registers shows a row of white circles outlined in black, with a
black dot in the center. Overall, the monochrome frieze is divided into neatly
measured registers and stripes.

   On the south side of the same wall (room B, northwestern side) was a
frieze consisting of two stylized flower and bud garlands painted entirely in
black on a white ground. The floral garlands are arranged in mirror image
with, between them, a narrow band decorated with a row of dot-centered
white circles outlined in black. One area of the wall forms a corner with the
adjoining wall (16); this latter wall was preserved to a height of about 2.20 m.
Additional painted decorations lined its upper surface. There, the extensive
black on white frieze was ornamented with three-stepped merlons at the top;
below them were several patterned bands, with a wider central one showing
a repeat of rosette-decorated circles.[32]

---

[31] Kühne 1984, pp. 172–173, Abb. 63 a-b, 64; Nunn, 1988, p. 133, Tf. 101–102.
[32] Kühne, 1989/90, pp. 320–321, Abb. 138; Nunn 1988, Tf. 103.

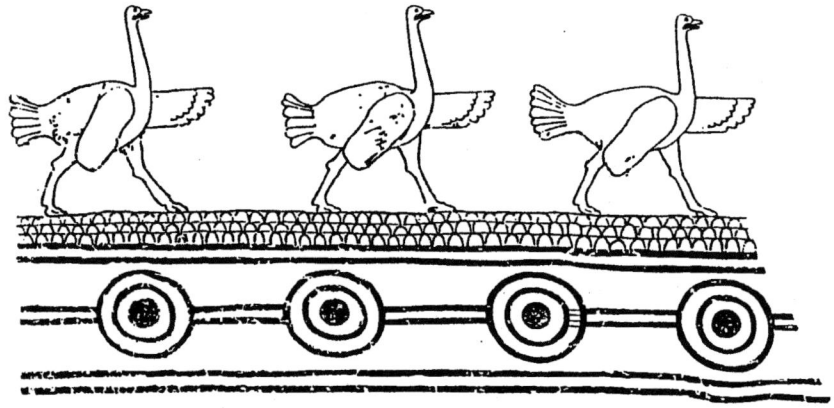

Fig. 5c. Wall painting with ostriches and band of
concentric circles, Dur-Katlimmu. Kühne 1993, fig. 6.

In the lower northwestern corner of room B, the wall surface immediately
below the garland frieze contained a monochrome decoration set within a
rectangular panel. Outlined in black on the white ground, a row of animals,
flowering shrubs, and trees are arranged along the angles of the two walls
(fig. 5b). In the center of the composition, above the curved roof of a structure
or tent, is a cuneiform epigraph ('das Gartenhaus'). In the narrow register
below the garden scene is a row of targeted circles connected by a double
striped band. A nearly identical row of targeted circles was discovered on
the northeastern wall of the same chamber.[33] All that remained on the wall
surface immediately above the geometric decoration was a pattern of scales
representing a rocky terrain, on which a line of ostriches with outstretched
wings stride to the right (Fig. 5c). Stylistically, the painted designs containing
the garden scene and the ostriches may be contemporary. However, the
excavators noted that they differ from the other ornamental wall paintings
and belong to a later phase in the late seventh century Assyrian period.

Fort Shalmaneser

Painted murals decorated the walls of the throne room suite (S3–5) at Fort
Shalmaneser. The best preserved were discovered in the throne room (S5),
on the walls of which were two sets of friezes, one above the other.[34] In the
lower frieze, on a panel 1.33 m high, a row of attendants advanced in a left

---

[33] Kühne 1993, pp. 77–78, Abb. 5–6.
[34] Mallowan 1966, pp. 443–444, figs. 307–308.

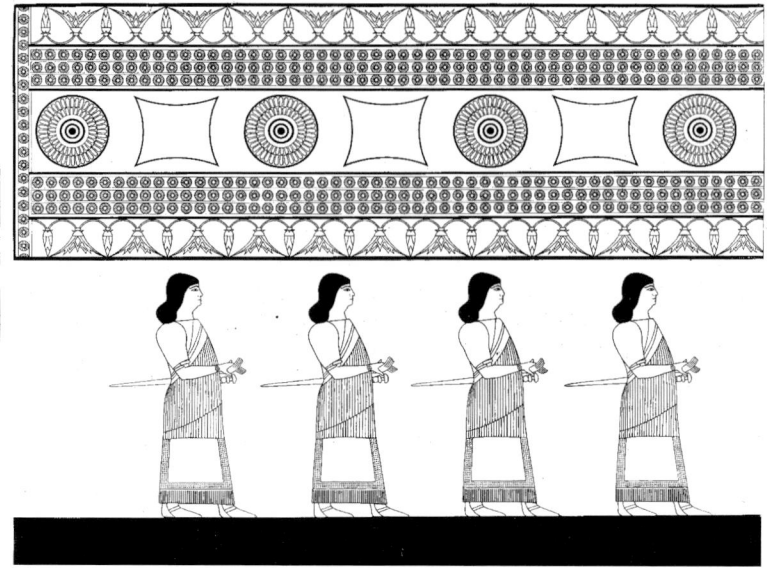

Fig. 6. Wall Painting from throne room S5, Fort Shalmaneser. Mallowan 1966, pl. 308.

to right direction. The attendants were drawn with a black line on a white ground, with traces of red still visible on the sandals. Immediately above this frieze was a patterned frieze 1.35 m high; the upper frieze consisted of five registers of floral and geometric motifs. The patterned frieze was drawn in a bold black outline with the application of red and blue to pomegranates and rosette petals. Based on style, the excavators attributed these wall paintings to the Assyrian king, Esarhaddon.

As reconstructed (fig. 6), the outer registers of the patterned frieze show a mirror image arrangement of a stylized lotus and bud garland. Three rows of repeated rosettes fill each of the second and fourth registers. Within the middle third register, a large rectangular panel, a square with incurved sides alternates with a circle decorated with two concentric circles filled with petals, and a target center. A single vertical row of rosettes completes the patterned frieze, a short distance from a doorway.

Overview of the Discoveries

Archaeological excavations have produced ample evidence for the decorative use of wall painting in Assyrian royal residences. In those chambers where the lower surface of walls were lined with carved stone slabs, painted designs were applied to the upper surface and in some instances to the ceiling. On occasion painted narrative subjects replaced the carved slabs, as exemplified by throne room S5 at Fort Shalmaneser. The ornamental designs were invariably outlined in black and the colors seem to have been restricted to red and blue on a white ground. During the last decades of the Assyrian Empire, however, single horizontal bands of red, green and yellow colored the plastered walls of chambers in the Acropolis Palace at Nimrud.[35] The pigments were applied as flat hues, and there is no evidence to suggest that pigments were mixed to produce shades of color within a given shape. Overall, emphasis was directed to the visual flatness of the ornamental designs.

Private residences excavated at Khorsabad and at North Syrian sites also furnish evidence for ornamental wall painting. The monochrome wall paintings discovered in the suite of two rooms at Arslan Tash, building E at Til Barsip, and building G at Dur-Katlimmu were rendered in a bold black outline on a white ground. The absence of color in those wall paintings raises the possibility that polychrome painted decoration was generally restricted to the residences of royalty and Assyrian officials of high rank, as well as to Assyrian temples. On the other hand, the black on white wall paintings discovered in the above-mentioned Syrian sites may reflect a stylistic taste that prevailed outside the sphere of the Assyrian royal court, during the late eighth and seventh centuries. Nonetheless, the black on white painted style seems to have reached Assyria proper, as evidenced by the modest wall painting discovered in the entrance chamber of a bathroom in the Governor's Palace at Nimrud.[36] In that area of wall the geometric design consisted of painted barred circles with a hollowed out central disk, set between four or five horizontal bands.

It is of further interest to note that the black-and-white style also dominated the pebble mosaics that covered the floors of several open areas at Til Barsip and Arslan Tash. At the former site, the exterior corridors surrounding several rooms were paved with a pattern of black and white checks. In the center of each square was a circle composed of the opposite color: black on white and white on black.[37] Plain black and white checks decorated the pebble mosaic courts discovered in the 'Batiment aux ivoires' and building E at

---

[35] Ibid, p. 293. Fragments of plain horizontal stripes of red paint, spaced at broad intervals on a white ground, survived in the Burnt Palace at Nimrud, and have been ascribed to the period of Assur-etil-ilani (626–621 B.C.). During the reign of Sargon II, the throne room in the Burnt Palace was decorated with geometric designs in green, red and cobalt blue on a white ground (not illustrated); ibid, p. 207.

[36] Ibid, p. 40, fig. 8.

[37] Thureau-Dangin and Dunand 1936, pl. XLII, plan B. A pebble pavement of squares of black and white was exposed at Ziyaret Tepe, a large mound overlooking the Tigris River. Several squares were divided into four by diagonal lines with opposing triangles of the same color, and a few others forming rosettes; see MacGinnis 2001, pp. 13–14.

Arslan Tash.[38] The absence of polychrome in the North Syrian floor mosaics is in contrast with the earliest known Phrygian pebble mosaic discovered in a large room of a residential building at the site of Gordion, dated to about the mid-eighth century.[39] In that mosaic a variety of geometric patterns in deep red, deep blue and white were used, and it was noted that the general effect was that of a rich ornamental rug or carpet. From the excavated evidence, then, one may conclude that the black and white ornamental style was a North Syrian phenomenon, during the seventh century B.C.

---

[38] See: Thureau-Dangin *et al* 1931, pp. 43–44, Plan; Bunnens 1992, 3–4, 6–7, figs. 7, 17; id. 1995, p. 23, fig. 4.
[39] Young 1965, pp. 10–12, illustrations on pp. 4, 6, 8, 10, 11.

CHAPTER THREE. TIL BARSIP

The ancient site of Til Barsip (modern Tell ʿAhmar) is located on the west bank of the Euphrates River. In the ninth century B.C. the Assyrian king Shalmaneser III, who re-named the city Kar-Shalmaneser, conquered it. The French excavated the ancient site in three campaigns during the years 1929, 1930, and 1931, and at that time an Assyrian royal residence was exposed. The structure consisted of over forty-three chambers, three courtyards, and several corridors (fig. 7; see p. 94). Wall paintings were discovered *in situ* in one area of the residence that the excavators identified as the royal apartments. However, in a number of places only traces of wall paintings remained. The wall paintings were mostly polychrome on white lime plaster and showed subject matter that fit into three main themes: narrative, ornamental, apotropaic. The pictorial evidence shows that the latter theme was restricted to the lateral walls of entranceways. Several rooms had both representational scenes and ornamental friezes on the same walls (rooms 1, 22, 24, 27, 47). In those instances the scenes were painted at eye level, above a band of bitumen that lined the base of the wall, and the ornamental friezes occupied the wall surface immediately above the scenes. An exception was room 1 (vestibule) where small fragments fallen to the ground were discovered. Several rooms contained ornamental paintings only; in all, seven ornamental friezes were recorded in drawings (rooms 21, 22, 24, 25, 26, 46, 47).

Through a combination of tracings, visual observations, reconstructions and partial conjectures, the architect Lucien Cavro made careful color copies of the wall paintings to the same scale on heavy paper, about 100 meters in total length, and these copies are presently housed in the Musée du Louvre. The accuracy of Cavro's renderings may be determined by comparing the painted versions with the original fragments in the Aleppo and Louvre Museums.[1] However, the publication of the Til Barsip excavations reproduces the wall paintings in black and white. Parrot's later volume on Assyrian art includes color reproductions of a substantial number of Cavro's renderings.[2] A Louvre registration number was assigned to each of the renderings, and

---

[1] Several of the existing fragments are reproduced in Parrot 1961, figs. 111, 114, 336, 337, 346. For a brief commentary concerning the differences in tone and texture in the reproductions, see p. 362.

[2] Cavro made tracings of the paintings; then in his Beirut studio he prepared the final version. The two shades of red/brown and blue in Cavro's original works were possibly due to the availability of the color pigments in Beirut (information courtesy of Elizabeth Fontan). Cavro's copies of the Til Barsip wall paintings were exhibited in 1930 in Paris, but afterwards were mislaid; they were found again in 1961. In Parrot's book, many of the wall paintings are reproduced in color. For a complete list of these illustrations, see pp. 336–337.

color negatives and black and white photographs of the paintings were made for the museum archives. Because of the fragile condition of Cavro's paintings, as well as the difficulty of examination, since each painted unit must be rolled out, the color negatives and photographs in the Louvre furnish a reliable means to study both the details of subject matter and color schemes. They are a major resource for the descriptions cited in the present study.

The French excavators divided the paintings into two styles: the first style was dated to the time of Shalmaneser III and Tiglath-pileser III, and the second style to the time of Ashurbanipal (663–631). Scholars have debated the dates for the specific Til Barsip wall paintings, and occasionally parallels with Assyrian palace wall reliefs are cited.[3] An extensive comparative analysis that includes other art media may help to determine which Assyrian king was responsible for the respective wall paintings at Til Barsip, particularly since repainting was noted by the excavators, thus confirming that the wall paintings were done over a period of time. Evidence of repainting can be seen in several of Cavro's renderings too.

Little attention has been given to the study of the ornamental wall paintings at Til Barsip. These paintings are thought to be contemporary with the narrative scenes, as well as with the apotropaic compositions, when both types appear on the same wall surface. The Til Barsip decorative paintings are outstanding for the variety of motifs that make up the respective designs, notwithstanding the similarity of overall arrangement. This observation suggests that at least several painted friezes were produced at different times. Another type of decoration that differs from the ornamental friezes is the pattern covering the garments of the winged genies that form part of the ornamental designs in room 25 and 46. Moreover in the narrative scenes the costumes of several Assyrian kings, officials of high rank, and those of the genies in the entranceways also show decorative patterns. The Til Barsip patterned cloths are multicolored and derive from the weaving technique, although a few patterns may represent embroidery or appliqué. The study of these textile patterns may lead to firm dates for several wall paintings and is therefore included in a separate section.

In the catalogue of wall paintings given below, an attempt is made to arrange the ornamental designs into groups, based upon a similarity of decoration or the inclusion of comparative motifs. Thus the rooms where the ornamental wall paintings were discovered do not follow the usual number sequence cited in the original publication. Although not always stated in the descriptions given below, it is important to note that black outlines always separate the colored areas.

---

[3] Nunn 1988, pp. 108–122. The author provides a convenient summary of the reasons given by the French excavators and several modern scholars for their respective proposed dates of

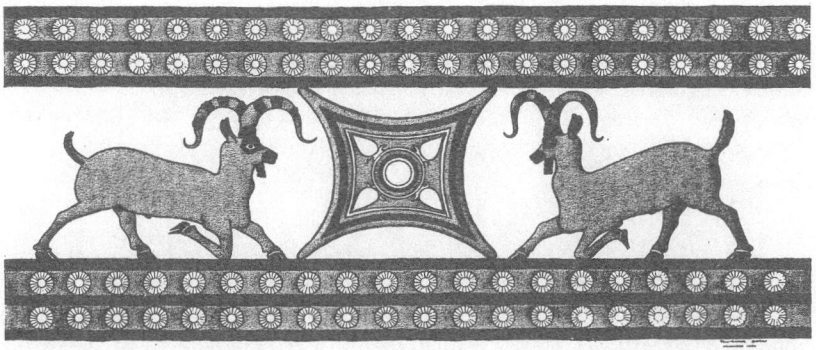

Pl. 9. Cavro, ornamental wall painting with goats. Room 26 in the Assyrian palace at Til Barsip. Thureau-Dangin and Dunand 1936, pl. XLVI.

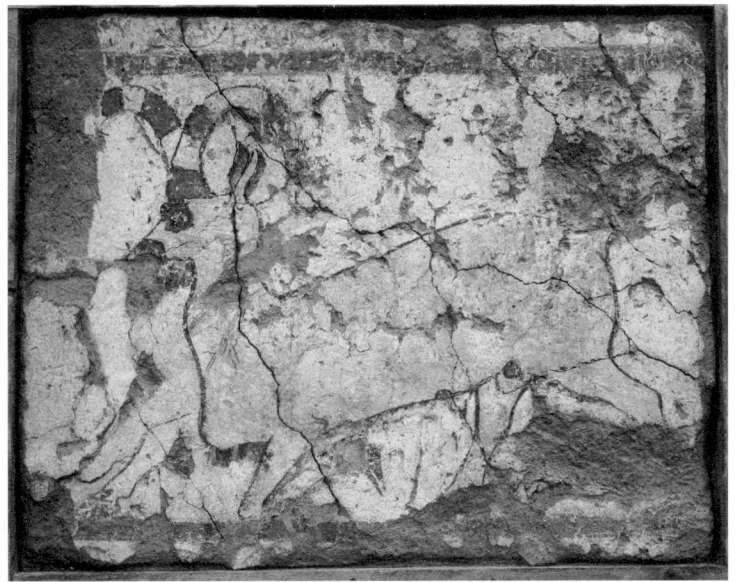

Pl. 10. Painted goat. Fragment of wall painting from room 26 at Til Barsip. Musée du Louvre AO 23010. Photo RMN, Chuzeville.

---

the Til Barsip wall paintings. For an earlier discussion on the same subject, see Tomabechi 1983/1984, pp. 63–74.

Room 26

Plates 9, 10.
Existing fragments: Louvre AO 23010; Aleppo Museum 250.
Publications: Thureau-Dangin and Dunand 1936, pp. 58–59, pls. XLIII 4,
    XLVI; Parrot 1961, figs. 336, 337; Beyer 1989, pp. 57–58; Fontan 1992,
    p. 83.

Room 26 was a long corridor that gave access to rooms 24, 25, 27. In this
corridor the frieze with goats was at a height of about 1.90 meters above the
level of the floor and was about 0.79 meter in width. The French excavators
noted that a red vertical band terminated the frieze near a doorway. The frieze
also decorated rooms 25 and 27, and passages 24/25, 25/26, 26/27. At a later
date several of the rooms and passageways were restored with different
painted decorations. The frieze represents the earliest known ornamental
decoration in the royal apartments.

Cavro's drawing of the frieze is now lost. The published black-and-white
ornamental design consists of two goats seen in profile flanking a large
square with incurved sides, framed by solid bands alternating with two rows
of rosettes. The existing color fragments show that the solid bands are red
outlined in black, and that the rosettes are white outlined in black. Each
goat is skillfully outlined in black and its body is entirely blue, except for
the addition of red on the muzzle and beard and around the visible white of
the eye. The animal's horns curve forward and backward, respectively. They
display a pattern of broad red and blue stripes outlined in black; however, on
the existing Louvre fragment the blue on the horns has mostly disappeared,
leaving the white plaster exposed. The blue color of the goat is probably
a decorative feature, although several other Til Barsip animals, including
an entranceway bull and the horse pulling the royal chariot represented in
room 27, are also painted this color.[4] The color scheme of the decorated
cushion-shaped square is unknown.

---

[4] Animals are known to have been intentionally painted blue or blends of that color, as a means
to enhance their value. Among the list of tribute from the West received by Tiglath-pileser III,
probably in 738 B.C. include 'live sheep whose wool is dyed red-purple, flying birds of the
sky whose wings are dyed blue-purple'; Tadmor 1994, pp. 69–70, 276. Tadmor considers these
items to come from a Phoenician or North Syrian ruler, but also to be considered is whether
the tribute comes from Zabibe, queen of the Arabs, who is mentioned in the text. Another text
mentions Samsi, queen of the Arabs, who probably gave tribute in 734 B.C. For discussion on
these female rulers, see I. Eph'al 1982, pp. 83–87. It may be pointed out that on the stone reliefs
of Tiglath-pileser III from Nimrud, one episode illustrates the battle and subsequent submission
of the Arabs that include a female, followed by a long procession of camels, cattle, sheep and
goats. Barnett considers the scene to represent the tribute of the Arab queen Samsi, whom he
suggests may be another name for Zabibe; Barnett and Falkner 1962, p. xvii, pls. XXIII–XXX.

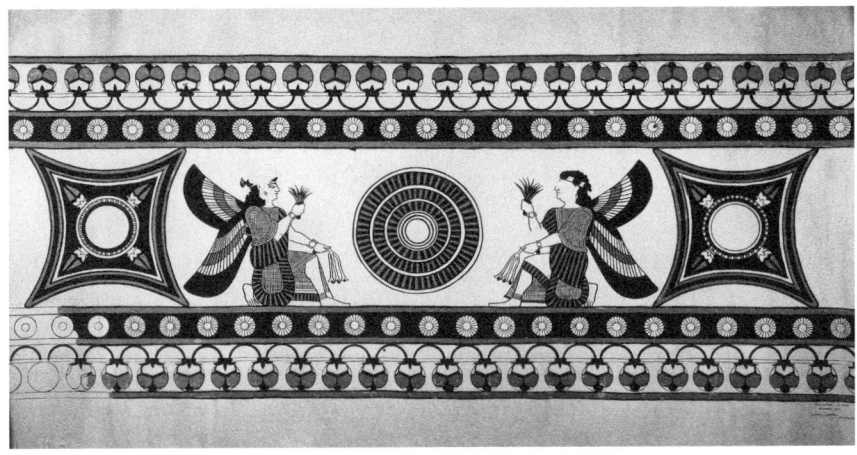

Pl. 11. Cavro, ornamental wall painting with winged female genies. Room
25 in the Assyrian palace at Til Barsip. Musée du Louvre AO 25067 K.

The goat is depicted at the moment of rising with its near foreleg bent
under the body, above the level of the ground, and the far foreleg extended
forward for balance. The body tilts upwards at the back and is supported by
the hindquarters. Parallels for the half-kneeling goat occur on a number of
carved ivories discovered in areas of the Northwest Palace at Nimrud, Fort
Shalmaneser, and the palace of Adad-nirari III in the outer town. The ivories
are dated to the end of the ninth and early eighth centuries B.C. Among
the horned animals and bulls kneeling on either side of a large palmette or
a flowering shrub are goats with horns bent forward and backward in an
arched curve, and a winged bull.[5] The latter animal is similar to that of the
painted version from the upper chambers at Nimrud, dated to the reign of
Adad-nirari III (pl. 3), with the notable exception that in the painted version
the placement of the near and far forelegs is reversed. Several of the ivories
are attributable to the reign of Adad-nirari III. One is tempted to attribute
to the same period the ornamental frieze with goats discovered on the walls
of several chambers in the royal apartments, but a date later in the eighth
century B.C. is also probable.

---

[5] See: Mallowan and Davies 1970, pp. 8, 12, 46–47, figs. 126–127, 134–139, 141, 201–202;
Herrmann 1992, pp. 24–27, 38–39, 53–54, 109–110, nos. 29, 30–31, 32, 34, 94, 351–354.

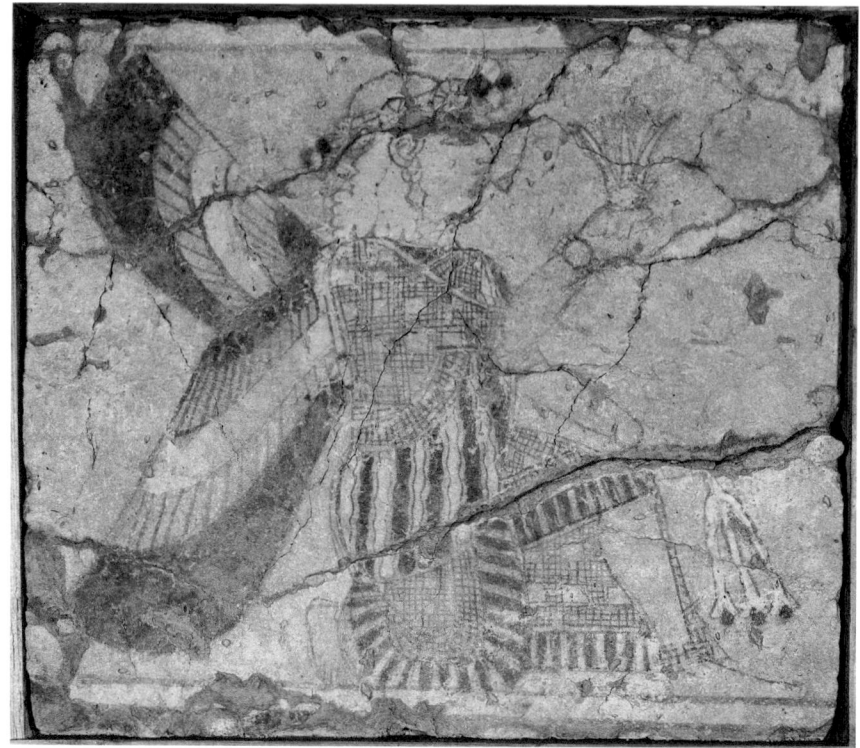

Pl. 12. Winged genie. Fragment of wall painting from room 27 at
Til Barsip. Musée du Louvre AO 23009. Photo RMN, Chuzeville.

Rooms 25 and 27

Plates 11, 12.
Existing Fragment: Louvre AO 23009.
Cavro's copy: Louvre AO 25067 K.
Publications: Thureau-Dangin and Dunand 1936, pp. 59–63, pls. XLIII,
    XLVII; Parrot 1961, p. xv (photo).

Room 25 was restored and a new frieze about 10 to 15 centimeters lower
than the earlier one, originally decorated with wild goats, measured about
1.04 meters from bottom to top. The excavators noted that the same frieze
recurred in rooms 26 and 27 (bathroom).

  Blue stripes alternate with the two decorated borders that frame the
principal register in mirror image. The inner border has a repeat of white
rosettes on a red ground and the outer border has a floral garland with a
flower emerging within a circle drawn in red to facilitate the artist's task. The

flower has two blue petals with a central red tip on a white base. The calyx and arcaded stems are red. The excavators described the garland flowers as 'fleurs de lis'; however, the blue-petal flower does not recur among the other published ornamental friezes at Til Barsip, nor does it appear elsewhere in Assyrian art. It may be that the exceptional flower in the garland and the one decorating the headband of the genie on the extant fragment represent two views of the same plant.

The principal motif in the central register consists of an antithetical pair of beardless, two-winged genies kneeling with one leg on the baseline with, between them, a large circle or roundel. Behind each genie is a cushion-shaped square. The upper bodies of the two facing genies are drawn in rotational symmetry and their lower bodies are in mirror image. In the raised right hand of each genie is a lotus flower in red and blue and in the lowered left hand is a triple-branched plant with small red flowers at the outer tips. The dress is plain, except for a pattern of vertical and horizontal striations in red, and the flounces of the shawl, outlined in black, alternate in red and blue. Attached to the white headband are red disk-like flowers. Plain striations demarcate the feathers of the paired wings of the respective genies, and across the wings are broad bands in red, white, blue, white, and red. On the exposed far leg of each genie is a broad ankle bracelet, an item of jewelry generally associated with women.

The fragment showing an entire winged genie facing right was disengaged from room 27 after Cavro's departure from the site, and this genie was in better condition than those from room 25. Several details in the painted fragment differ from those that appear in Cavro's copy. Thin black lines delineate the entire figure, but they are drawn over red lines that may represent the first sketches on the plaster ground. The dress is patterned with red horizontal and vertical lines surrounding large squares, and the wavy lines of the shawl are also red. The absence of blue, the appearance of white hair that was always painted black, and the thin black lines over the sketchy red ones, together indicates that the painted fragment, at least, is unfinished. The French excavators did observe that other details of the same frieze were sometimes simplified and drawn with red lines, while black was used for accents and the outlining of the main motifs, and they concluded that the painted frieze belonged to the second style, dated to the period of Ashurbanipal.

The roundel and the cushion-shaped square, the two large geometric shapes which in Cavro's rendering separate the genies, are in red, blue, white, and black. The roundel is decorated with three concentric circular bands framed by narrow white circles, each band filled with alternating red and blue bars, and in the center are black concentric circles on a white ground. The square shows concentric borders in blue, red, blue, white, black outline, white. Red serves as the background for the blue floral buds in the four corners.

39

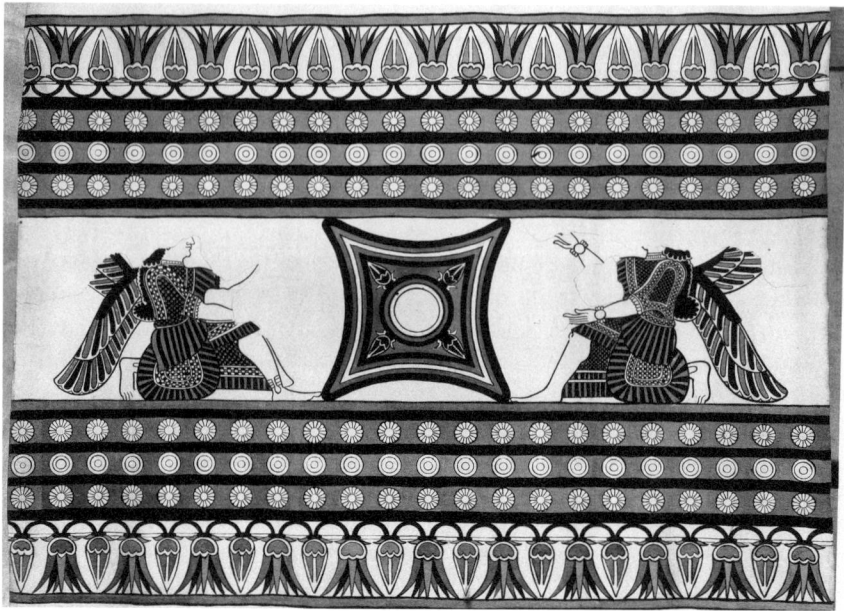

Pl. 13. Cavro, ornamental wall painting with winged female genies. Room
46 in the Assyrian palace at Til Barsip. Musée du Louvre AO 25067 M.

Room 46

Plate 13.
Cavro's copy: Louvre AO 25067 M.
Publication: Thureau-Dangin and Dunand 1936, p. 68, pl. XLVI.

Room 46 was a long corridor connecting rooms 44 (bathroom), 45 (courtyard), and 47. The frieze was at a height about 1.90 to 2 meters above the
level of the floor and about 1.27 meters in width. The French excavators
observed that the frieze resembled the one discovered in rooms 25 and 27,
but was not contemporary to it; rather it was probably earlier in date.

    The frieze is divided into three horizontal sections of equal widths. The
two framing sections are in mirror image, and are subdivided into solid
red stripes alternating with patterned bands of rosettes, concentric circles,
and lotus-and-bud garlands respectively. The rosettes and circles are white
outlined in black on a blue ground. The lotus-and-bud garlands are on a red
ground and, stylistically, they are identical to the garlands of room 21 with
one minor exception: white substitutes for pink.

    On the white ground of the central section, two genies with paired wings
half kneel in mirror image and confront a large cushion-shaped square. The

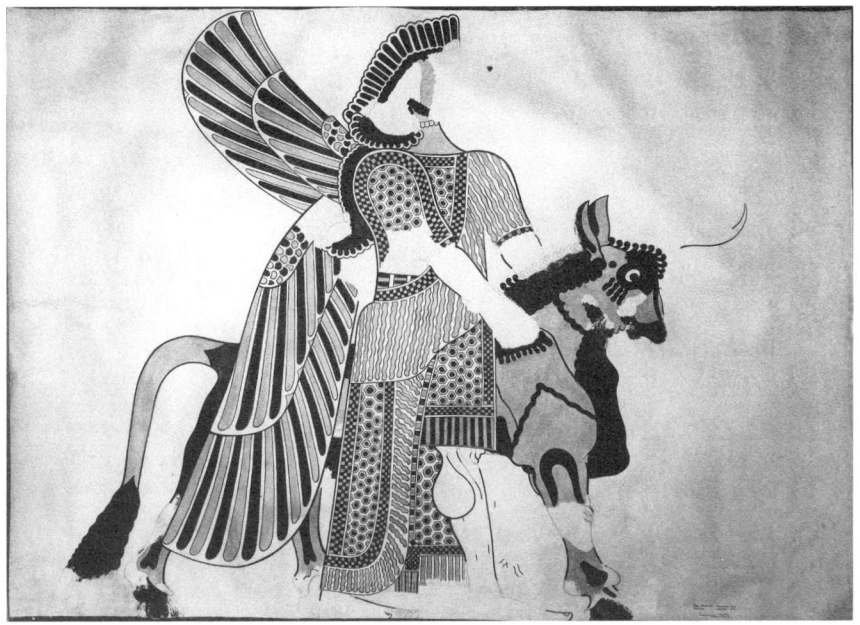

Pl. 14. Cavro, wall painting of winged bird-headed genie and bull. Passage 24/28 in the Assyrian palace at Til Barsip. Museé du Louvre AO 25067 S.

square is decorated with five concentric border bands in red, blue, white, red, and blue. The innermost band contains a red floral bud in each corner and these buds, in turn, rest upon the outermost of four concentric circles alternating in red, blue, white, black outline, and white.

The genies are beardless and female, similar to those represented in the friezes from rooms 25 and 27, but one genie is without the ankle bracelets. Still visible on the drawing of the now destroyed head of each figure is the shoulder-length hair, from which a thick long tress falls pendant at the back. The genies extend their arms forward, seemingly pointing toward the large geometric shape; no floral plant is held in either hand. Their respective costume, identical in style, consists of a knee-length dress beneath an ankle-length garment, over which extends a long tasseled shawl covering the far shoulder. The costume is patterned with checks alternating in blue and red, and the checkered trim shows a combination of blue, red, and white. The tassels are rendered as long stripes in alternating blue and red. The gracefully curved wings of the genies are divided into the upper wing, known as the covert, and two layered rows of large feathers in alternating blue and red on a white ground.

The genies from room 46 are distinguishable from the genies in the ornamental friezes painted in rooms 25 and 27 in two important ways. First,

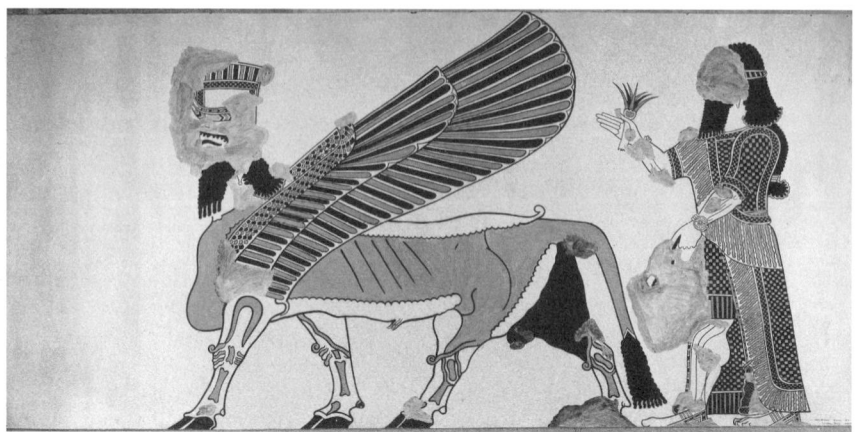

Pl. 15. Cavro, wall painting of winged bull and male genie. Passage 24/25 in
the Assyrian palace at Til Barsip. Musée du Louvre AO 25067 B.

in the room 46 the paired genies are depicted in strict mirror image, while
the published example from room 25 displays the proper 180º lateral rotation
of the torso. In both friezes, however, the lower body of the paired genies is
in mirror image. The second major difference is in the manner of depicting
the feathering of the wings. The feathering of each wing on the genies from
rooms 25 and 27 is reduced to a series of linear striations, with the colors
applied as broad bands that extend across the wing. In contrast, the careful
delineation of the individual feathers on each wing of the genies from room
46 is the typical method associated with the Assyrian style. At Til Barsip the
painted parallels showing the wings in the Assyrian style include the bird-
headed genie from passage 24/28 (Louvre AO 25067 S, pl. 14), the bearded
genie from passage 24/26 (Louvre AO 25067 F, pl. 16), the human-headed
bull from passage 24/25 (Louvre AO 25067 B, pl. 15), and the human-
headed bull in the ornamental frieze found in room 47 (Louvre AO 25068
D, pl. 19).[6] In these examples the similarity in the feathering of the wings
strongly suggests that the painted figures were produced during the same
period, but they are not contemporary with the painted genies from rooms
25, 27 and probably those from room 26.

---

[6] In contrast to the rendering of wings on Assyrian wall reliefs, where special attention is
given to the individual feathers, the broad color striations separating the rows of feathers on the
wings of the genies in rooms 25 and 27 seem closer to the rendering of wings on a number of
carved ivories from Fort Shalmaneser that belong to the Phoenician tradition. For comparison,
see: Paley 1976, pls. 14–15, 20; Albenda 1986, figs. 9–10, 14–15; Herrmann 1992, nos. 140,
200, 207, 231, 236.

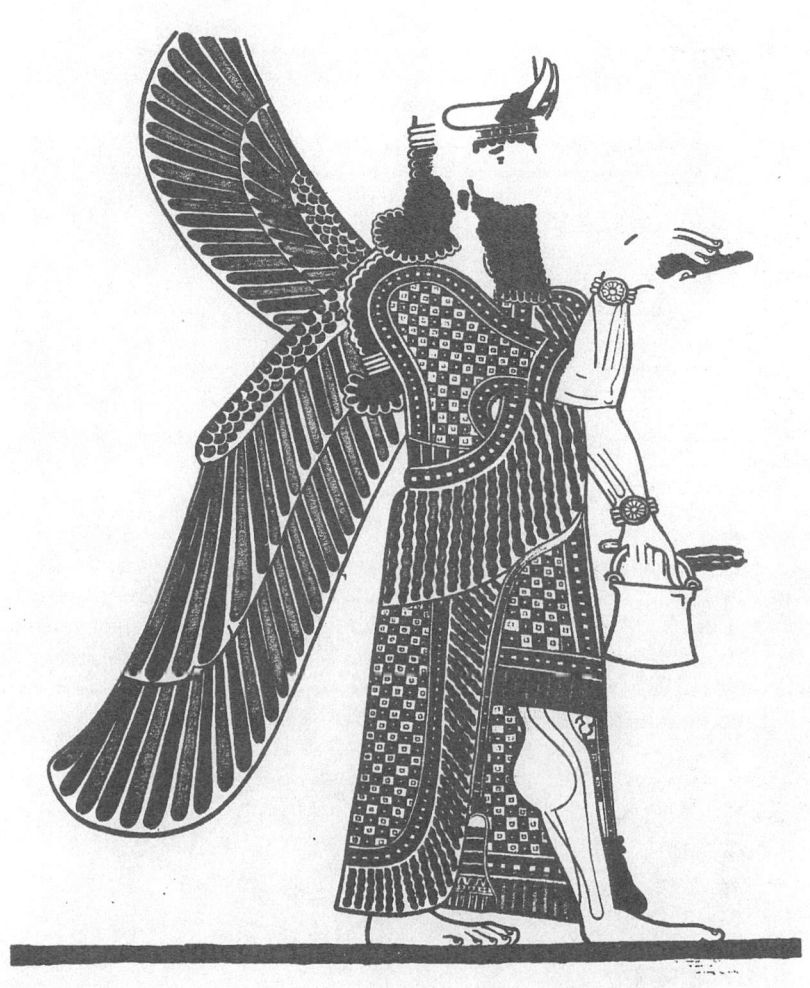

Pl. 16: Cavro, wall painting of winged genie. Passage 24/26 in the Assyrian palace at Til Barsip. Thureau-Dangin and Dunand 1936, pl. XLVII, 2. Musée du Louvre AO 25067 F.

Room 1

Publication: Thureau-Dangin and Dunand 1936, pp. 71–72, color plate facing title page.

The vestibule of the royal residence was extremely damaged and no paintings were found *in situ*. The debris on the floor contained fragments of decorative elements of a frieze that included the lotus, marguerite (rosette), circular

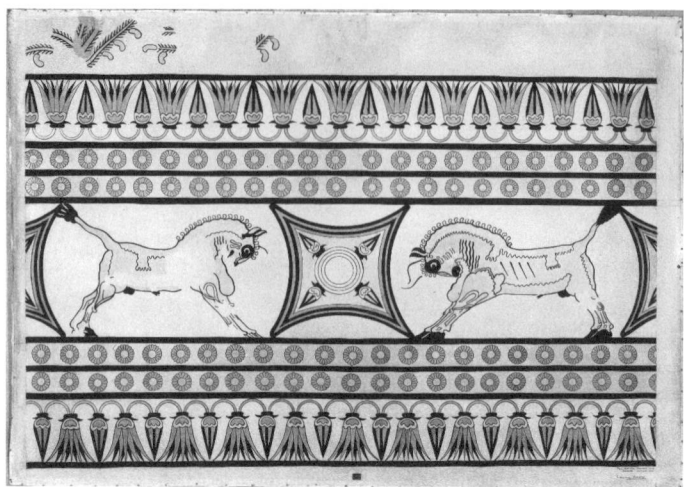

Pl. 17. Cavro, ornamental wall painting with bulls. Room 21 in the
Assyrian palace at Til Barsip. Musée du Louvre AO 25068 A.

motif, and part of the neck and shoulder of a bull. As they were detaching two
blocks of brick, which apparently came from a lower register, the excavators
found a painting showing a naval battle on one of them. The fragment was
published in the volume after a color photograph. No drawings were made
of the decorative fragments.

Room 21

Plate 17.
Cavro's copy: Louvre AO 25068 A.
Publication: Thureau-Dangin and Dunand 1936, p. 71, pl. XLVII; Parrot
    1961, fig. 342.

Room 21 was a long corridor connecting courts B and C. The ornamental
frieze was at a height about 1.90 meters above the level of the floor and
measured 1.23 meters in width. The principal motif of the frieze consists of
two confronting bulls on either side of a cushion-shaped square, and above
and below the animal motif are three decorated bands alternating with plain
red stripes. In the two inner bands are repeats of pink-centered blue rosettes
on a white ground. Each outer band contains a lotus-and-bud garland. The
various parts of the flower and bud are painted in red, light blue or pink, and
the arcading stem is light blue. The pink and light blue are probably faded
versions of the original hues. All the colors of the frieze are outlined in black.

Vestiges of floral elements, trees or shrubs, were recovered above the frieze and those fragmentary motifs indicate that the frieze with bulls covered an earlier painting. The French excavators assigned the ornamental frieze to the early style, noting the absence of the palmette, which they concluded occurs in the late style.

The two confronting bulls stand taut: the forelegs and hind legs are outstretched, the arched heads bend under to touch the chest, and the tails are raised upright at an angle. The animated bulls show a pinkish hide, with blue along the back and extending to the ears, dewlap, and belly. The blue areas on the painted bulls generally correspond to those parts of the winged human-headed bulls (*lamassu*) in stone that were covered with rows of ringlets. This correspondence between the painted and sculpted types indicates that the protective aspect associated with the *lamassu* is also given to the confronting bulls in the painted frieze.

Two other examples of bulls are known from the Til Barsip wall paintings. There was probably another bull led by a wingless genie that was depicted in passage 46/44, but in this instance animal was mostly destroyed at the time of discovery (Louvre AO 25067 H). The standing bull in the passageway connecting rooms 24 and 28, partially hidden behind a winged bird-headed genie (pl. 14), is blue with red filling the back, dewlap, belly and hindquarter. Moreover, small red curls extend outward from the forehead and across the back, and a similar row of ringlets exists on the bulls in the frieze from room 21. The winged human-headed bull in the passageway connecting rooms 24 and 25 (pl. 15) is painted with a blue body, with white on the back, belly, and hindquarter, and red on the far hind leg. The scalloped outer edge of the respective white areas on the body of the bull, together with the curled tip on the back, represent the outline of the ringlets that cover the same areas on the human-headed bulls of the Assyrian stone reliefs. Thus we can infer that the painted bulls at Til Barsip belong to the Assyrian style and the demarcation of ringlets on their bodies, indicated through color and contour, reveals their religious significance.

The cushion-shaped square set between the confronting bulls has two plain red and blue borders and concentric circles, and floral buds decorate the corners. The particular style of the floral buds recurs in the lotus-and-bud garland, where each blue flower rests upon a supporting ring base and is connected by arcaded stems that terminate outward, above the ring base. The open and closed flowers are distinctive for the plain triple arch shape of the blue and pinkish calyx. This detail of the calyx recurs in the lotus-and-bud garland from room 46, and in the flower held by the wingless bearded genie standing behind the winged human-headed bull in passage 24/25. There is a similar but not identical rendering of the lotus flower that is held in the hand of the existing fragment of the kneeling genie from room 27.

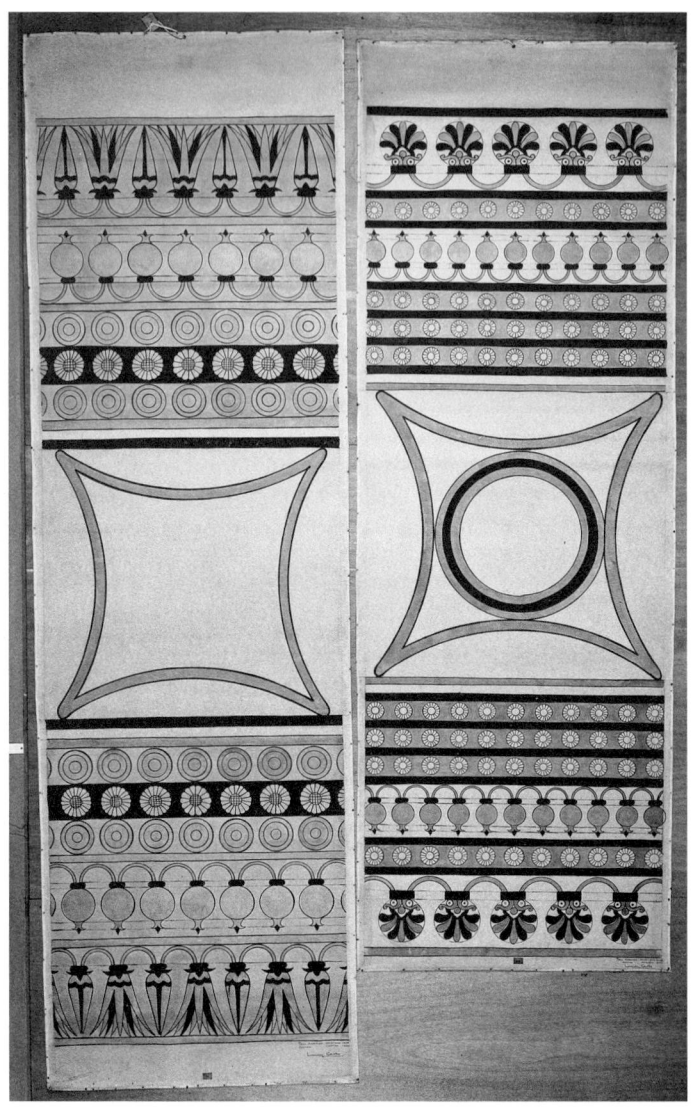

Pl. 18. Cavro, ornamental wall paintings from the Assyrian palace at Til Barsip: (left) room 22, Musée du Louvre AO 25068 F; (right) room 24, Musée du Louvre AO 25068 E.

Room 24

Plate 18, right.
Cavro's copy: Louvre AO 25068 E.
Publications: Thureau-Dangin and Dunand 1936, pp. 52, 57–58, pl. XLV;
    Parrot 1936, pl. 343.

Room 24 was 24 meters long and 7.85 meters wide. The height of the walls
was preserved to about 2.50 meters, except at the southeast angle where it
attained a height of about 5 meters. The room was decorated with painted
scenes and ornamental designs. The paintings in the lower register were 1.50
meters in height and they showed five separate compositions. The ornamental
frieze above the compositions was 2.30 meters in width. An identical frieze
appeared above the apotropaic panel in passages 24/25 and 24/28. Surviving
decorated fragments indicate that the frieze in corridor 28 was similar to
that of room 24. The excavators also noted that in passage 28/27 traces of a
palmette bordering a frieze was like that of room 24.

The ornamental frieze is divided into three sections of equal widths; the
two framing sections are each divided into bands of decorative motifs. A blue
stripe frames the central section, and the only motif drawn by Cavro is a large
square with incurved sides. The white square shows a blue trim and encloses
three narrow concentric circles in blue, red, and blue. The French excavators
distinguished traces of animals that formed the principal decorative motives,
specifically the front paws of a lion and the outline of the hooves of a bull,
and they suggested an alternating sequence between the groups of lions and
bulls. Since there is no indication of animal paws or hooves in Cavro's copy,
it remains unclear what the exact arrangement of the animals was in the
central register.

Each framing section is divided into seven red stripes that alternate with
six decorated bands. Within the three innermost bands are white rosettes
outlined in black on a blue ground; a blue pomegranate garland with red
accents fills the white ground of the fourth band; the fifth band repeats the
rosette motif of the innermost ones; a palmette garland on a white ground
fills the sixth band. Each palmette is inscribed within a partially visible black
circle that is not part of the design but served to facilitate the task of the
artist. The palmette consists of seven petals in alternating red and blue, and
the arcaded blue stems are connected to each flower by a red ring. Horizontal
blue stripes frame the entire ornamental frieze.

In the same chamber, the palmette recurs on the outer garment of a sandal-
footed Assyrian king who is depicted in panel d (AO 25967 C, pl. 20).
Palmettes, arranged equidistant from one another, trim the portion of the
garment that covers the king's left arm, above the red-and-blue twisted belt.
The petals forming each flower alternate in red and blue and there is a red

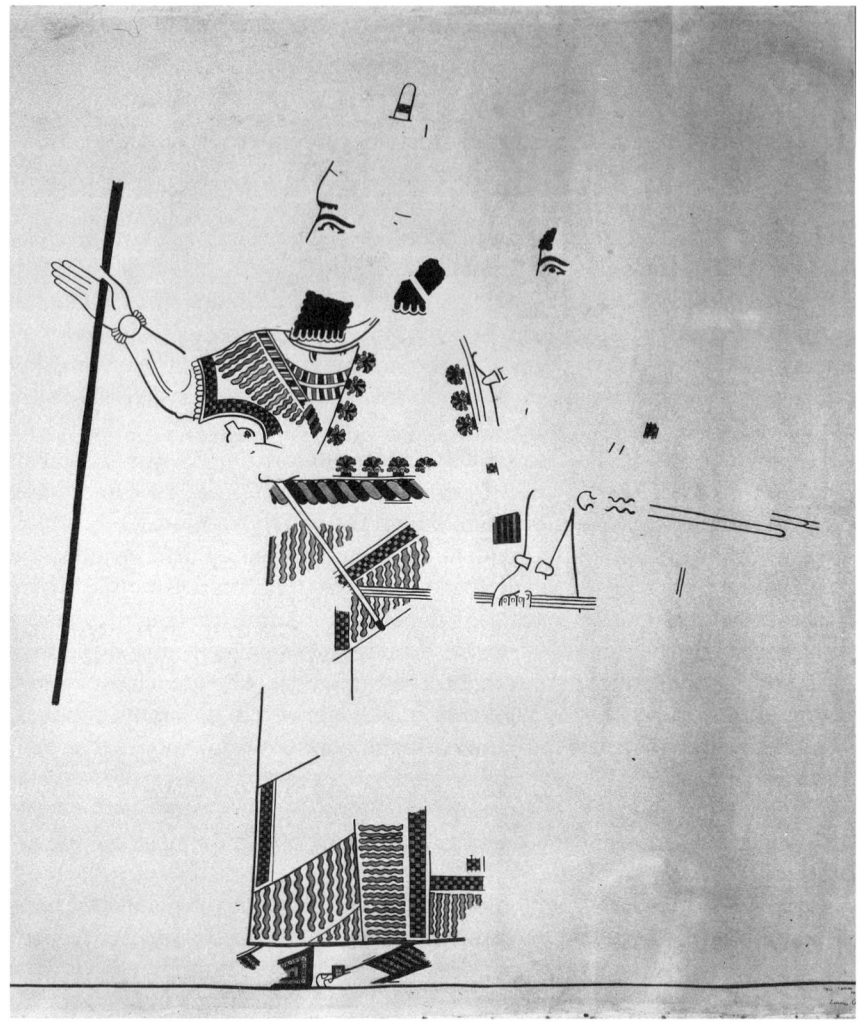

Pl. 20. Cavro, wall painting of an Assyrian king. Room 24, panel d, in
the Assyrian palace at Til Barsip. Musée du Louvre AO 25067 C.

ring at the base. The palmettes, which are not connected, rest upon the outer
edge of the cloth on three sides, producing a triangular effect. The palmette
trim on the garment of the Assyrian king is an unusual decorative addition,
and this detail indicates a contemporary date for panel d and the ornamental
frieze in room 24.

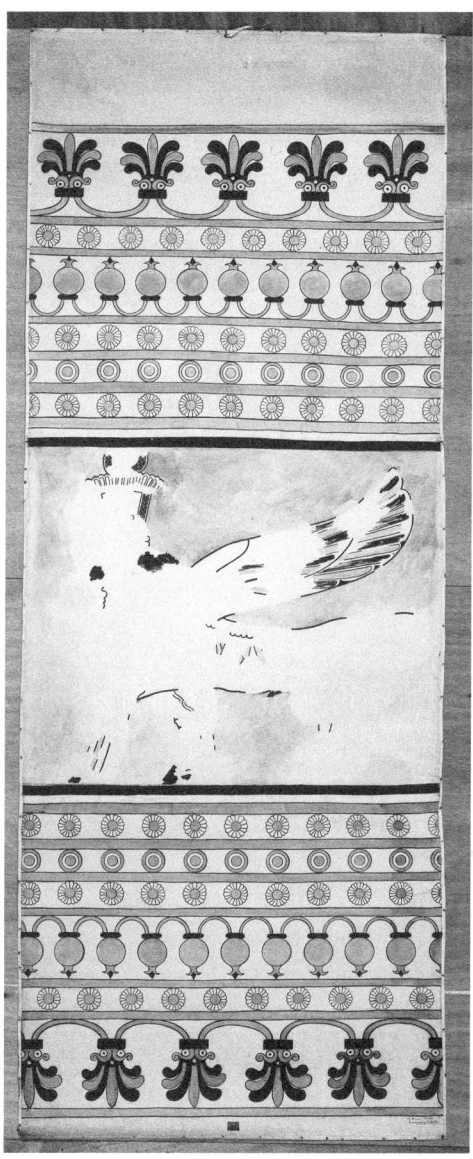

Pl. 19. Cavro, wall painting from room 47 in the Assyrian palace at Til Barsip. Musée du Louvre AO 25068 D.

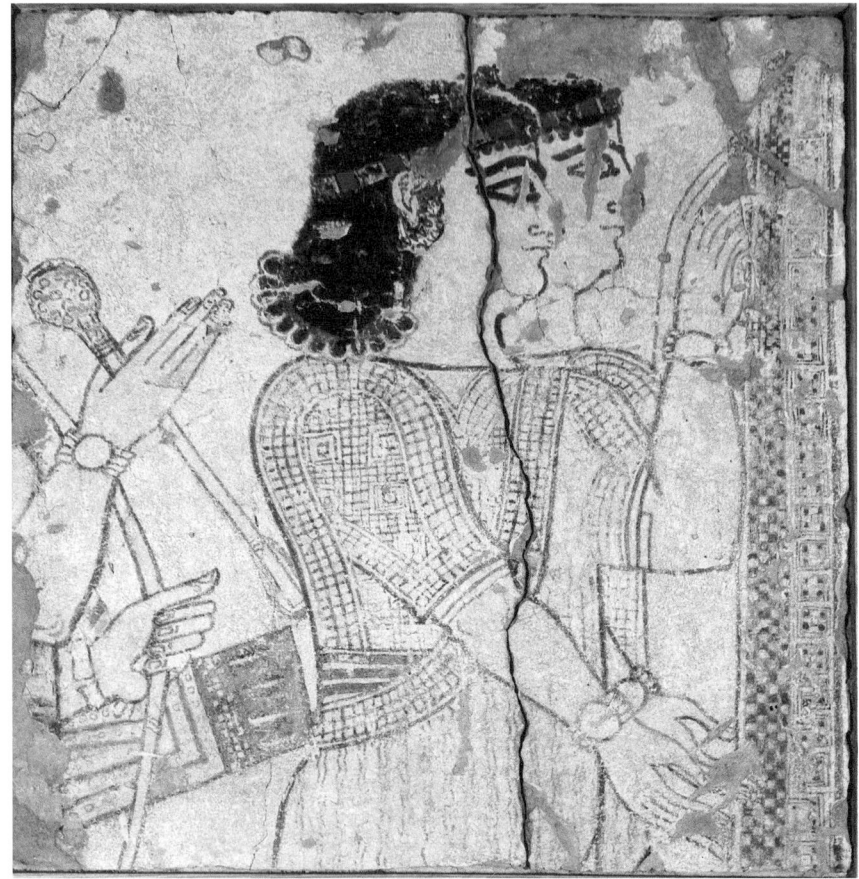

Pl. 21. Assyrian attendants standing behind the throne covered with
patterned cloth. Fragment of wall painting from room 47 at Til
Barsip. Musée du Louvre AO 23011. Photo RMN, Chuzeville.

Room 47

Plate 19.
Cavro's copy: Louvre AO 25068 D.
Publications: Thureau-Dangin and Dunand 1936, pp. 18, 57, 63–67, pl. XLV;
    Parrot 1961, pl. 343.

The large room was partially preserved and in places its walls reached a
height of 4.20 meters. The painted decoration consisted of two types. In the
lower decoration were four panels of narrative scenes about 1.30 meters in
height, and the upper ornamental frieze was about 2.20 meters in height. In

addition, above the 60 centimeters asphalt plinth at the base of the wall was a 10 centimeters high row of concentric circles framed by red stripes. The excavators give a brief description of the ornamental frieze. The principal motif consists of two winged human-headed bulls that stand and confront each other. The repeat of this hybrid group is described as 'two by two.' The border is framed by purely Assyrian elements: marguerites (rosettes), concentric circles, pomegranates, palmettes. The excavators attributed this frieze to the first style.

As drawn by Cavro, reaching to the full height of the central field is a fragmentary portion of a bearded (?) winged human-headed bull that strides to the left. The background is blue. The tall headdress is feathered at the top and surmounted by a large disk. The upturned wing has red and blue feathers, and it is stylistically similar to the wings found on the genies from room 46. Blue stripes separate the six bands of varying widths and decorations, which altogether form the framing sections in mirror image. All the bands have a white ground. In the three inner bands the designs consist of repeats of blue rosettes outlined in black, target circles in blue, and blue rosettes. In the fourth band is a blue pomegranate garland with accents of red. The fifth band shows blue rosettes. In the sixth band the flower of the palmette garland is composed of red and blue petals, and the arcaded blue stems are connected to each flower by a red ring. Minor differences, such as the long petals and the broad arches of the stems, exist between the palmette garlands from room 47 and 24.

Room 22

Plate 18, left
Cavro's copy: Louvre AO 25068 F.
Publications: Thureau-Dangin and Dunand 1936, pp. 15, 68–70, pl. XLV; Parrot 1961, pl. 343.

The French excavators identified room 22, the most spacious of the palace, as the throne room. It measured 9 meters in width and approximately 27 meters in length. In places at the base of the wall, above the 45 centimeters asphalt plinth was a 7 centimeters high double red stripe. A horizontal band of concentric circles appeared at the base of the throne and above it were recognizable traces of confronting lions; unfortunately, the last details are not indicated in the drawing. On several panels the narrative paintings, 1.75 meters in width, showed a procession of horses in groups of two, led by soldiers. On another wall were black outline drawings of six soldiers on horseback (four were reproduced) and traces of standing nude female figures.

The ornamental frieze intact measured 2.50 meters in height. It seems that the principal motif consisted of two confronting bulls on either side of a very simplified geometric shape. Tiny traces remained. As drawn, the ornamental frieze is divided into three horizontal sections of equal width. The two outer ones are decorated in mirror image and frame the central field, which has red border stripes. Within the central field, the only motif drawn is a plain cushion-shaped square delineated by a narrow blue border and outlined in black on a white ground. Blue stripes sub-divide the outer sections into three broad bands of decoration. The innermost band is itself sub-divided into three narrow bands in which respectively are concentric circles in solid blue outlined in black, white marguerites (rosettes) on a red ground, and blue circles. Of further interest, cross-hatching fills the center of each flower.

Two types of garlands fill the second and third outer bands. In the second band is a blue pomegranate garland, and at the base of each fruit a red ring connects the arcaded stems. A lotus-and-bud garland in red and blue fills the third band. The open flower numbers eight petals, in contrast to the seven petals of the lotus from room 46, and nine petals on the lotus from room 21. In addition, on each flower is a scalloped line between the connecting stems with down-turned terminals and the start of the petals. Stylistically, the renderings of the lotus-and-bud garland from room 22 and those from rooms 21 and 46 indicate that the two groups belong to different periods of production.

Discussion

Relying upon Lucien Cavro's renderings of the ornamental wall paintings, an overview of the Til Barsip decorative designs indicates that their production is not contemporary but corresponds to three periods of Assyrian rule. The earliest period is represented by the frieze in room 26, in which the principal motif consists of confronting goats. In the above discussion dealing with the rendering of the goats, comparative material was cited that supports a date between the early to the middle of the eighth century B.C.

The middle period of production is represented by the ornamental designs in rooms 21, 24, 46, 47, and passages 24/25, 24/26, 24/28. Specific motifs and details of the designs make it possible to connect the respective ornamental wall paintings, as follows: (1) the lotus-and-bud garland is rendered the same way in rooms 21 and 46; (2) the rendering of the palmette is similar in rooms 24 and 47, and on the garment of the king in room 24, panel d; (3) the feathered wings are stylistically similar on the figures in rooms 46 and 47, and passages 24/25, 24/26, 24/28. Thus the numbered rooms and passages show the following decorative connections: rooms 21 and 46 (lotus-and-bud garland), rooms 46, 47, and passages 24/25, 24/26, 24/28 (feathered wings), rooms 47, 24, and panel d of room 24 (palmette). From this observation, it is most likely that the ornamental wall paintings in the above-noted rooms and passageways were produced during the second period.

In assigning a probable date to this group of wall paintings, it is useful to look at the depiction of the later frieze from room 21, and to compare it with dated examples. Two monumental stone bulls with ringlets decorating their bodies are known from Arslan Tash, where they stood *in situ* and marked the entrance to a building complex. Each bull is carved from a basalt block, about 2.10 meters in height and 2.40 meters in length, and the inscription on one bull dates the pair to the reign of Tiglath-pileser III.[7] Each animal is compact and stocky, with the broad head on the shortened neck tilted down. Several fragments of a large relief (about 1.07 meters high) of the same period, discovered at Nimrud, represent the front portion of a winged human-headed bull.[8] Lacking from these sculptures is the animated quality existing in the Til Barsip painted bulls. On the other hand, the rendering of the bulls in room 21 finds close parallels with those depicted in the ornamental wall paintings from residence K at Khorsabad, dated to the reign of Sargon II. A winged bull represented in the vast maritime scene on the stone blocks that lined a section of wall in the main court of Sargon's palace at Khorsabad has a leaping pose, its head turned slightly downward and the oblique lines of the fore and hind legs accentuate its active movement.[9] Among the representations of standing bulls found on ivories one bovine animal, set within a cushion-shaped square, combines details seen on both the Til Barsip and Khorsabad bulls.[10] Presumably, the bull carved on the ivory with its distinctive shape reflects a knowledge of the Til Barsip and Khorsabad painted versions.

Earlier, mention was made of the painted fragment of a bull discovered in room 1 of the royal residence at Til Barsip. In all probability it should be attributed to the same period as the bull represented in the frieze from room 21. It is equally likely that the small fragments showing a sea battle were painted at the same time as the fragment of the bull. The probable dates cited for the battle scene range from the reign of Tiglath-pileser III, to Shalmaneser V, to Sargon II, that is, after the middle of the eighth century B.C. Tiglath-pileser III campaigned against the coastal towns along the eastern shores of the Mediterranean that included Sidon and Tyre, and he also fought a battle against a city on an island, which has been identified with

---

[7] Thureau-Dangin *et al* 1931, pp. 56–57, 60–64, plan facing p. 56, fig. 20, pls. IV 1, 2, V, 1. A new edition of the inscription carved on one existing bull is in Tadmor 1994, pp. 205–207. Albenda 1988, pp. 25–26, provides a brief study of the two bulls, which are housed in the Musée du Louvre.

[8] Sobolewski 1982, pp. 264–266, fig. 9.

[9] Albenda 1983, pp. 25–26, pls. 3, 9.

[10] Mallowan and Davies 1970, p. 41, fig. 125.

Arvad.[11] Shalmaneser V reigned five years (726–722), and during that time laid siege to Tyre on two separate occasions.[12] Relations between Tyre and Assyria changed when Sargon II assumed the rule of Assyria. Sargon's royal inscriptions record sea-battles against the Ionians (probably Greek pirates), in order to protect the northeastern Mediterranean Sea. Presumably, as the means to clear the sea of pirates, Sargon had to use a Phoenician navy, and Tyre put its ships at the disposal of the Assyrian king for the campaign.[13]

The fragmentary Til Barsip painted sea battle scene reveals an episode of close combat, since one attacking soldier (Assyrian?) grips the arm of an opponent who stands on the enemy ship. Of particular interest is the representation of a single bank of oars on the presumably Phoenician ship, and this differs from the two banks of oars on the ships or biremes that are illustrated in the maritime scenes depicted on the palace wall reliefs of the seventh century Assyrian king, Sennacherib.[14] It may also be noted that the merchant ships depicted in the maritime scene of Sargon II, in which the winged bull and other mythical and sea creatures appear, likewise show a single bank of oars. Thus, it seems unlikely that the Til Barsip painted scene is datable to Sennacherib's reign.

The ornamental friezes discovered in rooms 22, 25 and 27 represent the latest period of production. The one comparative motif that links the wall paintings is the flower of the lotus-and-bud garland. In room 25 the treatment of the bud in the four corners of the cushion-shaped square is similar to that given to the bud in the garland in room 22. In addition, the triangular projection at the base of the blue-petal flower in room 25 recurs in the red-and-blue lotus of room 22. This last detail provides the indication that both floral motifs are contemporary. A parallel for the rendering of the lotus flower occurs on the stone threshold slabs dated to the reign of Sennacherib (pl. 22).[15] On the carved stone slabs the terminals of the floral stems emerge above the ring base and curve down on each side, with a triangular projection between the ring and the scalloped line. In the Til Barsip paintings however the stem terminals, ring base and triangular projection merge into a unified shape.

---

[11] Tadmor 1994, pp. 176–177.
[12] On this subject, see Katzenstein 1973, pp. 225 ff.
[13] Ibid, pp. 233 ff.
[14] Barnett *et al* 1998, pp. 52–54, 71–72, pls. 38–41, 133–136, 139: nos. 30a–d, 31a, 39, 195a–b, 196a, 197,199.
[15] See: ibid, pp. 137–138, pls. 498–499: nos. 676–681; Albenda 1978, pp. 14–16, pls. 8–15.

Pl. 22. Bell, threshold slab from Kuyunjik (Nineveh), 'between winged
bulls and chamber C.' *Original Drawings* IV, 10. British Museum.

Til Barsip Textile Patterns

A conclusion made earlier is that the ornamental paintings from rooms 25
(pl. 11) and 46 (pl. 13) are to be dated to two different periods of artistic
production. The conclusion is based upon the way in which the wings of the
female genies are rendered, and on the lotus-and-bud garland of the frieze in
room 46, which is strikingly different from the unusual floral garland found
in the frieze from room 25. The assertion is made that the ornamental frieze
from room 25 is of a later date than the paintings in room 46 and is probably
datable to the reign of Sennacherib. If this assertion is correct, one wonders

whether the unusual flower may have been inspired by the cotton plant (see below), first mentioned in the royal inscriptions of Sennacherib, albeit the flower of the garland is painted blue and white with accents of red.

Another notable difference between the two friezes is the pattern on the dress of the respective winged genies. The pattern on the dress of the genies from room 46 is a checkered design in red and blue, and the checkered trim of the garment shows a row of red and white that alternates with a row of white and blue. The pattern on the dress of the genies from room 25 consists of vertical and horizontal striations in red; on the existing fragment the red striations form a kind of plaid design, which consists of large plain squares framed by closely spaced vertical and horizontal lines. Textile patterns also occur on the garments of several representations of one or more Assyrian kings, and on those of the winged and wingless genies and ranked officials. A description of these patterns and a comparative study of the textile patterns found on the stone reliefs dated to the reigns of the respective Assyrian kings, may furnish evidence for the dating of specific wall paintings at Til Barsip.

Textiles

Patterned textiles may be made in one of three ways: (1) the weaving technique, using multicolored threads, (2) embroidery, stitching the design onto a woven fabric, and (3) appliqué, in which decorations such as beads, buttons, and other materials including block printing are attached to the cloth. All three methods were already known in Pharaonic Egypt of the second millennium B.C.[16] Texts of the late Assyrian period list different kinds of textiles, and the textiles identified as *birmu*, meaning 'multicolored', must be patterned cloths. In the Near East, preserved patterned cloths made during the time of Assyrian prominence are extremely rare. One group of small finds comes from the tumuli at Gordion in Central Anatolia. Among the fragmentary textiles recovered from the Phrygian capital are cloths with geometric patterning, including stripes, lozenges, and meanders. The yarns of the plain and patterned cloths are made of vegetable and animal fibers. The Gordion textiles are dated to the end of the eighth century B.C.[17] Also dated to about the same time are the textile fragments from the excavated graves of royal women at Nimrud.[18] Laboratory analysis of several tabby woven fragments indicates that the yarns of the textiles discovered in the three coffins were made of flax; thus the fragments are linen cloths. In one coffin

---

[16] It is of interest to note that the textiles discovered in the tomb of the pharaoh Tutankhamun (1334–1325 B.C.) include pattern-woven and embroidered bands, and tapestry-woven fabrics; see Hall 1986, pp. 40–47. On the subject of textiles, two useful books that contain extensive bibliography are: Barber 1991; Geijer, 1979.

[17] Mellink 1981, pp. 269–270.

[18] E. Crowfoot 1995, pp. 114–118, fig. 5.

small fragments of well-preserved fabrics included areas of embroidery, and gold and carnelian beads lying in the folds of another textile may have been sewn to adorn a garment. Two little tassels, manufactured as separate items, are decorated with a lattice pattern in two colors, tan and white. Lists of garments and textiles in Assyrian texts include wraps that are embroidered (*ṣuppu*), wool of poor quality or felted (*biršu, bir*), linen (*kitû*), and a thin, fine garment (*qatattu*). A garment made of byssus (*būsu*) is also mentioned, and the fabric is linen of the highest quality.[19]

Cotton

One fiber not identified in neo-Assyrian texts is cotton. However, the fiber is described in the inscriptions of the Assyrian king Sennacherib; in one place he boasts of the variety of plants and fruit-bearing trees that were planted in his botanical garden at Nineveh, and mentions 'trees bearing wool.' He adds further, 'the wool-bearing trees they sheared and wove into garments.'[20] Although brief, this statement indicates a direct knowledge of the cotton plant, of its fiber-producing properties, and of the production of cotton cloth. The origin of cotton during that period would have been India, although the production of cotton may have already spread westward by the early first millennium B.C.; it eventually reached Egypt by the mid-millennium. The plant was probably brought to Assyria either as tribute from one of its eastern territories or from Elam, or through overland trade, perhaps by way of Nippur. The Babylonian city was an important caravan commerce center along the east-west trading route situated south of Assyria.[21]

The flower of the cotton plant (genus *gossypium*) is typically white or yellow, sometimes red, and may have purple-red spots. The flower blooms for a very short time, generally just for a day, wilts and is replaced by small green triangular pods, and after two or more months the pod bursts open and out pops a fluffy ball of cotton. The typical cotton plant has palmette-shape lobed leaves. Since cotton was known to the Assyrians by the start of the seventh century B.C., but not identified in the texts, A. Leo Oppenheim in his article on overland trade during the mid-first millennium B.C. argues in favor of interpreting either *ṭību* or *ṭumânu* as cotton, and the other word as silk.[22]

---

[19] Fales and Postgate 1992, pp. XXVI–XXIX. For additional discussion, see Oppenheim 1967, pp. 244–251.
[20] Luckenbill 1927, nos. 395, 402. The texts mention that the royal park contained plants that came from the mountains, Hatti (Syria), and Chaldea; the last-named region seems the most likely source for the import of the cotton plant.
[21] Cole 1996, pp. 62–67.
[22] Oppenheim 1967, pp. 251–253. Knowledge of silk and its method of production may have reached the Near East via caravan trade originating in Central Asia. Representations of bactrian

Within the scenes showing the transport of huge bull sculptures on the wall reliefs in room 6 of Sennacherib's palace at Nineveh, there is a botanical meadow of shrubs, coniferous and fruit-bearing trees growing upon the low lying hills nearby.[23] Readily identifiable are the pomegranate and grapes growing on their respective trees. One type of tree of particular interest that occurs several times within the same landscape has been identified as a fig-bearing tree. As illustrated on the bas-relief, this tree has broad leaves showing five fingerlike leaflets (quinquefoliolate) with slightly incised margins and unlike the fig, which is oblong or pear-like in shape, its small 'fruit' has a narrow elongated shape. The fruit may not be a fig at all, and one possibility here is that the Assyrian artist attempted to depict the cotton pod or capsule, in which case the tree would be identifiable as the cotton plant. In a few examples one can detect a triangular or modified zigzag line at the base; this could represent the triangular shape of the bracts supporting the pods or capsules containing the cotton fiber.[24] On another wall relief discovered in the throne room of the same palace, there appears a fortified foreign city and outside its walls is a long hedge of alternating fruit-bearing trees: grapevine, pomegranate, and the tree with the fruit of elongated shape or cotton pod.[25] The location of this landscaped scene must be in a territory to the west of Assyria, since the row of round shields placed along the top of the outer city walls is a protective device that occurs on other fortified walls of cities identified as Tyre (throne room) and Lachish (room 36).[26] The placement of the grove of trees at the base of the stone slab, in front of the fortified city, and the relatively prominent size given to the individual plants, all reaching to the same height, highlights the probable importance of the plants for the economy of this unnamed city.

Of further interest, trees with leaves somewhat similar in appearance occur among the groves of trees in the open fields surrounding the embattled city of Lachish, carved on another series of wall reliefs in room 36 of Sennacherib's palace.[27] However, on some of those trees the fruits are rounder and may represent cotton pods, but their shape also raises the possibility that the fruits are figs and the tree-type would then represent the Sycamore fig. Nonetheless, an identity with the cotton plant remains a viable option for the

---

camels in art works dated to the reign of Shalmaneser III may be instructive in this matter; see Mitchell 2000, pp. 187–190.

[23] Barnett *et al* 1998, pp. 67–68, pls. 110, 112–119, nos. 150a, 152a–b, 153a–b, 156a–156c, 157b.

[24] For close-up views of the fruit tree, see: Fuchs and Parpola 2001, fig. 22; Parpola, 1987, fig. 36.

[25] Barnett *et al* 1998, pp. 53–54, pls. 46–47, nos. 36, 36a–b.

[26] Ibid, pp. 52–53, 101–103, pls. 38–39, 328–330, nos. 30a–b, 430a, 431a. A drawing from room 5 shows an isolated view of a similar structure. Ibid, p. 57, pl. 57, no. 59a.

[27] Ibid, pls. 338–339, nos. 434a, 434c.

trees bearing the palmette-shape lobed leaves. This identification would add credibility to the suggestion that another possible source for the knowledge of the cotton plant, mentioned by Sennacherib in his royal inscriptions, is the cultivation of this crop to the west of Assyria, in the south-coastal areas near the Mediterranean Sea.

Assyrian knowledge of the cotton plant and of its use for the production of cotton fabrics, which incidentally can be more easily dyed than wool, may have inspired the design of the floral garland in room 25 of the royal residence at Til Barsip (pl. 11). The representation of the flower is unique and, after all, may be a decorative interpretation of the mature cotton capsule viewed from the side, which typically has four chambers when seen from above. If this interpretation is correct, one wonders whether the open flower adorning the headbands of the female genies in the central register of the same ornamental frieze, which also extended to room 27, is the cotton flower that blooms briefly before it dies, and is replaced by the triangular cotton pod.

Certainly, it was not unusual for the artists of the Assyrian kings to include specific plants and flora within the larger landscape compositions designed for the palace wall reliefs, and sometimes those plants are mentioned in the texts. Several administrative texts, dated to the reign of Sargon II, mention the transport of a substantial number of apple trees intended for the gardens of the king's new residence at Khorsabad and, according to the texts, the saplings of apple and other fruit trees came from the province of Laqe, and the cities of Shaddikani, and Nemet-Ishtar.[28] These named places provide a transport route that originates in the middle Euphrates region. Apple trees are identifiable among a wooded landscape scene depicted on the wall reliefs in room 7 of Sargon's palace at Khorsabad, and when the French excavators first exposed the stone reliefs, they noted that the round fruits of those trees were painted red.[29] A botanical garden with exotic flora is attested on Ashurbanipal's wall reliefs from the North Palace at Nineveh. The representations of flowering plants include the lily, sunflower, and mandrake (*mandragora*) – the latter flower is probably an import from Egypt – as well as grapevines wrapped around or 'wedded' to coniferous trees.[30] Unfortunately, since no decorative wall paintings were excavated in the North Palace, nor are there any wall paintings datable with certainty to that king's reign, there is at present no evidence that one or more of these flowers were included in the design of ornamental paintings that may have embellished the interiors of the royal residence.

---

[28] Parpola 1987, nos. 222, 226–227. For locations of the places mentioned, see map in folder; Parpola and Porter 2001, maps 3, 4, 9.
[29] Albenda 1986, p. 139, pls. 89–90. Apples on a branch are identified among the plant attachments that decorated Puabi's headdress, found in her tomb at Ur; see Miller 2000, p. 154, figs. 2, 7, 8.
[30] See: Barnett 1976, pp. 38–39, pl. XV; Albenda 1974, p. 5.

Silk

After his campaigns against Babylon and the Arab and Aramean tribes that had settled in the cities on the lower Euphrates, Sennacherib states that he received from the governor of the city of Hararate precious metals, animals, and *musukkannu* trees, which Luckenbill translates as 'great mulberry trees.'[31] The mention of a specific tree other than the date palm from a location south of Assyria is notable. Like the wool-bearing tree there must have been some importance associated with that plant, including its use for the manufacture of wood products.[32] The 'white' mulberry tree is necessary to the domesticated silk worm belonging to the moth family *Bombycidae*, since the insect feeds on the leaves of the tree. The fiber secretions made by the domestic worm, when it spins itself into a cocoon, produce the silk thread used to make a silk fabric. The worm is killed with boiling water before it leaves the cocoon, and the thread can then be wound off or reeled. The thread is known as 'cultivated' silk. This method of silk production was for many centuries known only in ancient China.[33]

Another family of silkworms, *Saturniidae*, feeds on a variety of plants and trees, including the juniper and oak trees, and if the worm is not killed in the cocoon and eats its way out, then the method of making a thread is to card and spin the fibers, the same way as with wool. Among the wild silkworm species of moths that produce silk while in the larva stage are the *Pachypasa otus* and *Saturnia pyri*, whose wings are patterned with wavy lines of varied hues and prominent 'eye spots' of differentiating tones.[34] The moths are a Mediterranean species found in several countries bordering the Mediterranean Sea, and as far northeast as Armenia.

However another identification for *musukkannu* tree has been proposed, and it is now considered to be the Dalbergia sisso. This tree has an origin to the Indus and a distinguishing feature is its hardness of wood.[35] Therefore, much more evidence is necessary before one can assert that the practice of obtaining cultivated silk in Western Asia began as early as the seventh century B.C. On the other hand, among the curses stated in the accession texts of Esarhaddon is the following: 'as a caterpillar does not see and does not return to its cocoon, so may you not return to your women, your sons, your

---

[31] Luckenbill 1927, nos. 265, 275.
[32] According to the Rassam Cylinder, mulberry and cypress trees, which grew large and were the products of the orchards, were cut down and used for the building of the royal palace. Luckenbill 1927, no. 402. It may be of interest to note that *musukkannu* tree is not among the tree-toponyms cited by Rowton 1967, pp. 265–274, nor is the mulberry tree mentioned.
[33] See: Geijer 1979, pp. 4–6; Barber 1991, pp. 30–32.
[34] For the identification of the winged insects on two vessels in the miniature flotilla wall painting from Akrotiri, Thera, which possibly derive from the moth *Saturnia pyri*, see Coutsis 2000, pp. 580–582, fig. 3.
[35] See: Postgate 1992, p. 83; Fuchs and Parpola 2001, p. 240, no. 248.

daughters, your houses.'[36] The description of the worm leaving its cocoon may be an indication that wild silk production was developed or known in Western Asia by the late Neo-Assyrian period.

Archaeological evidence for the wild silkworm comes from the site of Akrotiri on the island of Santorini in the Mediterranean Sea. Beneath the destruction level dated earlier than the mid second millennium B.C., a Lepidoptera cocoon was recovered. The cocoon was broken on the upper part as if the moth had emerged, and it has been identified possibly as *Pachypasa otus*. According to one scholar, the discovery of the wild silk cocoon thus confirms wild silk production at an early period in the Aegean. An explanation given for the existence of the cocoon in an urban area is its exploitation by the inhabitants of the settlement; however, the cocoon could have been imported from another center and processed on the island. At a much later date, Aristotle and Pliny discuss the production of 'wild silk', which they link with several Greek islands.[37] If one accepts the early cultivation of wild silk in the Aegean and its continuation through the centuries, it is then reasonable to surmise that later contacts with the Aegean region led the Assyrians to become aware of the importance of the silkworm, if indirectly, as reflected in the quote of Esarhaddon cited above. Cypriot, Syrian and seacoast cities furnished products for the rebuilding of the royal palace by that king at Nineveh, and luxury items, which were also sent to Assyria, may have included textiles containing silk threads.[38]

Patterns

In the Til Barsip wall paintings, the colors used for the textile patterns are limited to red, blue, black, and white. Laboratory analysis of the pigments found in the wall paintings confirms that the red is a natural ochre that occurs widely, the blue is a mixture of silicate, copper and calcium, known as 'Egyptian blue,' the black is a carbon of animal or vegetable origin, and the white foundation is a crystallized calcium carbonate.[39] In Assyrian texts the colors named for the dyed textiles are red, black and white. Several descriptions are cited for red, which is qualified as 'port,' perhaps a commercial red; as 'country,' perhaps of the mountain or natural red; a limestone red; and a scarlet dye for red wool. Madder is also mentioned, and this common red dye comes from the plant *Rubia tinctorum*. Kermes is a dye of animal origin

---

[36] Parpola and Watanabe 1988, pp. 53–54, no.79.

[37] Panagiotakopulu 2000, pp. 586–587, fig. 1. The author notes that the silkworm *Saturnia pyri* produces strong and glossy silk, dark brown in color, while the silk from *Pachypasa otus* is paler and finer.

[38] Pritchard 1969, p. 291. Several of the royal names and toponyms enumerated for the ten tributaries from Cyprus are identified with Greek names, confirming the presence of Cypriot Greeks; see Lipinski 1991, pp. 58–64.

[39] See: Thureau-Dangin and Dunand 1936, pp. 46–48; Beyer 1989, p 57.

which derives from certain species of scale insects (*kermo-coccus vermillo*) that feed on oak trees; it may be the scarlet dye mentioned in the Assyrian texts.[40]

Blue is not cited among the Assyrian list of colors. However, descriptive terms relating to blue do occur in Near Eastern texts of various dates, and two Akkadian terms of particular interest are *argamannu* and *takiltu*.[41] The two terms are well-known dyes that are produced from shell-fish or mollusks, and they are associated with the Phoenician purple dye industry.[42] The Tyrian purple or *argamannu* is a red-purple dye or crimson and *takiltu* is specifically of the blue-purple or hyacinth variety. Here, one may postulate whether the Assyrian 'red of the port' may pertain to Tyrian purple. Turning to the Til Barsip wall paintings, it should be pointed out that the blue and red, although separated by thin black lines, can optically effect the blending of those hues to produce a blue-red or red-violet that is a shade of purple. This optical phenomenon comes to the fore particularly when viewing the dress on the genie painted in passage 24/25 (pl. 15), which is decorated with a checkerboard pattern of small squares that alternate in blue and red. The same blue-and-red pattern of checks extends to the decorated trim of the garment. It may be pointed out that the border trim on the multicolored garments worn by various figures consists of three rows of checks in different color arrangements; for example, a horizontal row of red-blue-red alternates with blue-white-blue (pl. 16), or blue-white-blue alternates with white-red-white (pl. 14).

The textile pattern used for the tunic of the winged genie in passage 24/26 (pl. 16), holding a cone and bucket in the right and left hands respectively, consists of alternating blue and white squares and within each square is a small white square outlined in black. One wonders whether the absence of red may be an artistic attempt to emphasize the blue color of the garment, perhaps alluding to *takiltu*, while the white would of course provide the necessary contrast, so as not to produce too dark an appearance. In passage 24/28 the pattern on the garment of the winged bird-headed genie leading a bull (pl. 14) shows continuous rows of small hexagons outlined in black on a white ground, with alternating red and blue centers. An identical pattern of hexagons appears on the garment of the wingless genie leading a bull (mostly destroyed) in passage 46/44 (Louvre AO 25067 H). The unusual design embellishing the garments of the two genies indicates a contemporary

---

[40] Fales and Postgate 1992, p. XXVIII. Red dyes and dyes of other colors are discussed at length in Barber 1991, pp. 227–235.

[41] Landsberger1967, pp. 154–166.

[42] See: Ziderman, 1987, pp. 25–33, figs.1–2; Ziderman 1990, pp. 98–103. For arguments against the theory presented by Ziderman, with regard to the *Murex trunculus* as the source of tekelet, see: McGovern and Michel 1988, pp. 81–83; Saltzman 1988, pp 83–84; Elsner 1988, pp. 87–88. For response to the arguments, see Ziderman 1988, pp. 84–87.

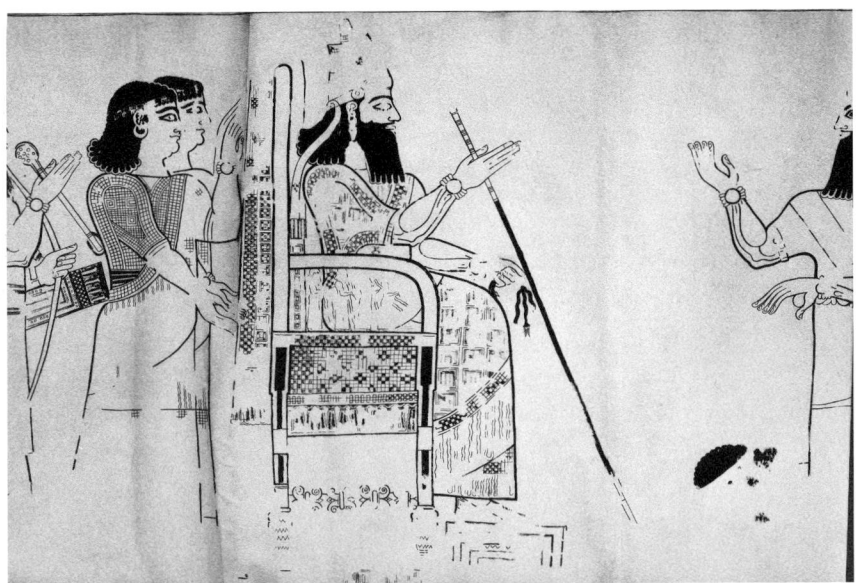

Pl. 23. Cavro, detail: wall painting of an enthroned Assyrian king. Room 47, panels a, b, c, in the Assyrian palace at Til Barsip. Musée du Louvre AO 25067 T.

date for the two wall paintings, as well as the probability that the same artist produced the paintings.

Less elaborate but equally interesting are the patterns displayed on the costumes of several Assyrian officials. In room 24, on panel i, is an official of high rank (pl. 24) facing the Assyrian king – unfortunately destroyed except for the lower portion – who is seated on a wheeled throne. His fringed mantle covering the arm and the dress is entirely patterned with rows of blue squares on a white ground, and within each square is a white square. The trim of the same garment consists of rows of similar but smaller squares. In the same chamber, on panels a, b, c, one of the Assyrian king's military guards is a mace-bearing soldier whose garment is decorated with a design made from black stripes on a white ground (pl. 25). The plaid-like design shows an overall pattern of vertical and horizontal bands that form large squares. The bands are divided into small squares with a dot in the center, and within each large square is a smaller square with a dot in the center. The absence of color on the soldier's costume in all probability is not an artistic oversight, since the evidence from the other Til Barsip wall paintings indicates that the use of multicolored garments in the Assyrian administration was restricted to persons of high rank, as well as to divine figures.

Mention should be made of the plaid design decorating the garments of the winged genies in the ornamental frieze from room 27. The motif consists

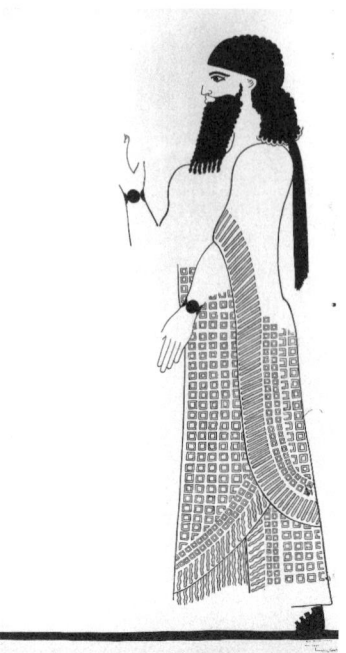

Pl. 24. Cavro, detail: wall painting of an Assyrian court official. Room 24, panel i, in the Assyrian palace at Til Barsip. Musée du Louvre AO 25067 D.

entirely of red horizontal and vertical lines, and may be compared to the plaid cloths discovered in ancient nomadic burials in central Asia, dated to the early first millennium B.C.[43] Another pattern that deserves attention is the stepped border decoration on the dress of a foreign woman member of a group of desert people represented in room 24.[44] The white cloth of the garment is decorated with an attractive woven design of an elaborate stepped motif in red and blue, with a broad red band near the outer fringes of the shawl covering the head and dress. A similar woven design appears on the garment of a woman who is represented on a wall relief discovered in the Southwest Palace at Nineveh.[45] She is among the captive people led away from a city that stands in the midst of marshes in Southern Babylonia.

[43] Barber 1999, pp. 133–141, pls. 13, 14A, points out the similarity of the twilled plaid design of several fragmentary cloths discovered in the Qizilchoqa cemetery with the Scottish kilt, and suggests that the mummies may have been ancestors of the historic Celts. A second class of plaid discovered in the cemetery consists of plain white cloth with warp and weft stripes in blue and red repeated at regular intervals.
[44] Thureau-Dangin and Dunand 1936, pl. LI.
[45] Barnett *et al* 1998, pp. 122–123, pl. 425, no. 549.

Probably the painted scene from room 24 showing Assyrian soldiers and the desert people, members of an Arab tribe, should be dated to the reign of Sennacherib.

The most elaborately patterned garments are those worn by the two representations of an enthroned king shown in the Til Barsip wall paintings. Modern scholars have debated the identity of the royal person. Added to the problem of identification is that originally nine depictions of an Assyrian king occurred among the Til Barsip wall paintings, and that probably several different kings were portrayed. One enthroned Assyrian king appears in the center of a long narrative scene, which shows a procession of tributaries advancing to the royal person, and behind him is a line of administrative and military personnel (room 47, panels a, b, c). Two patterned textiles associated with the royal person are particularly noteworthy (pl. 23). They are the king's shawl and dress, and the fringed fabric folded over the back of the high-back chair or throne, the open side of which is carved with upright figures, unfortunately mostly destroyed. Much of the design on the king's dress was destroyed at the time of discovery.

An examination of Cavro's copy of the painting reveals that the pattern on the king's garment consists of rows of squares. Each square has an outer blue border followed by a narrow white border that surrounds a motif of two white stripes connected by a third white stripe on the upper side, on a red ground. The motif is not readily identifiable, but seems to represent an architectural structure. The fabric on the back of the chair is a small flat woven blanket and may be the *dappastu* of the Assyrian texts, which sometimes served as a rug (pl. 21). The fabric shows a simple design of red and blue checks, bordered by a wide white trim that is likewise decorated. The design on the trim consists of a single row of individual squares outlined in blue, and within each square is a triple row of checks in a horizontal row of red, white, red, alternating with white, blue, white, alternating in turn with red, white, red.

In the second example of the enthroned Assyrian king (room 24, panels a, b, c), the royal figure is also at the center of a scene with a long line of subjugated foreigners advancing toward him, while his military personnel stand behind him (pl. 25). The king's shawl and dress are richly decorated with an identical pattern, which consists of rows of large red squares with a white outer border and a white rosette outlined in black in each square. The background surrounding the squares is blue, and this area is decorated with small white circles arranged around the squares. Visually, the overall effect of the king's complete dress, with its intense color scheme and integrated variety of patterned motifs, imparts richness assuredly suitable for royalty.

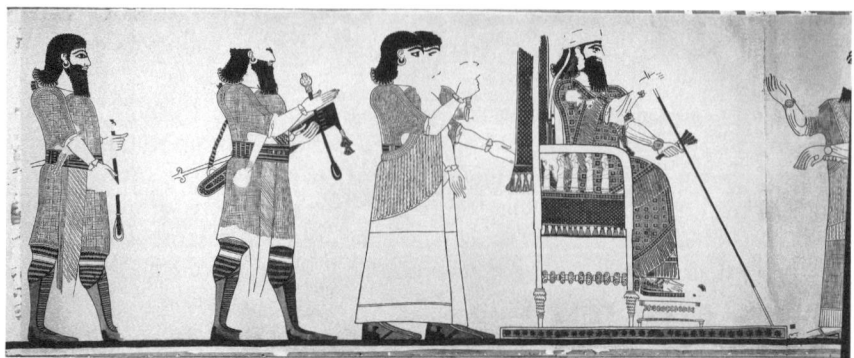

Pl. 25. Cavro, detail: wall painting of an enthroned Assyrian king. Wall painting from room 24, panels a, b, c, in the Assyrian palace at Til Barsip. Musée du Louvre AO 25067 N.

Discussion of textile designs

The variety of patterns found on the garments of the personages represented in the Til Barsip wall paintings are distinctive and may find parallels with textile patterns depicted elsewhere in Assyrian and non-Assyrian art. A survey of the decorative garments represented on wall reliefs, stone monuments, and glazed bricks, is therefore useful. The information that may be obtained would relate to contemporary tastes and the possible transmission of decorative ideas in textile art, and therefore help establish more precise dates for several of the Til Barsip wall paintings.

During the time that Layard excavated the ninth century B.C. Northwest Palace of Ashurnasirpal II at Nimrud, he made line drawings of the existing wall reliefs. Among his drawings are renderings of decorations that adorned the garments of the Assyrian king, court officials and genies.[46] The elaborate figural and floral motifs on the front of the garments must represent embroidery. Decorated border bands also appear on the respective garments used as edging for the flounced shawls, and as decorative trims attached to the garments. On the wall reliefs of Ashurnasirpal II, the decorated border bands are of two types, figural and patterned. The figural motifs included scenes of the royal hunt, animals flanking trees, winged genies, and lions and bulls in close combat.[47] The patterned bands show continuous repeats of individual motifs that include the rosette and concentric squares, and these motifs are

---

[46] For an example of Layard's drawing of the king's costume embellished with elaborate designs and views of the decorated bands on several existing reliefs, see Paley 1976, pp. 35–36, pls. 19b, 22a, 23c, 24a–c, 25a.
[47] Canby 1974, pp. 47–49, suggests that foreigners carved the figural motifs on the garment trims, and that the trims represent appliqué in metal. For a critical response and discussion of ancient textiles, see Barrelet 1977, pp. 51–90.

generally separated by a vertical line. It is likely that the decorative designs are woven patterns, or possibly embroidery on narrow woven cloths.

A stone stele discovered at Tell Abta, a site west of modern Mosul, depicts Bel-harran-belu-usur who served as palace herald under the Assyrian king Tiglath-pileser III and as governor of Guzana (modern Tell Halaf) under the king's successor, Shalmaneser V.[48] The stele is carved in a style that may be described as provincial, when compared to stone carvings from the royal workshop of Assyria. However, it is the dress of the official that commands our attention. The garment shows an all-over pattern of continuous concentric rectangles, and on one shoulder is a large ornament in the shape of a rosette or rayed flower. This prominent piece of jewelry alludes to the high status of the Assyrian official, since the rosette had symbolic meaning in Assyria. The emblematic use of the rosette for costume decoration was generally reserved for the Assyrian king and officials of high rank and genies, as shown in the visual arts; for example, rosette appliqués invariably decorated the royal headdress of Assyrian kings.

The all-over geometric patterning on Bel-harran-belu-usur's dress is new in monumental Assyrian art and, in this period, it is unusual for a ranked official to be shown wearing a richly patterned garment. By contrast, on his wall reliefs the contemporary Assyrian king wears a plain garment, and the only decorative feature is the repeat of rectangles on the narrow border band of the shawl.[49] Thus, it is likely that the patterned textile – probably multicolored – depicted on the stele of Bel-harran-belu-usur represents an imported luxury item.

A probable source for the imported cloth is Anatolia. On the large rock relief at Ivriz, near Konya in southwest Anatolia, the local king Warpalawas, a contemporary of Tiglath-pileser III, is depicted wearing a garment decorated with a grid design similar to the one found on the dress worn by the Assyrian governor.[50] Of further interest, the Ivriz garment shows a rectangular pattern with meander hooks near the bottom, and an identical motif occurs on one of the fragmentary cloths excavated at Gordion.

All-over geometric patterning on the garments of Assyrian kings first appeared during the reign of Sargon II, on the wall reliefs from his palace at Khorsabad. In several representations the late eighth century king wears a long dress, over which is a stylish fringed cloak[51] In these representations on the wall reliefs, the dress and cloak of the king are completely patterned, each with its own motif arranged in regular repeats. The cloak shows rows of

---

[48] See: J.B. Pritchard 1969, p. 301, fig. 453; Kataja and Whiting 1995, fig. 15. On the eponym dates, see Millard 1994, pp. 44–45, 58–59.
[49] Barnett and Falkner 1962, pls. XXII, LXXI, LXXXV, LXXXVII, XCVIII.
[50] Akurgal 1962, pp. 139–140, 278, pl. XXIV.
[51] Albenda 1986, pp. 128–129, 135, 140, pls. 44, 45, 70, 93.

double rosettes, one flower within the other, and the dress is patterned with either rows of a small square within a square or a rosette within a square. However, the most elaborately patterned textiles used for the dress and cloak of the royal figure occurs on one relief, now lost. The dress shows rows of rosettes within a square, and with small rosettes surrounding the squares. On the cloak, a rosette within a square alternates with a simplified walled city, and the two motifs are arranged in closely spaced rows. The walled city motif is presently unique in Assyrian textile art, and it may be what is represented on the garment of the enthroned king depicted in room 47 at Til Barsip. Of related interest, foreigners in a procession depicted on the wall reliefs of Sargon II are sometimes shown carrying the model of a city, an object that in this context is probably to be interpreted as an emblem of submission by a local city or region to Assyrian rule.[52] The model of a city may be the inspirational source for the modified version that appears on the royal costume.

In her study of western Asiatic jewelry, discussing the elaborate patterning on king Sargon's garments that include the walled city motif, Maxwell-Hyslop states that the designs are appliqué decorations.[53] It may be noted that a later version of the walled city or tower motif occurs in continuous repeat on a fragmentary woolen textile discovered in tomb 5 at Pazyryk, in the Altai region. The tomb has now been dated to the late fourth-early third century B.C. and the textile, which is a woven tapestry, is probably of the fifth or fourth century B.C.[54] Knowledge of the tapestry weaving technique as early as the second millennium B.C. is attested by several finds of fragmentary cloths from Pharaonic Egypt[55]; thus one may argue that the luxurious patterns of Sargon's garments were made by the weaving technique.

Later Assyrian kings were always represented on their palace wall reliefs attired in garments showing distinctive textile patterns. Sennacherib, the son and successor of Sargon II, seems to have favored cloths patterned with a repetitive motif of a circle within a circle, as exemplified by his portrayal on the series of wall reliefs illustrating the Lachish campaign.[56] There, the border bands on the costume of the enthroned king reveal a fine bead decoration, possibly this is an example of gold bead appliqué imitating granulation.

Ashurbanipal, the grandson of Sennacherib, was represented many times on the wall reliefs set up in his North Palace at Nineveh. He is depicted either

---

[52] Ibid, pp. 124–125, pls. 28–30, 32–33, fig. 79.
[53] Maxwell-Hyslop 1971, pp. 256–260.
[54] Lerner 1991, pp. 10–11, fig.10. In her article Bunker 1991, pp. 21–24, concludes that it is not possible to date the woven and embroidered silk finds in tombs 3 and 5 at Pazyryk earlier than the late 4th century B.C. For a detail view of the repeated tower motif on the Pazyryk cloth, see Barber 1991, color plate 4 (left).
[55] See: Barber 1991, pp. 157–159; Hall 1986, pp. 41–47.
[56] Barnett *et al* 1998, p. 104, pl. 335, no. 435.

wearing a long tunic belted at the waist or, during the hunt of lions, a tunic shortened to the level of the knee at the front, for ease of riding on horseback. A rich array of textile patterns covers the garment worn by Ashurbanipal.[57] The tunic below the belt is invariably decorated with rows of circles, each of which encloses an eight-pointed star, and on occasion the star-in-circle alternates with a circle enclosing three concentric circles with a dot in the center. It is of interest to observe that the two circle designs form a pattern that is placed obliquely on the tunic, and the resultant effect emphasizes the two motifs alternating with one another; on the other hand, a vertical alignment of the two designs would have produced a row of the star-in-circle alternating with a row of the concentric circle. Covering the chest of the king's tunic are narrow bands with repeat decorations, connected and arranged to form a large rectangle. The motifs in the respective bands include the rosette, lotus-and-bud, and stepped crenellation. Within the center of the rectangle, the double image of the king confronts a stylized tree, and behind each king is a large floral disk. The several renderings of the ornate design on the front of the king's tunic suggest that the design was made from a combination of woven bands sewn onto a cloth backing and embroidery that may have included the use of gold[58], and silk thread remains a possibility (see above).

Dating the Til Barsip wall paintings

The brief discussion of textile patterns found on the garments of Assyrian kings and personages of high rank or status, as depicted on the stone reliefs cited earlier, provides a framework for demonstrating that specific textile patterns were favored over a period of time by the Assyrian kings. The stone relief versions can now be compared with those found in the ornamental and narrative wall paintings discovered at Til Barsip. Thus, a more precise date of production may be assigned to several wall paintings, particularly since in the past scholars have cited one or more Assyrian kings responsible for the painted murals, although a date first assigned by the French excavators to the reign of Tiglath-pileser III is generally accepted for the narrative scenes.

---

[57] Barnett 1976, pp. 50–52, pls. XLVI–LIII; Barnett and Lorenzini 1975, pls. 116–118, 121, 122.

[58] Among the variety of treasures that Sargon II took from the temple of Haldi in Musasir, are '9 vestments, the garments of his divine majesty, whose embroidery (edges) was of gold.' See Luckenbill 1927, no. 173. Early direct evidence for gold-woven fabrics is a small assemblage of gold threads that were recovered in a Roman sarcophagus at the site of Philadelphia; see DeVries 1980, p. 137, fig. 4. Mention should be made of the discovery of four gold tassels, gold beads, and other small gold items in a cremation burial at Carchemish, which the excavators suggest dates to about 604 B.C. The gold beads are described as having been strung on fine threads used for weaving what was a 'cloth' of gold; see Woolley and Barnett 1952, pp 250–252, pl. 63 b.

A previous conclusion was that the ornamental and passageway paintings depicting animal and anthropomorphic figures with similarly rendered wings, showing layered feathering, belong to the same period of artistic production. In representations of the patterned garments, one textile pattern that recurs in a number of paintings is the checkerboard repeat, colored in red and blue and outlined in black. The garments worn by the winged genies depicted in the ornamental frieze from room 46 displays this pattern, in contrast to the genies depicted in the ornamental frieze from rooms 25 and 27, whose garments show a plaid design. One anthropomorphic figure whose costume is patterned with the checkered motif in red and blue is the wingless male genie in passage 24/25. He holds a plant in each hand and stands behind a human-headed winged bull. The animal's horned headdress is edged with a border of checks. The winged male genie in passage 24/26 holds a cone and bucket in the right and left hands, respectively. His costume shows an elaborate version of the checkered motif in blue and white, and in the center of each square is a white square outlined in black. The wingless male genie in passage 44/46 wears a costume patterned with continuous hexagons, while the border bands are decorated with the checkered motif. Checkered bands appear as accents of decoration on the garment of the bird-headed winged genie in passage 24/28, which is patterned with rows of small blue hexagons with a red center on the white fabric. A similar patterned garment is worn by the wingless male genie in passage 46/45. The pattern of checks on the respective costumes, as well as the application of the checkerboard border bands, is an indication that the above-mentioned paintings are contemporary.

The red and blue checkerboard woven blanket or small rug that covers the throne of each respective enthroned king in rooms 24 and 47, provides a supportive date for those Til Barsip wall paintings that include a similar textile pattern, once the identification of the two representations of the same Assyrian king is made. In the first place, the enthroned king must predate Sennacherib, since he wears open sandals, in contrast to closed footwear that is the style for later Assyrian rulers. Secondly, the elaborate patterns on the garments of the two enthroned kings find their closest parallels with those decorating the several garments of Sargon II, depicted on the wall reliefs at Khorsabad, as noted above. It was observed earlier that the fabrics of the garments worn by Tiglath-pileser III are plain, as shown on the wall reliefs. Unfortunately, no representation of Sargon II's predecessor, Shalmaneser V is known at present. Finally, parallels for the patterns of checks and their variants occur in the fragments of wall paintings discovered in the throne room at Khorsabad and on glazed bricks from the same site. The pattern on the garment of a soldier standing a short distance behind the enthroned Assyrian king in room 24 provides a notable example (see pl. 25). There, the decorative grid motif can be compared with a nearly identical motif on a

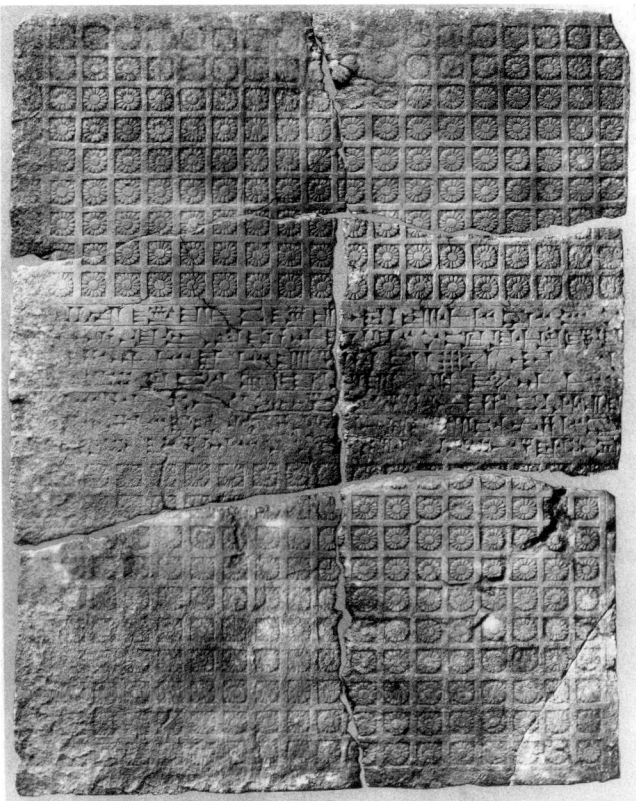

Pl. 26. Carved threshold slab discovered between room 116 and the central court of
residence L at Khorsabad. Inscription identifies Sinahusur as Sargon's
brother and grand vizier. Oriental Institute, University of Chicago A 17597.

fragmentary brick discovered at Khorsabad.[59] In addition, a modified version
of the pattern on the enthroned king's garment in room 24, which shows a
flower or dot within a square that is repeated in rows, occurs on the threshold
slab discovered in residence L at Khorsabad (pl. 26).[60] In this last example,
the flower is a large rosette within the square, and narrow bands frame the
square repeats. Missing from the pattern on the threshold slab are the single
rows of rosettes that surround the squares on the king's garment.

From the above comparative observations of the textile patterns, it seems
that the enthroned king represented in rooms 24 and 47 is most likely to be
identified with the Assyrian king Sargon II. The same Assyrian ruler may
also be represented in two other episodes, in room 24, labeled panels d and g.

---

[59] Albenda 1986, p. 153, pl. 151.
[60] Albenda 1978, pp. 12–13, pl. 4.

In both illustrations the king wears the traditional royal garment embellished with the checkerboard border. In one example (panel d) an additional border on the shawl consists of a row of rosettes, and open sandals on the feet. On the other hand, the identification with the Assyrian king Sennacherib should be made with the royal person in the poorly preserved wall painting in room 24, panel i (Louvre AO 25067 D). Although only the lowermost part of the painting remains, it represents the king seated on the wheeled throne with a pole at the top of which is a human head, and pulled by two attendants standing side by side. It is evident that the king wears closed footwear. In addition, Sennacherib is the only Assyrian king who is represented on the Assyrian wall reliefs sitting on a wheeled throne.[61] Of related interest, the high-ranked official standing before the same royal person is attired in a garment that consists of a white cloak and dress patterned with rows of small white squares within blue squares (pl. 24). It is tempting to identify this person with Hananu, the governor (*bēl pāhīti*) of Til Barsip, who was eponym holder in 701 B.C.[62] In contrast, the high-ranked court official facing the enthroned Assyrian king in rooms 24 and 47 respectively, wears the traditional eighth century costume and open sandals. The two representations of the court official, if he is the same person, therefore may possibly represent a governor of Til Barsip.

In summary, three periods of artistic production have been identified for the Neo-Assyrian ornamental wall paintings at Til Barsip: early, middle, late. The ornamental painting containing goats in room 26 represents the early period. This frieze is attributed to the first half of the eighth century B.C., and precedes the reign of Sargon II. The ornamental paintings of the middle period are dated to latter part of the eighth century B.C., and include those discovered in rooms 21, 24, 46, 47. To the same period belong the apotropaic figures, with or without bulls, who appear in the passages of room 24 that lead to room 25, 26, and 28 respectively. The checkerboard motif on the garments of the winged genies in the ornamental frieze from room 46, its recurrence on the garments of other anthropomorphic figures, and on the cloth covering the high back thrones of the two representations of the Assyrian king in rooms 24 and 47, indicates a contemporary date for the paintings in which this decorative textile pattern occurs. The enthroned Assyrian king has been identified with Sargon II, since it has already been established that the elaborate textile designs of the royal garments adorning the two seated figures find close parallels with the designs that embellish the garments of Sargon II in his representations on the wall reliefs from Khorsabad. To the late period of production belongs the fragmentary scene in room 24, panel i, which illustrates the king seated on a wheeled throne,

---

[61] Barnett *et al* 1998, pp. 91, 108–109, 112, 114, 479, nos. 148a, 148b, 152b, 660a.
[62] Millard 1994, pp. 49, 94.

with a court official attired in a patterned garment standing before him. In this example, the Assyrian king is identified with Sennacherib, based upon the type of throne upon which he sits. The ornamental friezes in rooms 25 and 27 are assigned to the same period.

Mention should be made of the several other Assyrian kings represented in the Til Barsip wall paintings. They can be placed within the several periods of production, based upon whether their costumes are plain or patterned, whether they are depicted with open sandals or closed footwear, and their placement within the larger composition. The Assyrian king wears a plain costume in room 24, panel g, and in room 47, panel d. A date to the eighth century B.C. is certain for these royal figures. In room 27, on panels c and e, the king on horseback and again in a chariot, during the hunt of lions, wears a costume that is decorated with circles. It is suggested that the two representations of the king are identifiable with Sennacherib, although they may also represent Esarhaddon, for whom unfortunately there are no datable comparisons; on his stelae from Til Barsip and Zincirli the king is wearing the official royal costume.[63] The composition style of the lion hunt scene in room 27 differs from those depicted on the rooms C and S wall reliefs discovered in the North Palace at Nineveh, dating to the later seventh century king, Ashurbanipal.[64] In the former example, the narrative scene containing the chariots and men on horseback unfolds in a simple one-direction arrangement, while in the latter examples the organization of the compositions are carefully structured and composed of episodic units. The last example of an Assyrian king represented in the Til Barsip wall paintings occurs in room 47, panel f. The king stands in his chariot, during a military procession but, unfortunately, the figure of the king was destroyed at the time of its discovery. One detail that makes it possible to identify the royal person is the presence of a soldier in the military procession wearing a broad headband with side flap. A person wearing a similar headband appears among other Assyrian military personnel on the wall reliefs of Sennacherib[65], therefore the Assyrian king standing in the chariot is identifiable with that ruler.

---

[63] For discussion of the steles from the two sites, with their different messages in both imagery and text, see Porter 2000, pp. 9–13. It is of interest to observe further that the Assyrian king on the Til Barsip stelae faces right, while on the Zincirli stele the king faces left. In general the initial reading of a line of text or picture is from left to right; thus in the display of the official royal portrait, as exemplified by Esarhaddon's monuments, the start of the visual movement is given to the image at the left side and ends with the image at the right side. On the Assyrian royal stelae and rock monuments the abbreviated compositions show a sequence of hierarchy: divine emblems, the Assyrian king and, on occasion, subjugated foreigners. Investigation into the re-arrangement of the sequence of hierarchy and placement in a given composition, as demonstrated by the Esarhaddon stelae, should also lead to a more precise purpose behind the respective royal portraits.

[64] For the design organization of the room C lion hunts and one episodic section of the room S lion hunts, see Albenda 1998, pp. 20–22, figs. 22–27, ills. 20–24.

[65] These soldiers, probably military personnel from Lachish who were incorporated into the

Although several of the Assyrian kings have been identified here with a high degree of certainty, nonetheless it must be remembered that the wall paintings at Til Barsip underwent repainting and, over time, new subjects replaced previously painted ones, as indicated by Cavro's renderings of the painted works. The dating of the ornamental friezes and figural subject matter can be accomplished by singling out details of motifs, as well as the respective stylistic tendencies, and by comparing them with works of art in other media, primarily the Assyrian stone reliefs, glazed bricks, and paintings. The few remaining fragments of wall paintings from Til Barsip are tantalizing examples of what must have been a wonderfully colorful and, in modern terms, sophisticated style of wall painting, in which the flat hues of large and small areas of the painted surface gained in clarity through the use of black outlines. The method of using fine lines for outlining purposes was particularly useful for the ornamental wall paintings, since many of the small details might have otherwise merged with the adjacent areas. Apparently, the Assyrian artists were quite aware that the ornamental designs were viewed from a distance, above the eye level of the person viewing those paintings, and by limiting the palette of colors and outlining the various shapes, large and small, the designs became clear and intelligible. The latter results were especially important since the ornamental designs originally extended across the entire surface of one or more walls, as demonstrated by the excavated evidence. The Til Barsip ornamental wall paintings therefore furnish model examples of a major category in the decorative arts that adorned the interiors of the Assyrian royal residence, in this instance during the eighth and early seventh centuries B.C. These wall paintings also provide significant data for the study of the ornamental wall paintings in Assyria, as they pertain to the selection of individual motifs, organization, and overall appearance. Assyrian wall painting in the decorative arts was not static but, as observed earlier, dynamic in the choice of motifs and in the complexity or simplicity of the designs. The study of Assyrian ornamental designs is the subject of the next chapter.

Assyrian army, are represented in a procession carved on stone slabs lining the passage leading towards the Ishtar Temple; see Barnett *et al* 1998, pp. 133–137, pls. 483–489, nos. 662–670.

CHAPTER FOUR.   THE ORNAMENTAL PAINTED DESIGNS

Archaeological evidence for the ornamental wall paintings that adorned Assyrian royal residences shows that they were in use during a period spanning from the thirteenth to the mid-seventh century B.C. This range of dates is documented by the Middle-Assyrian fragmentary paintings discovered at Kar-Tukulti-Ninurta and the Neo-Assyrian the wall paintings uncovered in the throne room and adjoining chambers at Fort Shalmaneser, the latter attributed by the British excavators to the reign of Esarhaddon. In addition, the latest ornamental wall paintings from the North Syrian site of Til Barsip are ascribed to the reign of Sennacherib.

Unfortunately, the ability to trace the evolution of the artistic tradition that produced the Assyrian wall paintings is hindered by gaps during periods between the thirteenth and early ninth centuries and the middle part of the eighth century. There is also a lack of archaeological evidence in the seventh century Southwest and North Palaces at Nineveh for wall paintings, which would represent the final phases of ornamental decoration in Assyria proper.

The seventh century wall paintings discovered in private residences at Til Barsip and Dur-Katlimmu disclose less elaborate but equally interesting decorative friezes. They show an affinity with the Assyrian method of structural organization, but their visual character is different. The departure from the Assyrian royal assemblage of decorative motifs at these North Syrian sites is an indication that new influences in the artistic sphere had taken hold in non-royal households. Whether the artistic impetus was local or regional or from a distant source is a question that deserves attention. A comparative study of the specific designs may provide insights into this matter.

In tracing the evolution of ornamentation in wall paintings produced during the Middle and Neo-Assyrian periods, it must be acknowledged that the excavated data derives from the royal residences, with the above noted exceptions. The artistic style was directed to satisfy the royal tastes and, therefore, whatever subject matter was selected and combined within an ornamental frieze, it had to meet certain criteria. The three types of subject matter – decorative, animal, and figural – occur in the overall designs according to pre-determined formulas, resulting in what may be described as the Assyrian royal style of ornamental wall painting. Probably several of the subjects depicted had religious or symbolic significance, while others may have been included for their visual appeal. The particular way in which colors were selected and applied to the designs is another important factor that contributed to this style, and one that should not be overlooked. Thus the structuring of the painted friezes and of the ornamental motifs had to have been carefully planned and executed to fit into the overall scheme of wall decoration, especially in those places where stone reliefs or narrative paintings also decorated the lower section of the walls in the same chambers of the royal residence. At times, another feature that must have been considered was painted ceiling decoration, some fragmentary evidence of which has been recovered.

Many of the published ornamental wall paintings are modern renderings of the original works, either replicating the painted fragments as found or re-constructions of the fragments into complete sections based on the excavated material. The last method was relatively easy for the excavators to achieve, once they became aware that in planning the large-scale ornamental designs the Assyrian artists oftentimes relied upon the rules of plane symmetry. This knowledge is borne out by the excavated evidence. Published photographs of wall paintings taken *in situ* at the sites of Arslan Tash, Fort Shalmaneser, Khorsabad, and Dur-Katlimmu provide a permanent visual record. One may want to consider whether some of the modern reconstructions of wall paint-ings that contain a great deal of ornamental detail may also include significant conjectural arrangements within the respective compositions. For the major-ity of the reconstructed ornamental paintings this consideration need not be pursued, since the excavated material remains central to the modern render-ings and empty spaces oftentimes appear in those areas of the renderings for which little or no evidence is available.

The Ornamental Compositions

The earliest evidence for Assyrian wall painting was uncovered at Kar-Tukulti-Ninurta with the discovery of thirteenth century B.C. wall paintings, in the painted style representative of the Middle Assyrian period. Isolated fragments and three reconstructions of sections of wall paintings were published in color.[1] The fragments were found on the north and south sides of the palace terrace built by Tukulti-Ninurta I (c. 1250–1210 B.C.). The three reconstructed sections of wall paintings, each one of which is based on an assemblage of isolated fragments, are not identical in appearance. This may indicate that, originally, the painted sections were treated as independent decorations within the larger compositions designed for the palace terrace. The reconstructed painting from the north side of the palace terrace shows rows of large square compartments, with backgrounds in blue, red, and white

---

[1] Andrae 1925, pls. 1–4.

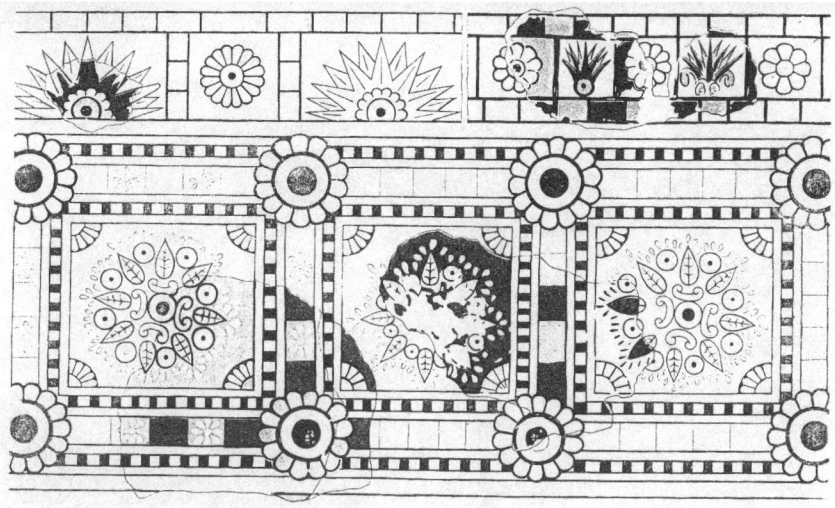

Pl. 27. Reconstructed wall painting from the north side of palace
terrace at Kar-Tukulti-Ninurta. 13th century B.C. Andrae 1925, pl. 1.

(pl. 27). Within each compartment is a 'star flower' composed of leaves,
circles, and branches. Surrounding the large squares are red and blue checked
border bands, edged with black and white strips. Where the border bands
intersect are large rosettes. Each rosette is composed of a central white circle
with a black dot in the center, surrounded by little red and white rosette petals.
Above the large square compartments and surrounding strips are bands of
rosettes, lotus flowers, and rayed rosettes. The other reconstructed drawings
represent sections of wall painting on the south side of the palace terrace.
One painting shows large rectangular panels of unequal widths arranged
alongside one another (pl. 28). The panels are framed by narrow bands of
continuous small plain squares. Above the panels is a large horizontal band
of squares inside which a rosette and flower alternate. Surmounting this band
is a prominent garland composed of alternating stylized plants. The third
reconstructed painting (pl. 29) is composed of two tiers of rectangular panels
of unequal lengths and widths. In the lower tier the panels are surrounded by
narrow bands similar to those found in the first painting, a decorative feature
that provides a connective link for the two paintings. In the upper tier the
panels are treated as separate and independent entities; moreover, they are
poorly integrated with the lower tier. Isolated fragments were also found and
recorded in a drawing (pl. 30). These fragments could not be fitted into the
three reconstructed paintings; however, it is evident from the isolated motifs
that they formed part of the large compositions that decorated the palace
terrace.

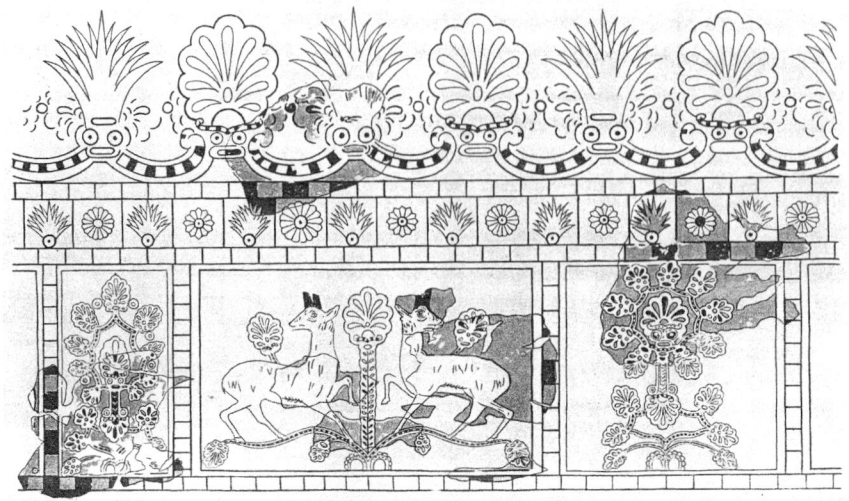

Pl. 28. Reconstructed wall painting from the south side of palace terrace at Kar-Tukulti-Ninurta. 13th century B.C. Andrae 1925, pl. 2.

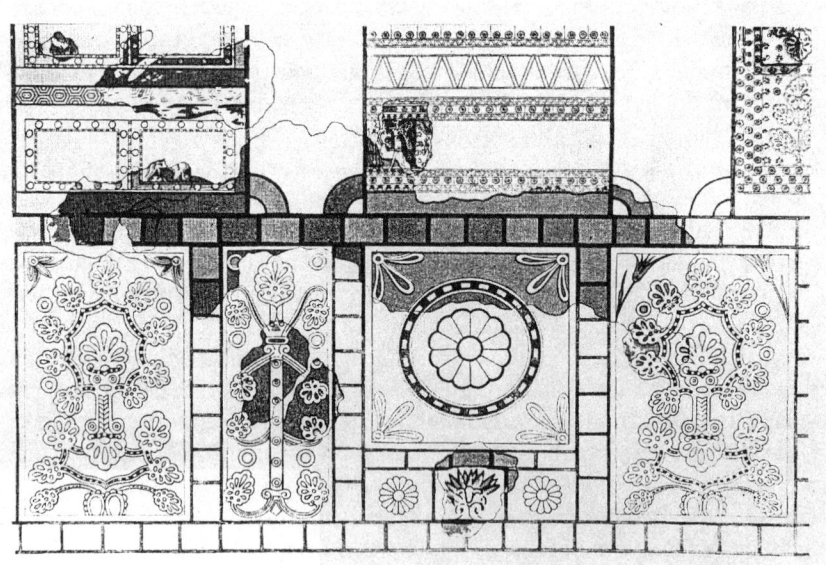

Pl. 29. Reconstructed wall painting from the south side of palace terrace at Kar-Tukulti-Ninurta. 13th century B.C. Andrae 1925, pl. 3.

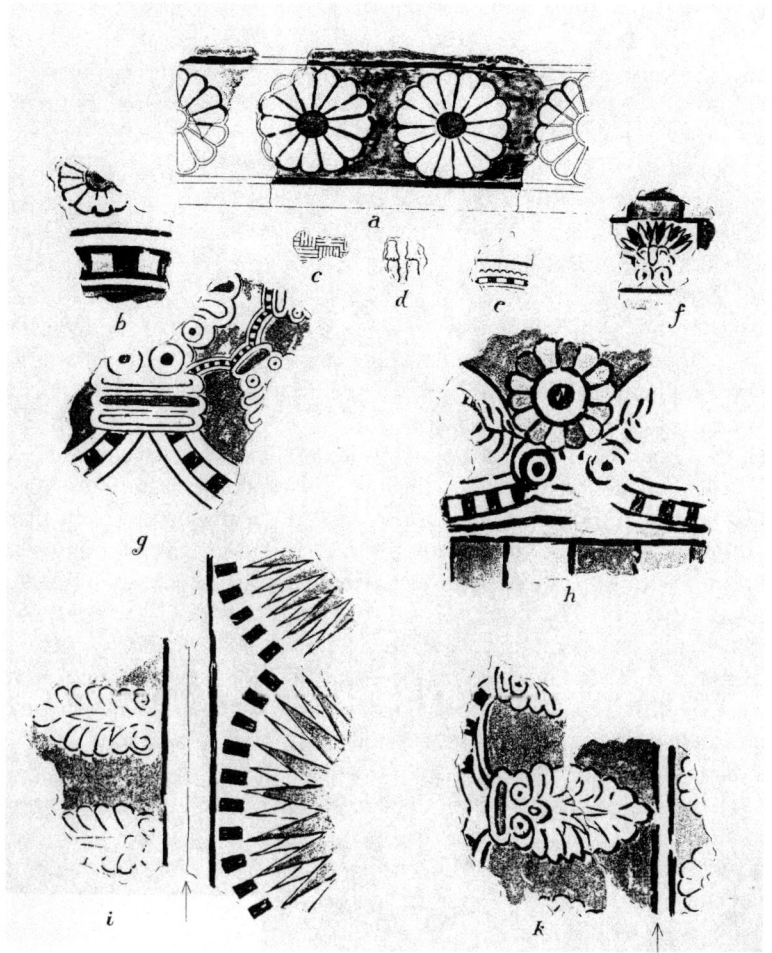

Pl. 30. Small fragments of wall paintings from the palace terrace
at Kar-Tukulti-Ninurta. 13th century B.C. Andrae 1925, pl. 4.

Analysis of the three wall paintings indicates that all the examples were planned as a series of compartments or panels of varying sizes, bound together by bands that framed them. As presented in the reconstructed drawings, the orderly placement of the individual panels within a given register establishes a unifying effect to the respective larger designs. The longitudinal direction of several bands tends to be offset by the vertical framing bands, producing a visual equilibrium in these paintings. It may be mentioned that the three paintings are heavily reconstructed and portions of the numerous details that make up the respective paintings are modern interpretations. Therefore, to some extent the original appearance of the

Assyrian wall paintings at Kar-Tukulti-Ninurta probably differed from the modern versions.

The decorative motives are compartmentalized within the respective large and small panels, and except for the decorated border bands, recurring motifs are not always coordinated according to a prescribed formula. The mirror image rendering of the goats on either side of the tree, the floral garland, the use of alternating motifs in the large framing band, and the limited palette of red, blue, black, and white are among the decorative features within the reconstructed paintings that must have been part of the original paintings. These decorative features recur in the ornamental wall paintings of the first millennium B.C., when their applications are reinterpreted to satisfy differing aspects of the planned designs. At present, there are no excavated examples of Assyrian wall painting that have been dated between the end of the thirteenth and the start of the ninth centuries B.C.

The wall paintings from the Northwest Palace of Ashurnasirpal II exemplify the use of painted decoration during the early phase of the Neo-Assyrian period. From the archaeological record and descriptions given by the various modern excavators of that impressive structure, wall painting was an important aspect of the artistic effort given to enhance the many rooms of the royal residence. Therefore it is unfortunate that no extensive portions of wall paintings discovered in the various chambers of the residence have been preserved or fully documented by the excavators. However, some fragments do exist, as well as modern renderings of painted sections. The study of these sources reveals that over time, between the thirteenth and ninth centuries, significant modifications occurred in the structure of the ornamental paintings. No longer are decorative motifs confined to rectangular compartments. Instead there is an emphasis on broad horizontal divisions of the painted surface, and within these divisions or registers specific motifs are repeated in several different ways. They include the continuous interlocking ribbons or bands forming a guilloche, and the garland composed of three floral motifs. In one of Layard's sketches of the ornamental wall paintings the outer decorated bands are depicted in mirror image, resulting in a composition based upon reflection symmetry (pl. 1).

In later periods geometric and figural motifs were combined to form a decorative unit that, in turn, was repeated across the surface of wall. An early example of this type of decorative unit appears among the fragmentary paintings discovered in one suite of rooms of Adad-nirari III's palace at Nimrud, as shown in Layard's sketches. Although incomplete, one sketch hints at the probable alternating combination of a winged bull with a decorated circle (pl. 3). Another sketch shows alternating circles and squares with incurved sides (pl. 4). The inclusion of battlements in the top register of three of Layard's sketches suggests that the façade of a lofty building was the intended image of the overall design.

Color also functioned as part of the planned painted designs. There are examples where the colors alternate, either within or between registers, particularly where the identical motif is repeated in one or more registers. Red and blue were the polychrome colors, black was used for the outlines and occasionally as a color, and the white plaster ground provided the contrast for the colors.

In the planning and execution of the ornamental wall paintings, a feature first observed in one painting of Ashurnasirpal II and developed further at a later date was centralization of the prominent ornamental design and framing it above and below with decorated border bands arranged in mirror image. This method is demonstrated in the paintings at Til Barsip. The ornamental wall paintings at Til Barsip and those found in residence K at Khorsabad represent the mature phase. These art works with their variant and rich array of decorations, which integrate the symmetries of repetition, alternate repetition and reflection on both a vertical axis and a horizontal axis, impart a sense of balance and harmony.

In the Neo-Assyrian period, a basic rule was to maintain the separateness of the individual registers. There is no instance where a motif extended across two registers, nor is there an occurrence where the longitudinal extension of the decorated register was restricted by a vertical band at given points, or by the intrusion of another set of motifs or patterns arranged perpendicular to the horizontal register. The all-over continuous repeat of a single motif was also utilized, but this type of pattern was used for the upper walls and ceilings. The motifs that were used for those surfaces are the circle and the hexagon (see fig. 2). Evidence indicates that the latter geometric shape was favored for ceiling decoration.

The seventh century B.C. wall paintings discovered in several private residences at North Syrian sites present modest designs and in several ways they are a departure from the Assyrian royal style. The use of horizontal registers aligned one above the other is common, with the decorative motif repeated in each register. But what is missing in general in the respective paintings are the individual designs composed of two or more motifs that are treated as a unit to be repeated within a given register. Reflection symmetry also seems to have been avoided in the planning of the seventh century painted designs. Polychrome is most often absent; thus black on white is the rule. Of related interest, the stark contrast of black on white also had visual appeal for the Assyrian artist working in Assyria proper, since there is evidence at Fort Shalmaneser for the black-on-white painted style which, based upon the ornamental design, is attributable to the seventh century B.C. The appreciation for the contrasting hues of black and white was not entirely a seventh century phenomenon in the art of Assyria. There is proof of its use early on, in the wall paintings at Kar-Tukulti-Ninurta. Moreover, chevron border designs in black and white appear in glazed brick paintings during the reign of Ashurnasirpal II. The same hues are also used as decorative fillings for floral plants on terracotta knobbed wall plates or plaques.[2]

Symmetries of the Ornaments

Turning to the painted designs, it is evident that several kinds of symmetries have been adapted for the ornamental designs. These symmetries provide the means that satisfy the requirement of visual coherence and which satisfy the orderly extension of the same design across the surface of the wall.[3] Emphasis upon the horizontal or longitudinal extension of the ornamental design is marked by the inclusion of solid narrow bands of varying thickness that separate the respective registers of the ornamental painting. Simple repetition or translation of a given motif is generally restricted to the rosette and circle with a center dot, both based upon the same geometric shape. There are examples where the chevron, three-stepped merlon, and vertical zigzag are repeated likewise in a given register, but these motifs occur infrequently. In addition the above-mentioned motifs serve a subsidiary role in the ornamental designs, particularly since the registers in which they occur are generally narrow and appear on the outside of one or both sides of the registers containing more elaborate decorations.

On occasion the extension or addition of lines connect the repetitive motifs, forming either a continuous ornamental design or a garland. For example the guilloche pattern is composed of repeats of the same motif, that of twisted ribbons or bands interlocking around a series of circles in one direction (S or Z). Similarly, a floral or geometric motif that is repeated at regular intervals and is connected by curved bands or stems forms a garland, which displays the symmetries of translation and mirror image. In the latter instance the geometric shape or flower is a reflection of the one preceding it, if one imagines a vertical axis midway between the two identically drawn motifs as the center of reflection. However, when two floral plants are included in the garland, the axis of reflection is in the center of the second flower. Only one known example exists of three plants making up the floral garland, and its symmetry is merely a repeat or translation (fig. 1a). Although subsidiary to the main central register with its elaborate decorations, band ornaments composed of garlands are oftentimes prominently displayed in the designs by placing them within large bands. At Til Barsip the floral garlands appear as the outer flanking motifs for the ornamental wall paintings.

Reflection symmetry is the geometric form that was oftentimes applied for the decorations in the main register of the wall paintings. When two

---

2 Albenda 1991, pp. 47–51, pls. I–X.
3 Albenda 1998, pp. 11–14.

identical subjects confront a motif, a vertical axis or plane of reflection within the motif provides the spatial configuration for bilateral symmetry. In the Assyrian wall paintings the subjects are restricted to animal and human figures, while the central motif consists of either a circle or a square with incurved sides. The choice of animals is restricted to the bull, which may be with or without wings or human-headed, and the goat. However, in the Neo-Assyrian period the latter example is known only from a wall painting at Til Barsip. The human-type figures found in the wall paintings are two-winged genies, male and female, which kneel on one leg, the other leg placed firmly on the ground (half-kneel). It is of interest to observe that, in the depictions of one group of winged figures whose respective upper body and arms display a rotation of 180° in the plane, the strict bilateral symmetry is relaxed (pl. 11). This is the only known example where the overall flatness of the ornamental paintings is replaced by the subtle notion of spatial depth.

Rotational symmetry on a plane is exemplified by the decorations within each of the circles and squares with incurved sides. The outer section of the square emphasizes a rotation on the order of 4, indicated by the introduction of a floral bud in each of the four corners. Within each of these circles or squares are concentric circles. Thus these circular bands containing repeats of decoration convey the notion of rotation into itself.

In later ornamental wall paintings, particularly those discovered in the royal residence at Til Barsip, one finds that two visual directions of symmetry are combined within each ornamental painting. One direction of symmetry derives from a horizontal axis of reflection centered in the main central register, which affects the arrangement of the upper and lower decorated and plain border bands. The other direction of symmetry derives from a vertical axis of reflection, also centered in the main register, which affects the lateral repetition of the figural/geometric grouping. To some extent the two visual directions provide a harmonious balance to the painted design that originally extended across a long surface of wall. At the same time the individual wall paintings are enriched not only by the interplay of symmetry but also by the selective placement of the respective motifs and the use of a limited palette to the various parts of the design.

The seventh century B.C. black-and-white wall paintings from North Syrian sites disclose a simple use of symmetry in the ornamental designs. Repetition of a single motif is the rule and, except for the painted stylized floral garland at Dur-Katlimmu (fig. 5b), other kinds of symmetries are avoided. A favored pattern seems to have been repeats of concentric circles with or without connecting horizontal lines. An elaborate version of this pattern occurs in a private residence at Til Barsip (fig. 4c). Solid horizontal bands are utilized and their arrangements not only serve to separate the motifs of the respective registers but also take on a degree of prominence within the decorative design.

The Ornamental Motifs

The various motifs that make up the designs of the ornamental wall paintings produced before and during the Neo-Assyrian period can be divided into three categories: single, bands and garlands, bilateral grouping. The specific motifs of ornamentation used in each type are identified and described, below. Furthermore, the occurrence of the respective motifs in other art media is also considered. This method of description and discussion will demonstrate the changing trends in the selection of motifs and their relative importance in the overall appearance of the painted designs. Moreover, viewed in other contexts, several of the motifs have religious or symbolic meaning, in addition to their decorative qualities. This aspect will also be considered, since it may help explain why certain motifs were favored in the painted designs.

Single motif

Rosette

The rosette flower (*ayāru*) is a common motif in Assyrian art. It is produced by the regular divisions of a circle, resulting in the arrangement of petals that radiate outwards from a central boss. The rosette occurs as early as thirteenth century B.C., on the stone altar of king Tukulti-Ninurta I that was discovered at Ashur.[4] On this monument the rosette is displayed prominently in the upper corners. In the painted medium the early use of the rosette is evidenced by the contemporary Assyrian wall paintings from Kar-Tukulti-Ninurta. The published versions depict three variants of the rosette. A rosette with thirteen or more white petals surrounding a small black center appears on one fragment (pl. 30). In a second instance, the rosette consists of a large circle with a prominent black disk or 'eye' in the center, surrounded by fourteen short rounded petals alternating in red and white (pl. 27). The third rosette resembles the second variant, but with the addition of a double row of large rays that radiate outwards from the flower (pl. 27). This unusual motif seems to impart the notion that the rosette itself is the source of the rays. A modest version of this particular motif occurs on another fragment depicted in the same published drawing. In this case the circle with dot center has a close arrangement of thin rays on the upper side, which may represent the leaves or ferns of a plant.

    The rosette does not recur in Neo-Assyrian wall paintings until the start of the eighth century B.C. Its absence from the ornamental painted designs between the end of the thirteenth century and the end of the ninth centuries is of course due to the complete lack of excavated material from that time

---

[4] Moortgat 1967, p. 120, pl. 246.

span. Moreover, the discoveries of wall paintings datable to the ninth century consist of small, isolated fragments. Examples of those fragmentary finds are from the wall paintings that were recovered in the Northwest Palace at Nimrud, on which the ornamental motifs are limited in scope. In contrast to its absence in the painted art works, the rosette does occur numerous times on the carved wall reliefs from the same palace. It is the main decorative element on bracelets worn by the king. Moreover, large disks in the form of rosettes are attached to headbands worn by Assyrian attendants and genies.[5] Each rosette varies according to the number of petals, ranging from eight to ten and at times to as many as sixteen that surround the ringed circle in the center. In many of the representations, the depiction of the rosette relates to a flower of the daisy family, albeit schematized.

The earliest known occurrence of the rosette in Neo-Assyrian wall paintings comes from Layard's painted versions of his discoveries in the upper chambers or suite of rooms in the palace of Adad-nirari III at Nimrud. Three variants of the rosette appear in these paintings. The plain rosette with twelve petals is used as a repeat in a narrow border band (pl. 3: right). The decorated rosette, set within a large disk with a patterned outer border, consists of twelve separate petals that extend outwards from ringed circles in the center. This rosette disk appears in the prominent registers of two paintings, and in both paintings it alternates with a decorated square with incurving sides (pls. 3: left, 4). In one of the paintings a rosette disk is lightly drawn in the upper register and alternates with a winged bull. The third and most elaborate rosette, set within a banded disk, shows twelve petals surrounded by a plain circle, with fifteen triangular rays between the circle and banded disk (pl. 5). This unusual variant seems to derive from a mechanical rendering of the motif. On the earliest wall painting from Til Barsip (pl. 9), attributable to the early or mid-eighth century B.C., two bands of plain rosettes and alternating narrow stripes frame the principal register showing goats kneeling on one foreleg.

Painted rosette fragments were discovered in the throne room of Sargon II's residence at Khorsabad. The white petals of the rosette are twelve in number, and extend outwards from a plain circle in the center. Although only a few plaster fragments with this motif were found fallen to the ground, a more permanent example appears on the monolithic throne base discovered in the same room, where two of the preserved sides are carved with scenes of warfare.[6] Below each scene is a band of rosettes that serves as a border. The petals of the individual rosettes whose centers show a large 'button' or boss,

---

[5] For good examples, see Barnett and Lorenzini 1975, pls. 2, 4–5, 9–10, 12.

[6] Loud 1936, p. 65, figs. 79, 80. Winter (1983, p. 24) interprets the two battle scenes on the throne base as a visual articulation of the boundaries of the Assyrian empire, East and West. With reference to the 'West' panel, it may be observed that the pile of heads set before the royal chariot recurs on a wall relief from room 2 of the palace at Khorsabad, now lost; the wall reliefs in that room deal with campaigns in eastern territories. See Albenda 1986, p. 89, pl. 111.

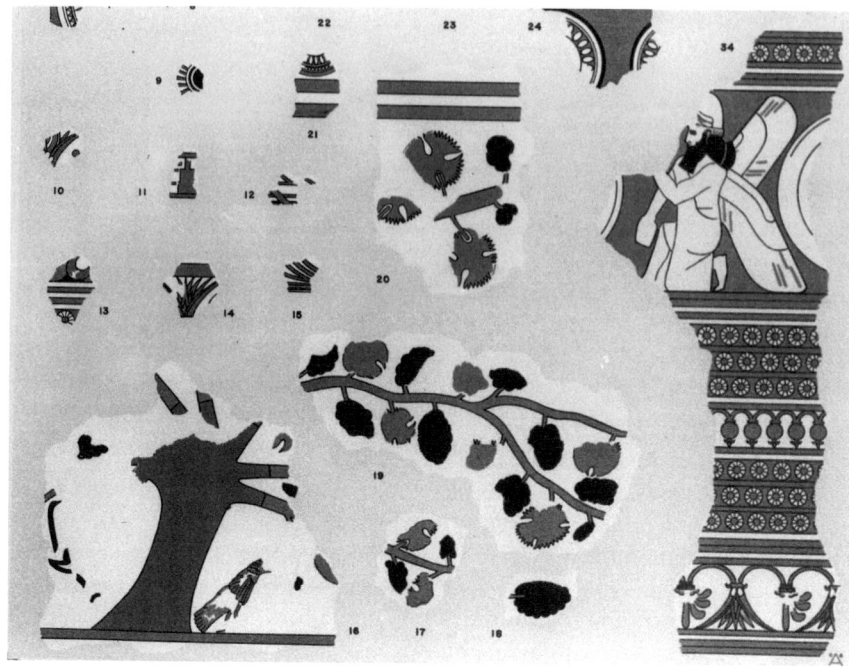

Pl. 31. Fragments of painted plaster from citadel buildings at Khorsabad.
Loud and Altman 1938, pl. 91. Oriental Institute, University of Chicago.

number from twelve to sixteen. Another painted ornamental fragment was discovered in room 12 (bathroom) of the royal residence. That design consists of bands of rosettes alternating with bands of target circles (fig. 2: bottom left). This particular fragment provides evidence that the addition of color was carefully planned within the overall decoration. The button centers of the white rosettes alternate in red and blue. At the same time the background colors for the rows of rosettes and circles are alternating blue and red.

In residence K on the citadel at Khorsabad the impressive decorative paintings, which still adhered to the mud-lime plaster walls at the time of discovery, include bands of white rosettes alternating with plain stripes of different colors (pls. 32, 33). The rosette bands are arranged within the larger wall painting in groups of three and frame a larger band containing repeats of a stepped merlon. Above this decorative arrangement is a palmette-and-lotus garland. Elsewhere in the same wall painting, the arrangement of five rows of rosettes and plain stripes serves to separate two prominent registers containing figural and geometric subjects. Among the painted fragments found in residences L and M, one example shows a symmetrical arrangement of three bands of white rosettes with a button center, separated by plain stripes, above and below a pomegranate garland (pl. 31).

86

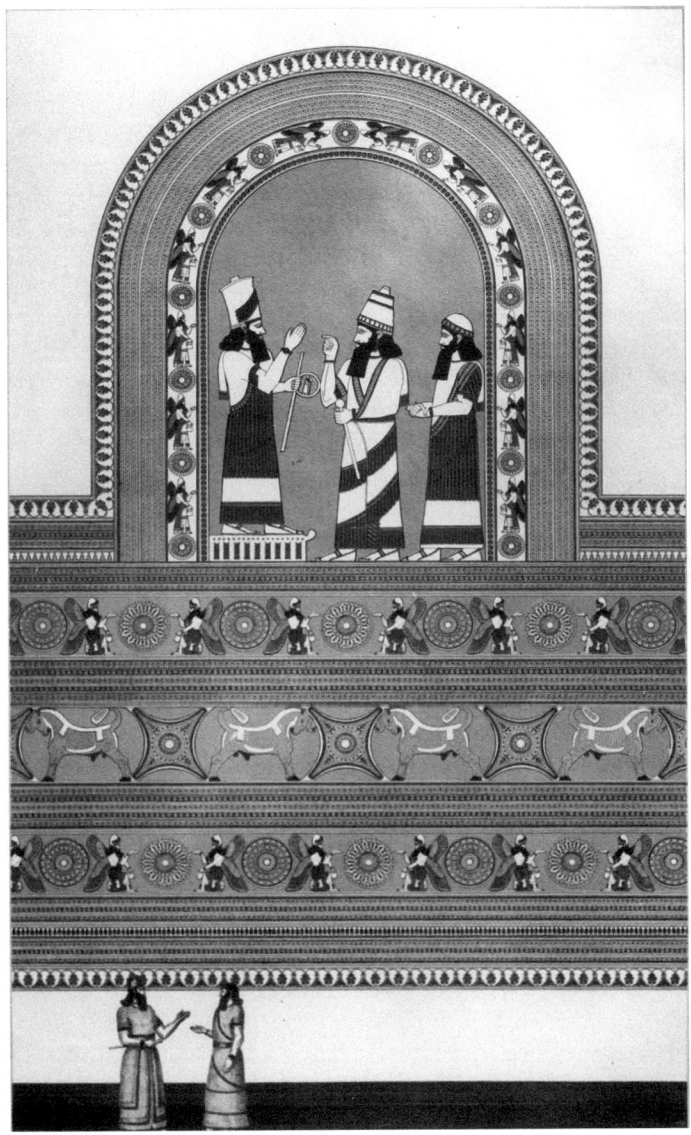

Pl. 32. Restored wall paintings in residence K at Khorsabad. Loud and Altman 1938, pl. 89. Oriental Institute, University of Chicago.

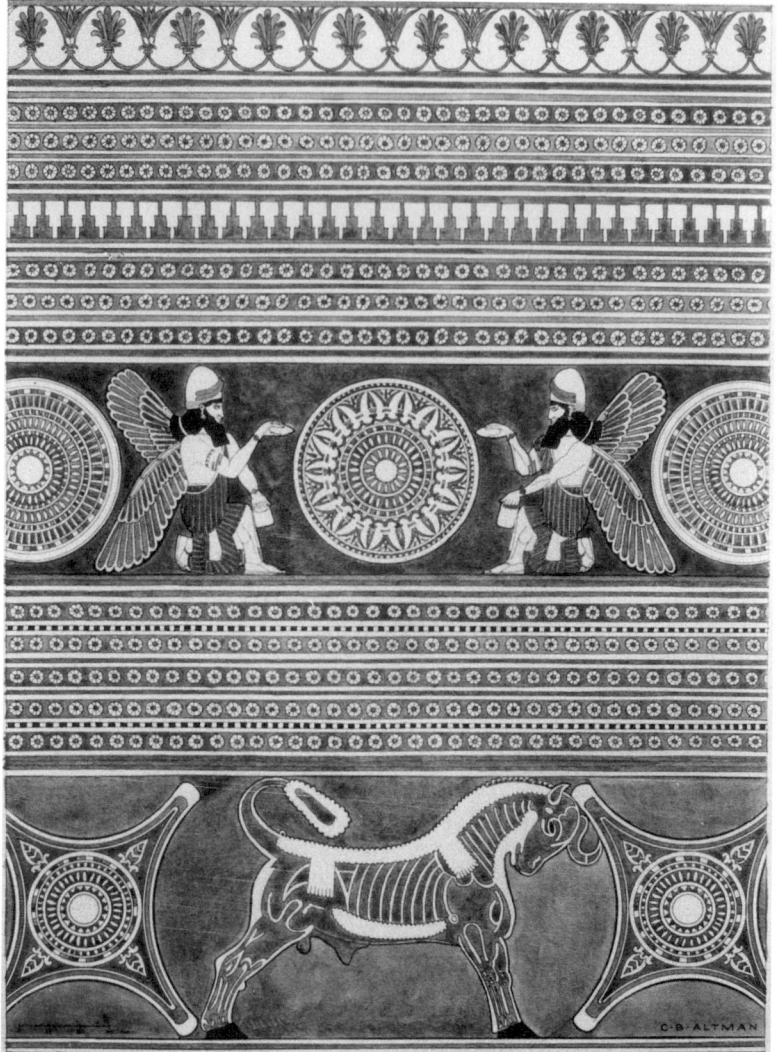

Pl. 33. Detail: restored wall painting in residence K at Khorsabad. Loud
and Altman 1938, pl. 89. Oriental Institute, University of Chicago.

At Til Barsip, all the ornamental wall paintings contain one or more bands
of rosettes that make up the framing decoration for the main central register.
Two bands of rosettes appear in the frieze from room 21 (pl. 17). Three
consecutive bands of rosettes form part of the framing decoration in the
frieze from room 24 (pl. 18: right). In rooms 46 and 47, two bands of rosettes
frame a band of target circles (pl. 13), an arrangement that is similar to the

one depicted on a fragment in room 12 of the royal residence at Khorsabad. All the above noted ornamental paintings are attributed to the reign of Sargon II. In those from rooms 22 and 25 at Til Barsip, attributed to the reign of Sennacherib, only one band of rosettes is included in the framing decoration (pl. 11). It may be noted that in the ornamental wall painting from room 22 bands of target circles frame the rosettes inside which the button center features a pattern of cross-hatchings. This detail in the flora suggests that a particular ray flower, such as the marguerite, may have been the intended image. In the later wall painting from Fort Shalmaneser, attributed to the reign of Esarhaddon, the triple framing bands of rosettes have a plain button center (fig. 6).

As demonstrated by the Assyrian wall paintings, the rosette was modified in the course of the ninth through seventh centuries B.C. The petals of the ray or disk flower are always drawn within a circular shape, and they vary in number from twelve to as many as sixteen. The larger number is the rule in later periods. Early on, the center of the rosette consists of concentric circles, which by the middle of the eighth century are replaced by a button center. Evidence for the further modification of the rosette in the late eighth century comes from the wall reliefs of Sargon II. Elaborate versions of the rosette resembling a flower of the Asteraceae family, which includes the daisy, chrysanthemum, and sunflower, occur as decorations on bracelets and headdresses worn by the king and his court officials.[7] In these representations the button center of the flowers is replaced by ray florets.

Later evidence for the decorative use of the rosette occurs on the stone threshold slabs discovered in Ashurbanipal's North Palace at Nineveh.[8] Both on the existing stone slabs and on those recorded in drawings, the center of the rosette shows a button center surrounded by a ring that, in turn, is surrounded by fifteen or sixteen petals. The carving of the rosette is in shallow relief, a modeled technique that gives a degree of solidity to the individual flowers. The rosette continues to be the essential ornament for the royal headdress. As shown on the stone reliefs belonging to the same king, the three rows of rosettes decorating the conical headdress probably consist of flat gold bracts.[9] In the lowermost row, each flower is rendered with much attention to detail and is a decorative interpretation of a member of the Asteraceae family. The sunflower is a likely candidate, since it is among the flowering plants that are depicted in the royal garden in room E of Ashurbanipal's palace.[10]

---

[7] Albenda 1986, pp. 150–151, pls. 139, 140. Mention should be made of an unusual version of the rosette inlaid in wood that appears on the face of two Phrygian serving stands of eighth century B.C. date. Simpson and Spirydowicz 1999, pp. 31, 39–43, figs.15–18, 24, 29–31. For discussion of the religious symbolism of the Gordion rosette, see Simpson 1998.
[8] See: Barnett 1976, pl. xx; Albenda 1978, pp. 16–18, pls. 16–26.
[9] Barnett and Lorenzini 1975, pls. 105, 127.
[10] Ibid, pl. 90.

As mentioned earlier, the rosette is the most common decorative motif represented in Assyrian art. In the course of centuries, from the Middle Assyrian period to the end of the Neo-Assyrian Empire, variants of the rosette were experimented with and applied to wall paintings, as well as carved into the stone reliefs. The basic geometric shape of the rosette is the circle, and whatever details were added to form a ray or disk flower is contained within the circular shape. In Assyrian wall paintings the plain rosette, with its petals surrounding a disk center, was generally used for band decorations, and therefore probably served a decorative purpose. However, when the rosette is viewed in broader contexts, such as the large painted circles decorated with patterned concentric circles, the rosette bracelets, and the bract attachments that embellish the headdress of the Assyrian king, the motif must be considered to have emblematic or symbolic significance.

The iconography of the rosette in the ancient Near East, from the Early Dynastic to the Neo-Assyrian and Late Babylonian periods is surveyed in an article published by E. Douglas Van Buren. There the author provides convincing evidence in the representational and decorative arts that the rosette 'symbolized the great goddess Innin, the later Ištar, and therefore the *motif*, whether typifying star or flower, was equally appropriate to her.'[11] Moreover, a late third millennium B.C. limestone seated statue of the Elamite goddess Narunte is decorated with the rosette that appears between two confronting lions at the front of the base of the statue.[12] The goddess seems to have had the reputation of being the goddess of victory. At a much later date, a text of the Assyrian king, Ashur-resha-ishi I (1133–1116 B.C.) states that the ruler restored the tower-gates of the great gate at the front of the main forecourt of the temple of the goddess Ishtar of Nineveh, and put stone rosettes all around the structures.[13]

In the Neo-Assyrian period there are examples where the rosette is directly associated with a female goddess. Goddesses wearing a horned headdress surmounted by a rosette disk are represented in several works of Assyrian art. One example is shown on a partially destroyed stone relief of Tiglath-pileser III, which depicts statues of goddesses taken as booty by Assyrian soldiers.[14] In another instance, on a stele from Til Barsip, the goddess standing upon a lion is identified by an inscription as Ishtar of Arbela.[15] On four rock reliefs at Maltai, among the procession of seven deities mounted on their respective animals, one goddess is shown standing upon a lion.[16] This goddess has

---

[11] Van Buren 1939, pp. 99–107.
[12] Amiet 1979, pp. 38–39, 129–130, figs. 36 a, b, c, d.
[13] Grayson 1972, nos. 951, 952, 955.
[14] Barnett and Falkner 1962, pp. 29–30, pls. XCII–XCIII.
[15] Thureau-Dangin and Dunand 1936, pp. 156–157, pl. XV 1. The inscription carved on the stele mentions that Assur-dû-pania of Kar-Shalmaneser dedicated it.
[16] Bachmann 1927, pp. 23–27, Tf. 26–29, 31.

also been identified as Ishtar of Arbela, whereas in the same procession the enthroned goddess supported by a lion has been identified with Ninlil or Ishtar of Nineveh. The representation of the enthroned goddess does not have the rosette disk on her headdress, unlike that of the standing goddess; however, the back of the throne is decorated with five plain rings, objects that have been associated with the goddess.[17]

On two wall reliefs dated to the reign of the ninth century B.C. king Ashurnasirpal II, beardless winged genies (*apkallu*) identified as female, wear necklaces composed of disks with rosette and star decorations.[18] On the relief from room L of the king's Northwest Palace, the four-winged genie is adorned with two necklaces. The necklace around the neck consists of two strands of beads connected to a flat disk at the front. The second necklace, which covers the chest, is composed of a thin chain and linked to it are two rows of decorated disks. The upper row shows rosettes and the lower one multi-rayed stars. On the relief from room I appear two female genies flanking and facing a stylized tree. They are two-winged; around their neck is an elaborate necklace composed of several elements. These elements include a chain of oval beads, a narrow pectoral with raised rim, and two rows of disks that are linked to one another by small rods. The decoration on the disks consists of an eight-pointed star.

An eight-pointed star enclosed within a ringed disk is one of the five divine symbols carved on the royal stele of Ashurnasirpal II; the same motif recurs on the disks with similar symbols that decorate the king's necklace.[19] On the same stele, the rosette-disk bracelet appears prominently on the king's wrist. The rosette and the star are similar, in that each motif consists of petals or rays that extend from a central circle. The rosette and the star are both identified with the goddess Ishtar; however, each motif probably represents a different attribute of the goddess. In a general way, the flower signifies the blossoming and fullness of life (aspect of fecundity), while the star represents the planet Venus (astral aspect) with which the goddess is associated.[20] On several Neo-Assyrian seals the second aspect of the goddess is depicted in human form; she stands in front of a large spiked nimbus – a circle of radiant light and astral brilliance.[21]

The star seems to have been generally excluded from the repertoire of motifs found in Assyrian wall painting. The unusual motif of the rayed-rosette that occurs in one of the fragmentary paintings of Tukulti-Ninurta I

---

[17] Albenda 1996, pp. 72–74.
[18] Ibid, figs. 1–2; Barnett and Lorenzini 1975, pl. 17.
[19] For a good illustration, see Barnett and Lorenzini 1975, pl. 2.
[20] On the astral aspect of the goddess, see Jacobsen 1976, pp. 138–141; Heimpel 1982, pp. 13–15.
[21] See: Herbordt 1992, pp. 165–166, Tf. I 7; Collon 2001, pp. 133–134, 138–140, nos. 253, 254, 270–271.

(pl. 27) may be an attempt to combine the two symbolic characteristics of Ishtar in the decorative arts. A later variant of this motif is the decorated rosette framed by rays, which appears in a wall painting from the suite of rooms in the palace of Adad-nirari III at Nimrud (pl. 5: right). Among a group of isolated details of wall paintings from the same palace at Nimrud, drawn in color by William Boutcher around 1854, are representations of three different stars (pls. 7–8). One star is similar to the example found in Layard's drawing. It is composed of a concentric arrangement of a flower with red and blue-tipped petals surrounding a white disk, a blue band, blue triangular rays, and a black circle that encloses the star. Another star shows radiating rays in black and white that surround a large disk with concentric circles, and these features are enclosed by a band of alternating red and blue squares. The black outline of a circle completes the design. The third star is closest to what may be described as a starburst. Extending outward from a large ringed disk in blue and white, are ten large blue rays with curved sides, and a red dot terminates each ray. Between the ten blue rays is the blue outline of a second row of triangular rays. From the private residence at Til Barsip a small plaster fragment, dated to the seventh century B.C., has painted on its surface what appears to be a segment of the starburst.[22]

At present, the pictorial evidence suggests that early eighth century B.C. examples of the painted starburst motif were the inspiration for the spiked nimbus that surrounds the goddess in Assyrian seal designs of the later eighth and seventh centuries, as noted above. What may be primarily a decorative rendering of the star motif occurs in a painted wall decoration discovered at Dur-Katlimmu, dated to the seventh century B.C. The wall painting includes a repeat of a black and white star with white rays, set within a solid black circle on a white ground (fig. 5a). Its arrangement with alternating registers of dot-centered circles, separated by black stripes, seems to echo earlier wall paintings from Assyrian sites; however, the visual impact is strikingly different.

Circle

The circle (*kippatu*) occurs in a variety of circumstances in Assyrian art. It is the most common geometric shape found in ornamental wall painting of the Neo-Assyrian period. Oftentimes additional details were added to this basic shape, in order to enhance or vary its appearance. In ornamental wall painting the circle appears early on, as evidenced on some of the painted fragments from Kar-Tukulti-Ninurta. One common feature added together

---

[22] Abbate 1994, pl. II, 21. The fragmentary section of the radiating circle (nimbus) may be compared with the complete version shown on a seventh century B.C. impression of a stamp seal from Nineveh; see Herbordt 1992, Tf. II, 2.

with this geometric shape is the central dot. In the Middle Assyrian examples, the dot-centered circle is used as part of a larger floral motif, either a rosette or a 'palmette' plant. Among the fragmentary ninth century wall paintings from the Northwest Palace at Nimrud, the dot-centered circle is used as the central filler for the twisted ribbon or guilloche. In this instance, however, the circle is composed of a solid black and a solid white ring with prominent black dot in the center, forming a target motif. The target recurs on the upper surface of a number of contemporary clay cones.[23] It also appears on decorated wall attachments as exemplified by a number of fragmentary glazed bricks discovered at Fort Shalmaneser in Nimrud.[24] Inscriptions inscribed on several of these bricks date them to the reign of Shalmaneser III. Visible on the decorated surface are four concentric semicircles in a row that were probably completed into whole circles on the adjacent bricks. On a few bricks the colors of the concentric circles are white, black, and white, with a black center, while on several other bricks they are white, yellow, and white, with a yellow center. Both groups of targets are on a blue background. It may be noted that a brick with similar design appears among the fragments of bricks illustrated in one of Layard's drawings (see the upper right side of pl. 2).

Among Layard's renderings of the fragmentary wall paintings from the suite of rooms in Adad-nirari III's palace at Nimrud, there appears a row of four white circles outlined in blue with a prominent blue dot center (pl. 5: left). The inclusion of an arched line connecting two of the circles indicates that, originally, the dot-centered circles formed a garland. In addition, one circle has a tri-petal extension, an indication that the geometric motif represents a flower. It may be noted that the particular way in which the circles are rendered recalls the eyestone (*ēnu*), an agate or chalcedony stone that was considered semi-precious and used for jewelry.[25] There are also existing eyestones with dedicatory text or curses inscribed on the surface.[26] A second variant of the circle garland is depicted in another of Layard's renderings of the wall paintings from the same palace. The garland consists of a solid blue circle with a narrow white border (pl. 3: right). The floral aspect of the circle

---

[23] For examples, see Albenda 1991, pls. VII, IX d; Curtis and Reade, 1995, figs. 50–52.

[24] Curtis *et al* 1993, pp. 25–26. figs. 23–25.

[25] Maxwell-Hyslop, 1971, pls. 55, 164. Among the treasures found in the graves of Assyrian queens, discovered at Nimrud, include jewelry inlaid with eyestones; see Elmer-De Witt 1989, pp. 80–81 (color photographs). Other color photographs of the jewelry are on the Internet; see www.aina.org/aol/nimrud (2003). Of interest, an Assyrian text mentions that the headdress of the god Nabu was fashioned with eyestones; see Parpola 1993, no. 41, fig. 11 (jewelry pendant with eyestone).

[26] Amiet 1979, no. 244. Eyestones are included among a list of precious and semi-precious stones with Assyrian royal inscriptions; see Galter 1987, nos. 2, 9, 40, 42, 79.

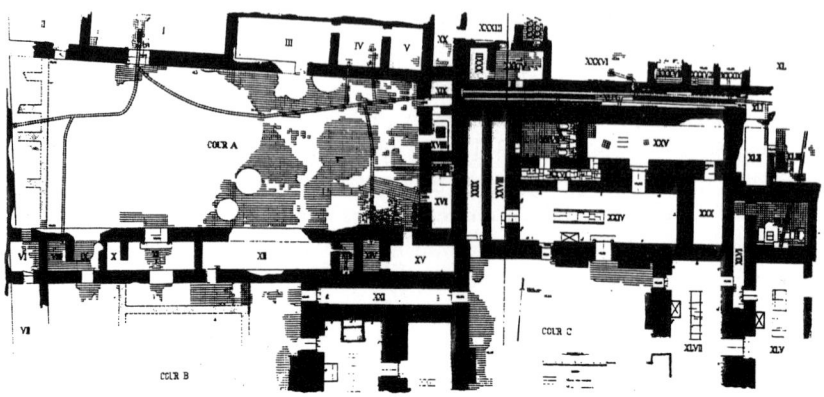

Fig. 7. Plan of royal residence at Til Barsip.
Redrawn. Thureau-Dangin and Dunand 1936, plan B.

is indicated by the tri-petal extension at one end. It may be that here, too, the circle itself represents an eyestone.

The plain dot-centered circle was a common motif in the wall paintings discovered in the royal palace at Khorsabad. Several painted fragments excavated in the throne room of the palace show repeats of the dot-centered circle arranged in two and probably more rows, and there is evidence that the pattern of circles was a favorite decoration for the ceiling beams. The individual rows of circles painted on the plaster fragments that were discovered in room 12 (bathroom) of the royal residence include those decorated with a dot center, a target, and a rosette (fig. 2). In contrast to the modest decoration on the circles from room 12, the most elaborately decorated circles in Assyrian wall painting are those that were applied to the walls of the private residences at Khorsabad. The circles are assuredly masterfully designed with all their intricate details, for they impart a sense of balance and richness in pattern (pls. 32, 33). On the other hand, at Arslan Tash one finds a modified version of the decorated concentric circle, within which are two barred circles. The circle alternates with a decorated cushion-shaped square, together forming the central design of the continuous frieze that was painted on the walls of the chambers forming the royal suite (fig. 4a). A horizontal band in the center of the register connects the respective motifs. This added detail indicates a possible late eighth or, more likely, an early seventh century date for the Arslan Tash wall paintings.

Dot-centered, concentric, and target circles were common motifs applied to the black-and-white painted wall decorations in the non-royal residences in North Syria, dated to the late eighth and seventh centuries B.C. In addition,

94

one finds a connecting stripe in the center of the register that contains the row of circles framed by solid stripes. A simple design of five thin concentric circles, but without a center dot, decorated the walls of two small chambers at Arslan Tash (fig. 4b), in a building that probably housed an official attached to the royal household. This wall painting may be contemporary with those that adorned the royal residence, or slightly later in date. The combination of the target motif and connecting stripes forming a modest but attractive design is encountered in the wall painting reconstructed from painted fragments discovered in residence E at Til Barsip (fig. 4c). The subdivision of the register into two equal sections is unusual, with the upper and lower ones containing a target on either side of the large central target. A unifying feature of the overall design is the use of triple stripes that frame the upper and lower registers and connect the central targets.

The wall reliefs discovered *in situ* at Dur-Katlimmu show that dot-centered circles predominated and varied somewhat, within the various registers that were separated by three or more solid stripes. The eyestone motif and a circle, the dot center of which is surrounded by a thin circle, occur in one wall painting (fig. 5b). A single register of targets framed by a pair of stripes, which are also connected to one another by another pair of stripes, was part of the painted decoration on the walls of another chamber in the same building (fig. 5c). In these two instances the single register of targets is placed below a landscape scene in one case and a row of ostriches in the other.

The circle in ornamental wall painting was favored over other geometric shapes, such as the triangle and square. One may deduce that this shape had special meaning, beyond the purely decorative contexts of the visual arts. In Assyrian art, the circle forms the symbol for three astral features: moon, sun, and morning/evening star. Their symbols represent the three deities Sin, Shamash, and Ishtar. On the stele of Ashurnasirpal II, the three circles are among a group of five symbols representing different deities.[27] One circle has the inclusion of a curved line that delineates a crescent, the symbol of the moon god Sin. The two other circles show a ringed center. Surrounding the ringed center of one of these circles is a series of transverse lines forming a cross of the formée type, the symbol of the god Shamash. The circle itself is small and framed by two rows of striations representing birdlike wings and tail. Surrounding the ringed center in the other circle is a series of diagonal lines forming a star, the symbol of the goddess Ishtar. A winged disk on which the figure of a bearded deity, the god Shamash, appears in lieu of the cross is represented in a ritual setting on two wall reliefs from the throne room of the Northwest palace of Ashurnasirpal II.[28] Turning to representations

---

27 Barnett and Lorenzini 1975, pl. 2.
28 See: Ibid, pl. 13; Meuszyński 1975, pp. 55–56, pls. II (B-23), VI (B-13), fig. 6. Two additional

on Assyrian cylinder seals, several examples show the winged circle with or without a button-like central dot.[29] At a much later date, in the reign of Ashurbanipal, the ornament on the pole of the king's chariot shows a three-ringed circle surrounding the figure of a goddess, Mullissu of Nineveh. Prominent rays with ringed tips extend from the outermost circle.[30]

Carved on their surface of boundary stones (*kudurru*) of the Middle Babylonian period are symbols of various deities, and the disks of Shamash and Ishtar are readily identified by the standardized designs.[31] Neo- and Late Babylonian seals provide further evidence that the circle with a dot center represents the symbol of a deity. In two cylinder seal examples, a worshipper or priest stands before two divine symbols, each one surmounting a large pear-shaped stand that, in turn, rests upon an altar.[32] The context of both scenes confirms that the divine symbols represent concrete objects. One symbol is the crescent of Sin and the other is a disk with a dot and the four lines of a cross is the symbol of Shamash. A more detailed version of the disk symbol of Shamash, decorated with the four-pointed cross and radiating wavy lines, occurs on the ninth century B.C. stone tablet of Nabuaplaiddin and on the sixth century B.C. stele of the Babylonian king, Nabonidus.[33] From the several examples mentioned above, it seems that the wings attached to the disk of Shamash, a common feature during the Neo-Assyrian period, were omitted in the Neo- and Late Babylonian periods.

In Assyrian ornamental wall painting, the circle with a dot in the center is a decorative motif. In some instances it is the basis for the sign or symbol of one or more deities, as exemplified by its occurrence in other art forms. An all-over pattern of circles with a dot in the center embellishes the garment worn by Sennacherib, the Assyrian king represented on the wall reliefs illustrating the Lachish campaign.[34] The motif may have importance beyond its decorative aspect. It is also used for celestial signs, either a planet or star, as demonstrated by three star calendar fragments of clay tablets from Nineveh.[35] Two of the fragments show the circle representing a planet (*Bibbu*) and the

---

depictions of a deity in a winged disk hovering above the Assyrian king appear in scenes of battle on the wall reliefs in the throne room. One deity is bearded and holds a bow in the lowered left hand. Behind the deity, who emerges from a narrow ring, are the rays associated with the god Shamash. The other deity is beardless and is surrounded by a broad ring. This deity shoots with bow and arrow, and may represent the war goddess Ishtar. For illustrations, see Barnett and Lorenzini 1975, pl. 39; Winter 1983, figs. 11, 12; Livingstone 1989, fig. 2.

[29] For discussion and illustrations of the winged disk, with and without god, in seal designs, see Collon 2001, pp. 81–82.

[30] Barnett and Lorenzini1975, pl. 107.

[31] Pritchard 1969, p. 311, pls. 519, 520.

[32] Collon 2001, pp. 193–194, nos. 389, 390.

[33] Pritchard 1969, pp. 318, 379, pls. 529, 837.

[34] Barnett and Lorenzini 1975, pls. 76, 77.

[35] Hunger 1992, figs.1, 6, 9.

third the star (*kakkabu*), and both astral signs have a similar arrangement in the respective calendars. Thus it may be that the choice of motif for the patterned dress of the Assyrian king may also indicate an association with celestial symbolism.

A variant of the circle with dot center is the concentric circle, that is, a series of circles within a circle. The motif occurs in Assyrian wall painting, although less frequently before the seventh century B.C. (fig. 4b). There is less direct evidence that the motif of the concentric circle can be equated with a celestial sign or symbol of a deity. The representation of the goddess in the triple ringed circle, mentioned previously, may be an indicator for such an association; however, at present the association remains an open possibility. Nonetheless, it should be observed that on the wall reliefs of Ashurbanipal, where the patterning on the dress of the king consists primarily of repetitive rows of star-disks, there are two notable exceptions among the episodic scenes from room S. In this instance the pattern consists of alternating rows of star-disks and concentric circles that may be viewed as three rings.[36] As an astral sign the star is generally associated with the Venus goddess Ishtar. It may be that in the context of the patterned fabric of the royal costume, at least, the motif of the concentric circle is also to be interpreted as an astral sign. If the last notion is accepted, one needs to consider the interpretation of the concentric circle. Perhaps the circle represents the halo and radiance associated with celestial phenomena. Among the celestial observations of the sun and the moon are 'the sun at its rising carries red radiance,' 'the sun surrounded by a halo' and 'the moon surrounded by a halo.'[37] Brief phrases such as these can be rendered in the visual sphere simply as a series of circles – or rings – one within the other. Thus it may be that the two motifs on the dress of Ashurbanipal are astral signs associated with specific deities. The star-disk represents the Venus Ishtar, and the most likely deity represented by the concentric circle is either Shamash (sun) or Sin (moon).

Ostrich

The ostrich (*lurmu*) occurs in a wall painting from Dur-Katlimmu, dated to the seventh century B.C. (fig. 5c). The painting shows three repeats of the bird in black outline, advancing to the right. The running gait of the ostrich is depicted with simplicity of line. Its movement is correctly indicated by the outstretched near and far wings, which are respectively extended downward and upward. The bird moves upon a flat rocky terrain indicated by three bands of a scale pattern. Evidently the ostrich is a late addition to the repertory of motifs used in Assyrian wall painting.

---

[36] Barnett and Lorenzini 1975, pls. 122, 124.
[37] For examples, see Hunger 1992, nos. 6, 20, 68, 44, 308, 413.

The ostrich is known to have existed in Mesopotamia from early periods through very recent times, when it became extinct in that region. Early representations of the ostrich occur on cylinder seal designs from Ras-Shamra and Minet-el-Beida in Syria, and are dated between the sixteenth and fourteenth centuries B.C.[38] Of a later second-millennium date, the ostrich appears among astral signs and images on a Babylonian boundary stone, as well as on several Assyrian cylinder seals, on which the bird is shown fleeing a human hunter.[39] Ostriches are mentioned in the inscriptions of several Assyrian kings who reigned from the twelfth to the ninth centuries B.C., describing the royal hunt and killing of wild animals. Tiglath-pileser I (114–1076) states that he brought down every kind of winged birds of heaven.[40] However, the killing of ostriches is first mentioned by Ashur-bel-kala (1073–1056).[41] On the other hand, Adad-nirari II (911–891) states that he formed herds of different animals in the Inner City (Ashur), which included ostriches.[42] Presumably, the Assyrian king established a royal zoo, an event that recurred in the reign of his grandson, Ashurnasirpal II.[43] Tukulti-ninurta II (890–884) mentions in one text that he killed ostriches on his hunting expedition and that he also captured the young of the ostriches, during his campaign along the Middle Euphrates region.[44] In the same general region, Ashurnasirpal II killed twenty ostriches and captured twenty others alive.[45] However, the inscription on the so-called banquet stele mentions that the same Assyrian king slew two hundred ostriches and captured one hundred forty of them.[46] The large numbers of birds listed by the ninth century B.C. Assyrian kings are an indication that ostriches thrived along the desert and forest regions of the Middle Euphrates region.

The ostrich is a large flightless bird, attaining a height of about 2.4 meters (8 feet) from crown to foot. It is a rapid runner, and can attain a speed of about 40 miles per hour (65 km) for up to thirty minutes. The ostrich spreads its wings when running, and its powerful legs are used for purposes of defense. The male ostrich is black with white wings and tail; the female is a dull brown. The characteristics of the ostrich must have made it a formidable object of the hunt for Assyrian kings. Representations of the ostrich are known in other media produced during the Neo-Assyrian period, such as garment decoration, glazed ware, cylinder seals, and carved ivories.

---

[38] Schaeffer-Forrer 1983, pp. 82 (R.S. 4.162), 130 (R.S. 24.403), pl. XVII 19 (R.S. 6.051).
[39] See: Hunger 1992, fig. 17; Frankfort 1954, figs. 159, 160.
[40] Grayson 1976, no. 45.
[41] Ibid, no. 248.
[42] Ibid, no. 436.
[43] Ibid, no. 598.
[44] Ibid, no. 472.
[45] Ibid, no.581.
[46] Ibid, no. 682.

Two ostriches with outstretched wings flanking a palmette are depicted among the ninth century B.C. decorated garments recorded by Layard, and similar birds also appear on a large blue-green glazed vase, discovered in a room of the Northwest Palace at Nimrud, which is decorated with a hunting scene.[47] In the latter example, dated to the seventh century B.C., a mounted horseman runs down three ostriches in open terrain, next to a river with fish, with a winged sun disk hovering above. Each ostrich assumes a different gait: one bird strides forward, the second flees rapidly with outstretched wings, and the third pauses to look back at the scene from the safety of the opposite side of the river. The renderings of the ostriches disclose that the seventh century B.C. craftsman had observed knowledge of the movements of these birds.

One group of seals has representational scenes showing an ostrich pursued by an adversary on foot. This group has been studied for one particular theme, which illustrates a method used by nest robbers of enticing away an ostrich from its eggs.[48] Other interesting designs found on carved cylinder seals depict a three-part, heraldic arrangement of the capture of ostriches. Two of the seals have similar representations. Both, one of which was discovered at Nineveh and the other, also thought to be from the same site, include an inscription stating that it is the seal of Urzana, King of Musasir.[49] These seals are datable to the late eighth century B.C. and probably originate from the same workshop, although several details in their compositions do differ. The two seals show a four-winged genie clutching an ostrich by its long twisted neck in each hand. Each bird turns its head back to face the genie and stands submissively, as indicated by the position of the wings, which are kept at the side of the body. However in one scene only the near wing is visible, while in the other both wings are depicted. The scene on a third seal shows a hero standing with one foot on a recumbent goat while, at the same time, clutching an ostrich by the neck in each hand.[50] The birds have open beaks and turn toward the heroic figure who lifts them off the ground. Their bodies hover obliquely and their wings are spread in a fluttering motion.

The third seal may be compared with a small ivory group carved in the round that was discovered at Fort Shalmaneser. It represents an Asiatic carrying a goat on his shoulders, with at his side an ostrich that he grasps by the neck.[51] The ostrich with open beak walks in a fluttering gait, indicated

---

[47] See: Layard 1849b, pl. 47; Mallowan 1966, p. 120, fig. 61.
[48] Collon 1998.
[49] For these seal impressions, see: Collon, 1987, pp. 77, 141, nos. 350, 405; Moortgat 1940, p. 73, Tf. C 7; Dorow 1820, pp. 3, 6–7, Tf. I. (The photograph of the Urzana seal impression is reversed in Collon.) Dorow states that the Urzana seal was found before 1820, and is said to come from the mound at Nineveh.
[50] Moortgat 1940, p. 141, no. 613.
[51] See: Mallowan 1966, pl. 445; Herrmann 1992, pp. 101–102, pl. 62, no. 303.

by the upward wing touching the human figure and the downward wing, a fragment of which is broken, kept at side of its body. The ivory group has been dated to the seventh century B.C. The seal design just discussed may likewise belong to the same general period. A detail of particular interest on the carved ivory is the position of the ostrich's wings, which is similar to respective outstretched and down-turned wings of the birds depicted on the wall painting from Dur-Katlimmu. Thus both the ivory group and Dur-Katlimmu wall painting were produced during the seventh century B.C., although their different artistic merits must be acknowledged. One may surmise that a more permanent decorative object, such as the carved ivory, inspired the painted version of the ostrich. Mention should be made of a fourth seal, probably Babylonian and datable to the same period.[52] The scene carved on that seal depicts a hero flanked by ostriches, which he grips by the neck. The birds spread their wings and kick at the man with one foot, the other leg standing on the ground. The vigor of their actions is in defense of their young, as shown by the two ostrich chicks beneath each adult bird.

Large birds with outstretched wings and running in a row appear in several designs on Neo-Assyrian seals, and despite the cursory linear style they are probably identifiable as ostriches.[53] The subject matter of this group of seal designs is comparable to that on the wall painting discovered at Dur-Katlimmu, which suggests that the motif of running ostriches enjoyed some popularity in the seventh century B.C. Interestingly, the motif of the running ostrich also appears on a group of eight small trapezoidal plaques in ivory discovered at Fort Shalmaneser. They form a unified group in the Assyrian style of carving.[54] Each ostrich runs to the left with open beak, extended feathered wings, and one foot off the ground. The probable date of production is attributed to the ninth century B.C., in the reign of Shalmaneser III or slightly later. However the finding of mural paintings in the same and adjoining rooms, which are attributable to the reign of Esarhaddon, raises the possibility that the ivories showing ostriches are of contemporary date. A seventh century B.C. date for the Fort Shalmaneser ivories would add to the number of examples of known late representations of ostriches in Assyrian art.

It is likely that the depiction of the ostrich in Assyrian art was originally inspired by the hunting exploits of the Assyrian kings. During the later period of Assyrian rule, live ostriches may have been imported from the Middle Euphrates region and from as far as Egypt, if the above-mentioned

---

[52] Collon 2001, p. 171, no. 334. For other seal impressions showing a hero grasping an ostrich in each hand, see Herbordt 1992, pp. 235, 245, Tf. 8, 1–2. An unusual seal design depicts two ostriches flanking a 'rosette tree'; see Collon 2001, p. 104, no. 197.
[53] See: Moortgat 1940, pp. 148–149, nos. 712–714; Collon 2001, pp. 57–58, nos. 90–92.
[54] Herrmann 1992, pp. 51–52, pl. 2, nos. 10–17.

carved ivory in the round is an indication. Overall, stylistic differences are observable among the respective renderings of ostriches in the various art forms, since they were made at different times by different hands in different places.

Guilloche

The basic motif of the guilloche is a twisted braid of two or more strands or ribbons. In the painted examples found in Assyrian art of the ninth century B.C., the guilloche is a modest version, limited to two twisted ribbons. The Assyrian guilloche is composed of a series of circles with a prominent dot center and the equidistant spaces between them determine the width of each of the two ribbons. The twisted ribbons follow the over-under pattern, typical of twisted strands. The Assyrian guilloche seems to have been planned according to a simple mathematical formula that imparts a visual sense of balance. Taken from one fragmentary extant painted guilloche from Nimrud, the measurements are approximately 18 cm, 20 cm, 18 cm for the respective widths of the upper ribbon, the circle, and the lower ribbon; the ratio is 9/10.1.9/10.[55] Since the width of each ribbon is slightly narrower than that of the circle, this measured detail may have been an artistic refinement to offset an otherwise visual weightiness. Generally, the published painted fragments from Nimrud show the ribbons with an S-twist, and each ribbon is decorated with a chevron pattern. The colors are limited to red, blue, black, white, and yellow ochre. Set against a blue background, the visual impression of the large guilloche produced by the bold combinations of color and pattern has been described as dynamic.

The guilloche on a fragmentary wall painting recorded in one of Layard's drawings, made during his excavations in the Northwest Palace of Ashurnasirpal II, is a plain version (pl. 1, fig. 1a). As reproduced in color, the two ribbons are red and blue, and form a Z-twist around the black-and-white circle with its prominent black dot center. A narrow white border on the inner and outer edges of the twisted ribbons outlines the guilloche. This last detail adds a contrasting sparkle to the overall appearance of the guilloche. Another painted plaster fragment showing an S-twist guilloche with a target center is a more recent discovery, and came from the debris of throne room of Ashurnasirpal's palace.[56] Reproduced in color, one ribbon shows black chevrons on a white ground and the other ribbon shows alternating red and blue chevrons on a white ground.

Aside from the examples discovered in the Northwest Palace at Nimrud, the use of the guilloche in Assyrian wall painting is otherwise unknown.

---

[55] Tomabechi 1986, pp. 51–52, fig. 5.
[56] Illustrated on the Internet; see www.learningsites.com (2003).

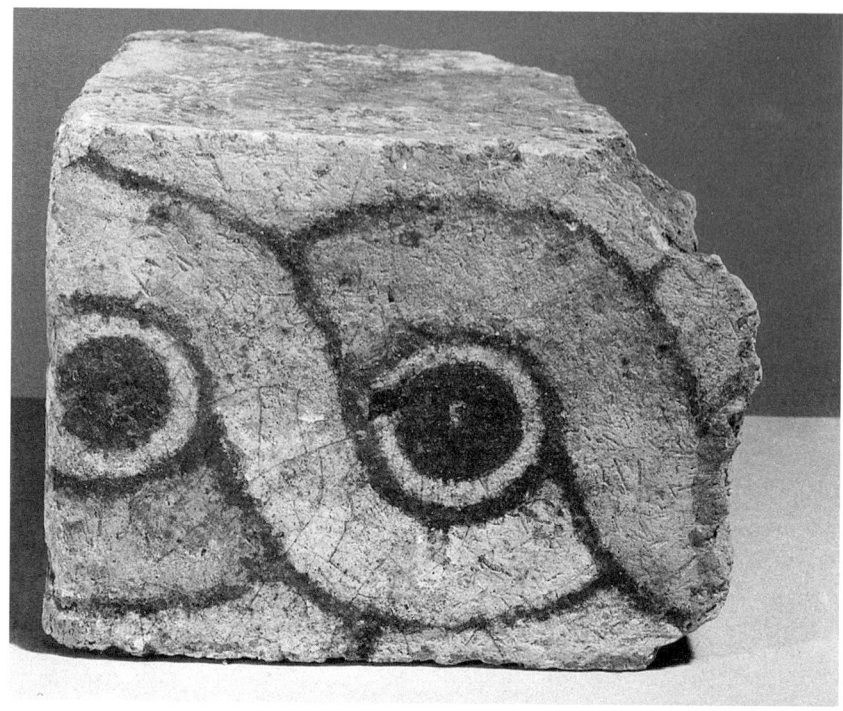

Pl. 34. Glazed brick fragment with guilloche design. Nimrud, 9th century
B.C. Metropolitan Museum of Art, Roger Fund, 1958, 58.31.58.

However, the guilloche does occur in other art forms dated to the ninth
century B.C. A painted glazed tile, originally forming part of a narrative
scene representing the Assyrian king and military attendants, shows a large
guilloche that probably serves as the lower decorative border (pl. 35).[57] The
guilloche is outlined in black, its two Z-twist ribbons are white with yellow
edges, and in the center is a prominent black dot. The extant lower portion of
another glazed tile discovered at Ashur, showing a similar narrative scene,
also displays a large Z-twist guilloche.[58] The tile was taken from a dwelling
house near the temple of Nabu, where it may have been set up originally.
Other ceramic examples in which the guilloche occurs include ninth century glazed bricks from Nimrud, decorated on one narrow side (pls. 34, 36),
and wall attachments or knobbed plates discovered at several Assyrian sites.[59]

---

[57] The glazed brick is reproduced in color; see Reade 1983, fig. 41.
[58] Andrae 1925, pp. 28–29, fig. 6.
[59] See: Moortgat 1959, p. 18, Tf. 18; Albenda 1991, p. 51, pls. III b, IV, VI, fig. 7; Curtis and
Reade 1995, no. 52.

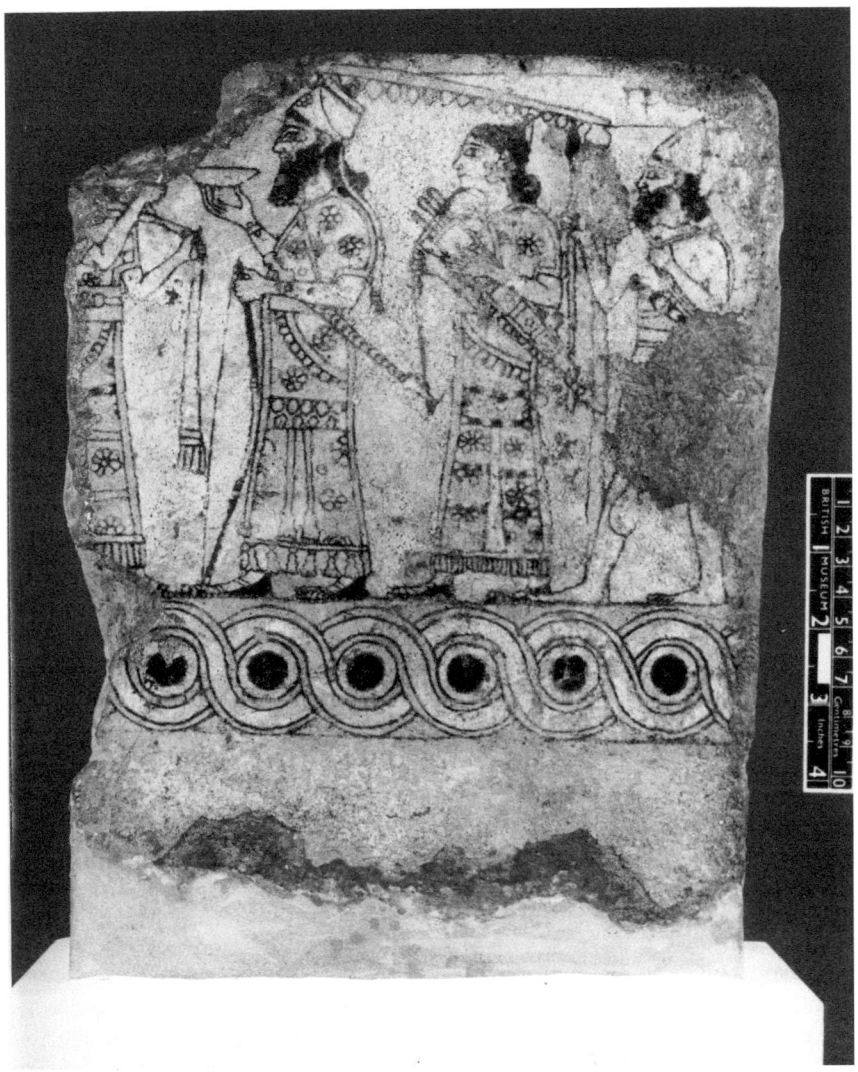

Pl. 35. Glazed brick with painted narrative scene and
guilloche border. 9th century B.C. British Museum WA 90859.

On the last group of objects the guilloche consists of two plain ribbons, often
in black and white, surrounding a dot-centered circle. In another example the
ribbons are cream and beige on a white ground, and in yet another example
the ribbons of the guilloche are beige with chevrons in black and white.
S-twist and Z-twist ribbons of the guilloche occur on the wall plates, an
indication that the choice of the twist reflects the preference of the ceramist.

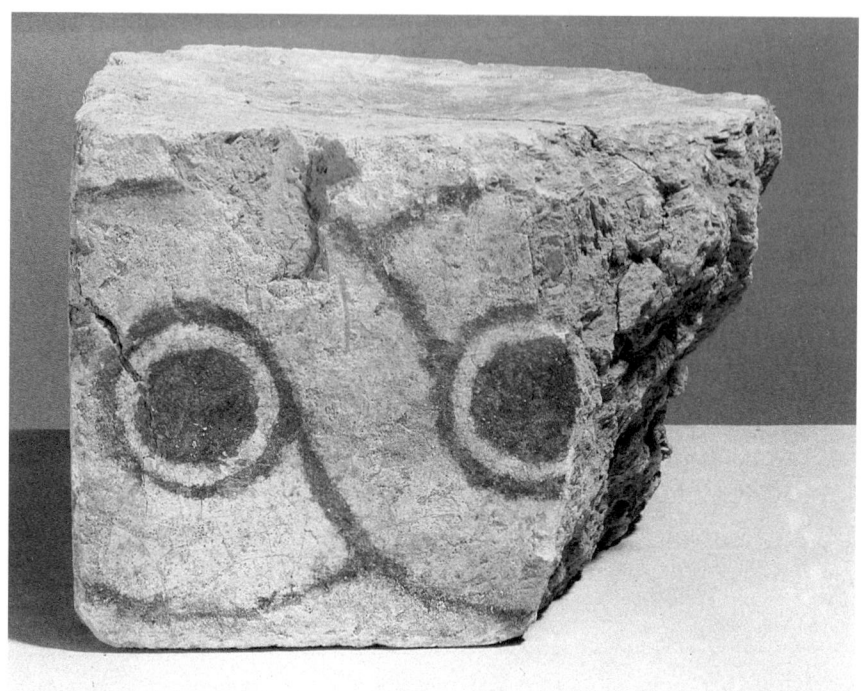

Pl. 36. Glazed brick fragment with guilloche design. Nimrud, 9th century
B.C. Metropolitan Museum of Art, Roger Fund 1958, 58.31.59.

Decorated ivory carving in the Assyrian style also furnishes examples of
the guilloche, where it is used as a divider or border decoration.[60] Generally,
the guilloche consists of two plain ribbons surrounding a circle with dot
center, either in an S-twist or a Z-twist. Most of the Assyrian style ivories
are dated to the ninth century, in the reign of Ashurnasipal II. However, one
interesting example of the guilloche carved on a fragmentary ivory plaque
is datable to the late ninth century or later. The guilloche serves as a divider
for the upper and lower representational scenes, has a Z-twist, and the two
ribbons between the respective prominent dots are spaced rather closely.
Consequently, the under ribbon does not always appear continuous, when it
becomes the upper ribbon. A particularly attractive example carved on four
fragments of an ivory frame shows eight-petal rosettes surrounded by the
ribbons of the guilloche; however, this example is identified as belonging to
the North Syrian tradition of ivory carving.[61] Mention should be made of a
group of ivory fragments carved in the Assyrian style, which are decorated

---

[60] Herrmann 1992, pp. 3, 27, 50, 57, 58. 129, nos. 7–10, 58, 62, 126, 475–476.
[61] Ibid, p. 126, nos. 458–459.

with a double guilloche; that is, two connected strands of the guilloche pattern.[62] The facility with which the double guilloche is carved suggests that this particular version was utilized in other works of the decorative arts.

In Assyrian wall painting the guilloche no longer occurs after the ninth century B.C. By the late eighth century, there is no evidence of its use in the various forms of Assyrian art. Yet, it did not disappear entirely from the repertory of decorative motifs, since the guilloche was used to embellish the yoke pole of the royal chariot that is represented on a wall relief dated to the reign of Ashurbanipal.[63]

The guilloche has a long history in Mesopotamian art. Seal impressions from Uruk in southern Mesopotamia, dated to before the third millennium B.C., show braid patterns alternating with birds in a variety of combinations. Other seal impressions have braid patterns made from entwined snakes.[64] In the third millennium B.C., a fine example of the interweaving band forming a guilloche occurs on a stone plaque from Tello (ancient Girsu).[65] In the second millennium, the guilloche occurs in cylinder seal designs produced at different times and originating from a number of sites to the west of Assyria, as far as Cyprus.[66] The guilloche is represented in a wall painting from the governor's palace at Nuzi, in a work of the Mitannian period dated to the fifteenth century B.C.[67] The early use of the guilloche in Assyrian art is represented in several seal designs discovered at Ashur that have been dated to the end of the fourteenth century B.C.[68] A possible inspirational source of the interweaving bands on these seals may be the example depicted in the wall painting from Nuzi. In the Neo-Assyrian period the guilloche as a decorative pattern seems to have enjoyed a brief period of popularity during the ninth century, and used particularly for wall painting and artifacts produced by the Assyrian royal workshops. It is not clear whether the guilloche is purely decorative or has symbolic significance. One may mention that on a number of stylized trees carved on the wall relief in Ashurnasirpal's Northwest Palace paired stems or ribbons extending from the central pole to the outer floral garland include a complete swirl of the guilloche.[69]

---

[62] Ibid, pp. 58–59, no. 61. The fragments were discovered in room S4, and may be contemporary with the wall painting in the adjacent throne room (S5).

[63] Barnett and Lorenzini 1975, pl. 107.

[64] Collon 1986, pp. 13, 15, fig. 9.

[65] Moortgat 1969, fig. 117.

[66] See: Schaeffer-Forrer 1983, pp. 35, 49, 55, 62, 66, 90, 132, pl. XXXVI 1–7; Collon 1986, pp. 59, 62, nos. 1–2, 4, 6, 18, 21, 23–24; Collon 2000, pp. 288–290. Several representations of the guilloche show double and triple twisted strands.

[67] See: Moortgat 1959, pp. 13–14, Tf. 15; Moortgat 1969, p. 109, fig. 77.

[68] Moortgat 1940, p. 62, Tf. D 2, 3.

[69] For illustrations, see: Paley 1976, pls. 5, 8, 12–15; Albenda 1994b, figs. 1–4, 8 a, b. Albenda's study shows that two of the four variant styles of the stylized tree, described as rayed, lattice, double-garland, and ornate double-garland, include swirls of paired stems.

A possible stimulus for the revival of the guilloche as decoration in the ninth century B.C. may derive from the major works of art that the Assyrian kings came into visual contact with, during their military campaigns to northern Syrian cities, as well as from small decorated objects that were received as gifts or tribute. A city known to have utilized the guilloche in its art is Carchemish. The guilloche serves as a border at the base of stone slabs that were carved with figural subjects and set up along a long wall of sculpture associated with the Hittite palace.[70] The pattern is composed of paired ribbons that twist around a central dot. The stone reliefs have been dated to the tenth century B.C. At the same site, an unusual variant of the guilloche border band occurs on a fragmentary stone relief of a lion.[71] The pattern consists of triple ribbons that twist around a central dot. This relief is datable to the Middle Hittite period, and exemplifies the early use of the guilloche in Hittite art. Among the decorated objects discovered at Carchemish, datable to the Late Hittite period, are fragments of steatite pyxis that are carved with figural subjects and the characteristic double guilloche.[72] These small objects may represent the types of gifts that were presented to the ninth century Assyrian kings, in particular Ashurnasirpal II who marched to Carchemish and received lavish gifts from its ruler.[73] We may assume that Assyrian contacts with the cities of northern Syria brought to the attention of Assyrian craftsmen an ornate motif that was thereafter included in ornamental wall painting and other decorative arts.

Arcaded garlands

A common decorative design in Assyrian wall painting is the arrangement of one to three floral elements in a continuous repeat pattern, connected by plain or decorated narrow stems. The choice of floral elements seems to have differed in the course of the Neo-Assyrian period. Several examples of the garland occur only in the reign of a given Assyrian king, thus leading to the suggestion that artistic experimentation might have been sometimes encouraged. In a later phase of the Neo-Assyrian period, however, the floral elements that form the garland are restricted to a few examples. Although the limited choice of flora reveals a conservative outlook, over time that tendency is offset by the refinement in the rendering of the various floral specimens.

Arrangement of plant motifs into a continuous garland occurs early on, in Assyrian wall painting. The earliest is found in the Middle Assyrian

---

[70] Woolley and Barnett 1952, p. 166, pls. B 37, B39 b, B 40 a, b, B 41 a, b, B 42 a, b, B 43 b, B 46 a, b.
[71] Woolley 1921, pp. 116–117, 240, pl. B 31 c, fig. 35.
[72] Woolley and Barnett 1952, pp. 250–151.
[73] Grayson 1976, nos. 584, 601.

wall paintings from Kar-Tukulti-Ninurta. In one reconstructed illustration (pl. 28), the garland shows two prominent plants connected by curved stems decorated with black and white squares. The plants are shown essentially in outline form and differ markedly from each another. One plant seems to derive from a cluster of long pointed leaves rising upward. The other shows a broad scalloped border and within it are what appear to be individual leaves radiating from a central area. This plant replicates the upper part of the tree represented in the lower right side panel of the same painting.

Floral garland

The painted floral garland discovered in the Northwest Palace of Ashurnasipal II is unusual because of the three different plant elements of different shape and size that alternate in a balanced arrangement (pl. 1, fig. 1a). The plants appear similar to the pinecone, palmette, and lily, but have been reduced to simple outline forms. Within each plant, however, a combination of pattern and color provides the visual richness that is a characteristic feature of the garland. The boldness of the rendering is accentuated by the black outline surrounding the individual plants and their connecting stems, which are also patterned. The connecting stems are somewhat flattened and frame the outer edge of the broad middle band containing the guilloche. The arrangement of the floral garland in mirror image, above and below, may be an innovation during this period. The floral garland designed for wall painting in the Northwest Palace of Ashurnasirpal II seems to have been a favored decoration. It occurs on contemporary wall reliefs from the palace, where it embellishes border bands of costumes, as well as a broad necklace.[74] At this juncture it is useful to discuss separately, each of the three plants forming the painted garland.

Cone

The shape of the cone suggests that a tree of the pine family (*pinaceae*) is its original source. The all-over scale pattern within the cone-shape makes this identification likely, since scales are characteristic of cones or 'fruits' belonging to evergreen conifers. Except for the wall painting recorded in Layard's sketch, no other example of the pinecone occurs in that art form. A cone does occur with other plants as a textile border pattern, and on an ivory in the Assyrian style of carving the pinecone appears together with the pomegranate in an alternating pattern.[75] Embroidered plant motifs on garments show the palmette with sprouting stems that end in a cone, and stylized trees whose long linear branches terminate in a cone.[76] On carved

---

[74] Paley 1976, pls. 23 c, 25 a.
[75] Mallowan and Davies 1970, p. 19, no. 10.
[76] For convenient detail illustrations of Layard's drawings, with references, see: Bleibtreu 1980, pp. 58–59, Abb. 17–21.

stone threshold slabs dated to the eighth and seventh centuries B.C., the cone combines and alternates with a lotus in a quatrefoil arrangement to form an elegant design. [77]

When held by winged genies depicted on the ninth century wall reliefs, the cone or an object resembling that fruit takes on significance as it may relate to a religious event, or as a symbol with special meaning.[78] One reason for its significance is perhaps that the cones of the pine tree are of two kinds, male and female. The male cone, which is small, produces the pollen that is received by the ovules on the upper sides of the female cone – the pinecone. After fertilization the cone grows and eventually opens, and this allows the seeds to drop out. Since pine trees have both sexes on the same tree, they are monoecious. Several interpretations have been given to the scenes on the wall reliefs in which the winged genie holding the cone confronts the stylized tree, the so-call sacred tree, or stands behind the king, or stands alone. An original past conclusion which has recently found renewed acceptance is that the tree scene represents the pollination of the date palm and, furthermore, that there is a connection of the date palm tree to Ishtar, the goddess of sexual fertility.[79] An aspect of the goddess as paradox is her androgyny: she embodies both femaleness and maleness.[80] Similarly, the fertilized pinecone embodies the two sexes that are grown on the same tree, and one wonders whether the cone depicted in Assyrian art may be a symbolic reminder of one of Ishtar's characteristics. The association between the cone and palm tree is treated within a religious context on the ninth century wall reliefs. Interestingly, on the seventh century B.C. wall relief of Ashurbanipal the cone has now evolved into the pine tree that alternates with the date palm in a natural setting as a backdrop for the banqueting royal couple in the garden.[81]

Palmette

The palmette represented in the wall painting of Ashurnasirpal II is drawn with six fronds arranged symmetrically on either side of the seventh, central one. The plant rests on a triple ringed base that, in turn, connects to the two stems whose ends extend outward and curve upward above the ringed base. In addition each frond, which is broad and rounded at the upper ends,

---

[77] See: Barnett 1976, pls. XXVII, XXXVII; Albenda 1978, pls. 2, 3, 9–18.
[78] See the remarks of Paley 1976, p. 22.
[79] Porter 1993, p. 138. Parpola 1993, pp. 165–168, reasons that the 'Tree' is an imperial symbol, that it symbolizes the divine world order maintained by the Assyrian king.
[80] On this aspect of the goddess, see the discussion of Harris 1991.
[81] Barnett 1976, pls. LXIII–LXV. It may be that within the context of the garden scene, the alternating conifer and date palm trees convey a political statement; that is, the control over the northern (conifer) and southern (date palm) lands. Thus the grapevines wedded to the conifer trees allude to the wine-producing territories to the west of Assyria. The political interpretation strengthens the significance of the inclusion of the trophies in the garden setting, as discussed by Albenda 1977.

is patterned with chevron stripes in black and white. At a later date, in residence K at Khorsabad, the palmette alternates with a lotus flower to form a garland that occurs in the uppermost register of an elaborately designed wall painting (pls. 31–33). As restored, the fronds of the palmette alternate in solid colors of red and blue. The ends of the two stems form the base of the plant. A garland consisting of the palmette only occurs in two wall paintings discovered at Til Barsip. Both paintings are datable to the late eighth century B.C. In one example the fronds of the palmette, with their broad and rounded ends, alternate in solid colors of red and blue (pl. 19). In the second example, the fronds of the palmette extend to the edge of a pre-determined circular shape (pl. 18: right), thus modifying the general appearance of the palmette. This plant, too, shows the fronds in alternate red and blue colors.

The palmette plant does not occur among the seventh century B.C. wall paintings presently known from excavated sites in Assyria and northern Syria. In other forms of the decorated arts, however, the palmette does occur as early as the ninth century B.C. A palmette garland appears on an ivory fragment.[82] Among the painted decorations that were applied to the glazed wall plates discovered at several Assyrian sites, mentioned previously, the palmette alternates with a bud to form a palmette-and-bud garland. Assuredly, as a decorative motif the most refined renderings of the palmette garland are the examples carved on several stone threshold slabs discovered in the North Palace of the seventh century Assyrian king, Ashurbanipal.[83]

There are instances in the visual arts where the palmette, either singly or repeated into a garland, takes on a meaning that goes beyond pure decoration. A royal figure whose costume displays a prominent palmette resting on a ringed base on the shoulder is found on a ninth century B.C. fragmentary glazed tile from Nineveh.[84] The royal figure wears a mural crown, which in other works of art was shown to be worn only by the Assyrian queen.[85] It should be mentioned that the fragment on the left side, with a beard, does not join the larger fragment on the right side. The rendering of the palmette on the royal figure's garment has stylistic parallels with those found on several decorated wall attachments or plates originally placed in the temple of the goddess Ishtar at Nimrud. It may be inferred, then, that the palmette on the costume of the royal personage alludes to that goddess and represents a sign of cultic importance.

The palmette also occurs as part of embroidered designs with flanking animals (bull, goat, ibex) on costumes carved on the reliefs of Ashurnasirpal

---

[82] See: Mallowan and Davies 1970, p. 20, no. 14; Mallowan 1978, no. 21. For the palmette attached to the guilloche, see nos.180 a, c.
[83] See: Barnett 1976, pls. XXVII, XXXVII; Albenda 1978, pp. 17–18, pls. 22, 25, 26.
[84] Reade 1987, p. 139, fig. 1.
[85] See the remarks of Albenda 1998a.

II, and on ivories carved in the Assyrian style.[86] On the ivories, the composition shows half-kneeling goats confronting a large palmette. This particular design is a later development of a similar scene in which goats confront a tall tree. An early example exists in the thirteenth century B.C. fragmentary wall paintings from Kar-Tukulti-Ninurta (pl. 28). The extant fragments of the tree show compact fronds surrounding the upper part of the trunk, and small leaves are indicated within each frond. The palmette-like tree may have its origins in the date palm tree. The date palm is depicted rather realistically in an Assyrian cylinder seal impression dated to the twelfth century B.C.[87] The scene depicts a winged bird-headed genie who plucks the fruit from the tree. By the ninth century, the tree is on occasion reduced to a palmette on a low trunk. In one ornamental garment design, its obvious religious or symbolic aspect is indicated by the mirror image of the Assyrian king with both knees on the ground confronting the shortened tree, as well as by the winged disk that hovers above the scene.[88] Elsewhere, the combined motif of the winged disk set above the palmette is included in a ritual scene that originally decorated a glazed vessel.[89] The two descriptive ritual settings for the plant motif support the conclusion that the palmette has a symbolic meaning, since the winged disk is identified as the symbol of the god Shamash.

However, the most developed version of the palmette-type tree occurs on the wall reliefs from the Northwest Palace of Ashurnasirpal II at Nimrud. Originally, over one hundred representations of the tree were carved on the stone slabs that decorated the various chambers of the royal residence. Although they are similar in appearance, three main variations of the stylized palmette tree have been identified.[90] In spite of their differences all the trees consist of single or double palmette garlands surrounding the central trunk, with bands connecting the garlands to the trunk. Invariably, a prominent palmette surmounts the tree trunk. Later variants of the stylized tree surrounded by a palmette garland occur on fragmentary reliefs from the reign of Tiglathpileser III, discovered at Nimrud, and on a now lost wall relief from the palace of Sargon II at Khorsabad.[91] In the latter example only half of the tree is recorded in a drawing, but presumably the entire tree was originally carved on the L-shaped slab that was set up in one corner of the chamber.

Modern scholars generally describe the stylized palmette-type tree as the sacred tree. Its religious or symbolic importance is emphasized in the visual arts by the inclusion of winged genies or the Assyrian king positioned on

---

[86] See: Layard 1849, pl. 43, 2, 4, 5; Herrmann 1992, nos. 351, 355.
[87] Moortgat 1969, pl. K 7.
[88] For convenient detail illustrations of Layard's drawings, with references, see Bleibtreu 1980, Abb. 17–21.
[89] Pritchard 1969, p. 325, fig. 628.
[90] Albenda 1994b, pp. 124–132.
[91] See: Belibtreu 1980, Tf. 6 a, b; Albenda 1986, pl. 76.

one or both sides of the tree. These figures often face the tree and stand in a pose that may relate to a ritual ceremony. In a seventh century B.C. Assyrian text dedicated to the goddess Ishtar of Nineveh, is the following: 'O palm tree, daughter of Nineveh, stag of the lands! She is glorious, most glorious, the finest of goddesses … the crown on her head gleams like the stars; the luminescent disks on her breasts shine like the sun.'[92] These brief descriptions of the goddess Ishtar disclose her association with the palm tree, as well as with the rosettes and star-symbols that occur in the visual arts, including Assyrian wall painting. Early on in the Neo-Assyrian period, the so-called sacred tree represented on the wall reliefs consist of palmettes surrounding and surmounting the trunk. In the late seventh century, an example of the palm tree and rosette into a single image occurs in a ritual scene on a cylinder seal presently housed in the British Museum.[93] Thus, accepting the palm tree and rosette (see above) as iconographic symbols, one may conclude that an aspect of the multifaceted Ishtar that is not generally discussed by modern scholars is her attribute as the goddess of fecundity and vegetation or, briefly stated, the goddess of fertility.

Flower

The floral motif is a schematized version of a particular flower known to the contemporary artist. However, the flower is patterned imaginatively with chevron bands. In his brief description of the garland, Layard identified the flower as a lily (genus *lilium*). He probably based his identification upon the outline of its shape, which includes a zigzag at the top, indicating the tips of the petals that extend downward to the stem of the garland. It is not until the seventh century B.C. that the lily is readily identifiable in depictions of the royal garden on the wall reliefs from rooms E and S[1] in Ashurbanipal's North Palace.[94] On the reliefs from room S[1], one female attendant plucks the flower from a shrub and another carries the plucked flowers on a tray. Therefore it is unfortunate that the lily does not recur in Assyrian wall painting after the ninth century B.C. However, the lily does occur on several plaques of ivory discovered at Fort Shalmaneser. On these plaques, dated to the eighth century, the subjects are carved in the North Syrian style.[95] The inclusion on the plaques of a lily as a flowering plant, although still not rendered realistically, indicates that the flower enjoyed some popularity, during that period.

---

[92] Livingstone 1989, no. 7.
[93] The rendering of the tree and other similar examples are described as the 'rosette tree'; see Collon 2001, pp. 84–85, nos. 173–181.
[94] Barnett and Lorenzini, 1975, pl. 90.
[95] For the formalized rendering of the lily, see Mallowan and Herrmann 1974, pp. 18–19, 73–74, 85–87, nos. 38–39, 42. A lily and bud garland also occurs on ivory fragments; nos. 145–146, 148.

Floral sprigs are sometimes held in the hands of winged genies represented on the wall reliefs found in the Northwest Palace of Ashurnasirpal II. A variety of flora and plant – flower, several types of rosette, pinecone, and palm frond – are attached to the smaller branches of the sprig yet, except for two possible examples, no lily is identifiable among them.[96] In one example, a winged genie holds a sprig with five small branches in his lowered left hand. [97] Each branch terminates in a single flower. In two other renderings of a floral sprig held in the raised right hand of a winged genie, there are also several branches, each one supporting a flower of the same type.[98] In these examples the flower is shown as a rounded body with pointed tips that extend slightly outward. Chevron striations are indicated on each flower. Admittedly, the flower seems to have little resemblance to the unique type found in the contemporary wall painting and textile band designs that decorate the costumes of Assyrian officials. Generally, modern scholars identify the plant on the above-noted sprigs as the pomegranate (genus *Punica granatum*), that is a fruit rather than a blossom. The pomegranate is round and heavy. If one accepts the identification of pomegranate, then the image of the sprig in the hands of the genies should impart a visual heaviness. This visual effect is lacking. It seems more reasonable to consider the plant as a blossom. Because the stylistic renderings between the painted and sculpted versions of the plants differ, it remains unclear whether they are intended to represent the same flower, probably the lily or a blossom.

Perhaps the flowers on the garland depicted in a small section of wall painting discovered in a suite of chambers in the palace of Adad-nirari III at Nimrud belong to the same floral family as those shown on the sprigs (pl. 6). In the sketch that Layard made soon after he uncovered the fragmentary painting, two complete flowers of an arcaded garland are illustrated, as well as the faint outline of a third flower. The two flowers are shown as closed buds with petal tips that curve slightly outward. Both flowers are red and outlined in gray; one has two gray-black concentric circles in the center and the other a double ovoid-shaped line. The rendering of these flowers is somewhat naturalistic, and a departure from the more abstract floral versions that appear in the earlier art of Ashurnasirpal II. Nonetheless, the arcaded flowers probably represent a later version of the flowers on the sprigs held

---

[96] The list of the types of floral sprigs that are held by the genies and the wall reliefs on which they appear is given in Bleibtreu 1980, pp. 60–70. For a selection of the Ashurnasirpal II reliefs that show the floral sprig, see: Ibid, Tf. 3, Abb. 23–25; Mallowan 1983, figs. 8–10; Paley 1976, fig. 21a.

[97] Barnett and Lorenzini 1975, pl. 14.

[98] See: Crawford *et al*, 1980, fig. 10, no. 15; Kolbe 1981, Tf. VI 3. A similar flower appears on a low-lying shrub, with kneeling goats on either side, which is carved on an ivory dated to the 9th century B.C. The two types of flora that alternate on the branches are described as a stylized pomegranate and bud flower; see Mallowan and Davies 1970, p. 46, no.163.

in the hands of the genies on the wall reliefs of Ashurnasirpal II, mentioned above. The red color is noteworthy, if it is an indicator of the actual hue of the arcaded flowers rather than a decorative addition. A flower mentioned in Assyrian texts as *illūru* whose identity, unfortunately, remains uncertain, has been identified as red in color.[99]

An unusual floral garland that occurs only once appears in a wall painting from room 25 at Til Barsip (pl. 11). The flower derives from a circle drawn in red, and shows two blue petals with central red tip on a white base. Red occurs on the calyx and arcaded stems. In the previous discussion of the garland flower (see Chapter III), it is suggested that the blossom is a decorative interpretation of the mature cotton capsule viewed from the side. Production of the cotton plant was known in the reign of Sennacherib, the period to which the painted frieze with its unusual floral garland has been dated.

Pomegranate garland

Among the band decorations depicted in the sketches of wall paintings discovered in the palace of Adad-nirari III at Nimrud, are two examples of particular interest. They may represent an early version of pomegranate garlands (pls. 3, 5). Both arcaded garlands consist of circles extending down from the stems, as discussed above. Each circle has a small tri-petal projection at the lower end. The addition of the modified petals makes it likely that the circles are intended to represent a plant of some kind. In this instance the pomegranate is the proposed identification; therefore, the tri-petal addition may represent the calyx that crowns the base of the fruit.

The pomegranate garland appears among the isolated fragments of wall painting that were discovered in a residence of the citadel at Khorsabad. In this version (pl. 31) the red fruit hangs as a pendant from the connected blue stems, and the circle shape of the pomegranate shows a three-petal projection at the lower end. An additional feature is the ringed band that connects the fruit to the stems. A similar version recurs in three wall paintings – rooms 22, 24, and 47 – discovered at the North Syrian site of Til Barsip (pls. 18, 19). In the three painted examples the fruit is solid blue, with red on the tri-petal of the calyx and ringed band. The choice of colors increases the decorative aspect of the pomegranate garlands, especially as they form part of more elaborate ornamental designs with their restrictive color palette.

A garland of alternate pomegranates and flowers does appear on a carved ivory. The fruit is depicted simply as a circle with a tri-petal crown.[100] Of related interest, it may be mentioned that on some of the wall reliefs of Tiglath-pileser III and Sargon II wingless genies are represented holding a

---

[99] CAD, vol. I-J, pp. 87–88.
[100] Mallowan and Davies 1970, p. 19, no. 10.

three-prong sprig with vegetation that resembles the pomegranate.[101] This identification is generally accepted. An alternate identification, however, is that the vegetation represent the pods of the poppy (genus *papaver somniferum*). Against this identification, it has been argued that there is no archaeological evidence for the poppy in the Near East in ancient times.[102] A counter argument is that the depictions of the plant on the wall reliefs most resemble the poppy pods, particularly in the Sargon examples where the shape is oval rather than round. Moreover, this identification is consistent with the type of plant form shown on the sprigs that are held by genies, that is a blossom rather than a fruit. Nonetheless, two fragmentary wall reliefs dated to the reign of Tiglath-pileser III depict the remaining sections of stylized trees framed by a plant arcade. The eroded surface of the stone makes it difficult to identify the particular plants. They may represent a blossom-and-bud arcade, a pomegranate-and-cone arcade or, perhaps, a poppy-and-cone arcade.[103] Fruits similar in appearance to those depicted on garland plants on the Tiglath-pileser III reliefs are included in the trays of food brought by attendants on the seventh century wall reliefs of Sennacherib.[104] The fruits are identifiable as pomegranates, and one is prone to make the same identification for the framing plant arcade on the reliefs of Tiglath-pileser III. Moreover, individual trees with fruit identifiable as the pomegranate do occur within the landscape of several narrative scenes carved on the reliefs of Sennacherib and Ashurbanipal.[105] To summarize, it may be that when held in the hands of genies on eighth century wall reliefs, the sprigs show the poppy pods, while on the garlands framing the tree it is the pomegranate and/or blossom that is represented.

Garland with lotus flower

The earliest known representation of the water lily or lotus flower in Assyrian wall painting occurs among the many registers of an elaborate design that

---

[101] See: Beliebtreu 1980, Tf. 8a, b; Albenda 1986, pls. 4, 53–54, figs. 16–17, 19–20, 22–23.

[102] Krikorian 1975, pp. 99–113, argues against the identification of poppy on three points: there is no known Akkadian word for poppy; no seeds identifiable as the opium poppy have yet been found in the archaeological plant material; the rendering of the plant on the Assyrian wall relief is not convincing 'to a botanist.' On the last point, Krikorian relies upon a photograph of a wall relief of Sargon II (incorrectly dated by the author) to demonstrate that certain details are 'unrealistic.' However, one may counter-argue that 'realistic' does not pertain to Assyrian art, which re-interprets or summarizes observed existing forms to satisfy a particular style of imagery.

[103] Bleibtreu 1980, Tf. 5 b, 7.

[104] Barnett *et al*, 1998, pp. 123–124, nos. 563–567.

[105] See: Ibid, pp. 53–54, nos. 36, 36 a, b; Barnett 1976, pls. LXIII, LXIV. Note that on the Sennacherib slab, the tree with pomegranates appears among a grove of trees planted outside a foreign city. This is the earliest known representation of the tree in Assyrian art. However, the pomegranate is mentioned as an item of food in the inscription on the so-called Banquet Stela of Ashurnasirpal II; see Grayson 1976, no. 682.

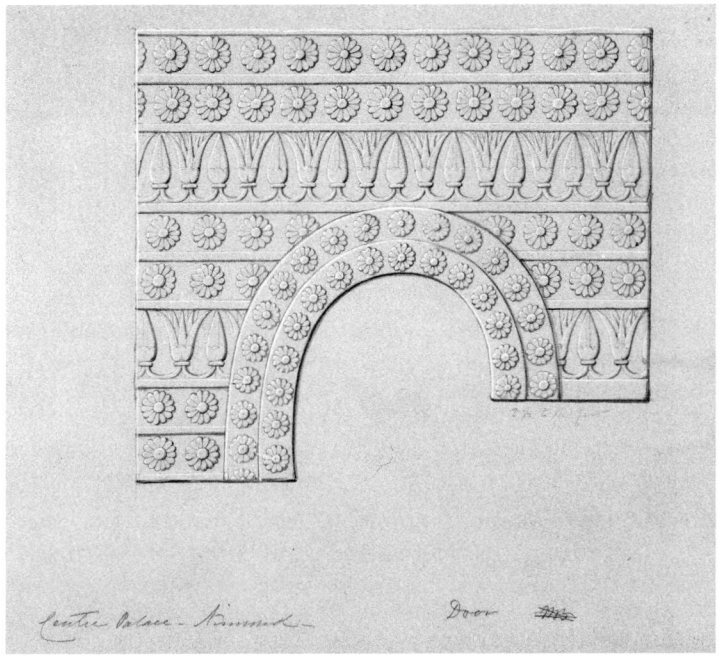

Pl. 37. Layard, threshold slab from 'centre palace' (central palace) at Nimrud.
Period of Tiglath-pileser III. *Original Drawings* VI, 37. British Museum.

filled the walls of one room of residence K at Khorsabad (pls. 32, 33). It forms part of a floral garland composed of alternating lotus and palmette. This particular garland type is unusual, since it does not re-appear in any other type of Assyrian art. In this regard the lotus-and-palmette garland is an innovative design.

However, the Khorsabad example does not represent the first time that the lotus was used for a garland design in Assyrian art. A lotus-and-bud garland was included in the carved decoration of a stone threshold slab discovered at Nimrud, which has been dated to the reign of Tiglath-pileser III (pl. 37).[106] Although the slab survives only in a drawing made at the time of its discovery, the lotus-and-bud garland is represented prominently and alternates between two rows of rosettes. The flowers on the garland are supported by a ring base and connected to scallop-shaped stems. Without extant archaeological evidence, one can only surmise that a painted version of the lotus-and-bud garland once colored the walls of the Central Palace of the Assyrian king at Nimrud.

---

[106] Albenda 1978, pl. 1.

115

The lotus-and-bud garland does re-appear on some of the wall paintings that were discovered in the royal residence at Til Barsip. The floral garland is an important feature of the framing band decorations included in the painted designs in rooms 21, 22, and 46 (pls. 13, 17, 18: right). Two distinct renderings of the lotus flower are observed. The distinction between the two flowers indicates that they belong to different periods of production. The lotus of the garlands painted in rooms 21 and 46 show details that are stylistically identical. Based upon comparative analysis of the wall paintings in these rooms, discussed previously, the lotus-and-bud garlands were executed during the reign of Sargon II. It has been further noted that parallels for the lotus-and-bud garland in the painted decoration of room 22 provide a date of production to the reign of Sennacherib. In rooms 21 and 46 the open and closed flowers are blue, while in room 22 the lotus-and-bud garland is colored red and blue.

The wall painting that extended around the throne room S5 at Fort Shalmaneser was a decorative mural 1.25 m high depicting a procession of Assyrian soldiers wearing court dress, surmounted by a patterned frieze of about 1.35 m in height.[107] The most likely assumption is that the paintings were executed on the orders of Esarhaddon. The excavators photographed the wall painting; their photograph was published together with a reconstructed line drawing (fig. 6). The patterned frieze above the procession consists of four decorated bands framing the large central register. The designs in the bands include buds and flowers, as well as rosettes with concentric circles. Within the central register squares with incurving sides and circles alternate. Each circle is decorated with a double band of petals and target center. The floral and geometric designs were done in bold black outline with red and blue colors for the buds, flowers, and rosette petals. Arcaded stems connect the alternating buds and flowers in the outermost framing registers. The flowers, although stylized, represent the lotus.

The earliest known appearance of the lotus in Neo-Assyrian art occurs during the reign of Tiglath-pileser III. Mention has been made of its presence on the threshold slab dated to that period, which illustrates its decorative use (pl. 37). On the other hand the lotus held in the hand of the same Assyrian king, represented on the wall reliefs, suggests that the flower had some meaning in the context of the narrative scene.[108] Furthermore, there is an elaborate version of the lotus-and-bud sprig held in the Assyrian king's lowered left hand on one of the wall reliefs of Sargon II.[109] The triple-branched plant shows a bud between two lotuses. Another wall relief of the same period depicts a wingless genie or priest grasping a wild goat or ibex to

---

[107] Mallowan 1966, pp. 380–381.
[108] Mallowan and Falkner 1962, p. 36, pls. XVIII–XIX (relief 12), LXIX, LXXI (relief 36).
[109] Albenda 1986, pls. 71, 93. For the king in his chariot holding the flower, see pl. 89.

the level of his chest, and in his lowered right one is a triple-branched plant composed of a lotus between two buds.[110] Of later date, on the wall reliefs of Ashurbanipal, the Assyrian king is once depicted holding the lotus flower, while reclining on his couch in the royal garden.[111]

The lotus is of course not indigenous to Assyria; however it is a flower that was well known to the ancient Egyptians. Of the two main types of lotus, white (genus *Nymphaea lotus*) and blue (genus *Nymphaea caerulea)*, the latter was a favorite flower, partly for its colors but chiefly for its scent. In Egyptian paintings the flower is represented in garden scenes, and there are also examples of lotus bouquets.[112] The Egyptian hieroglyph sign lotus is a symbol of the sun, of creation and rebirth, and as such it is a sacred flower. The importance of the lotus, a desirable and 'exotic' flower with symbolic connotation, may have been brought to the attention of the Assyrian kings, during the second half of the eighth century B.C. This knowledge would have occurred as a consequence of Assyrian military incursions to the West and direct contacts with Egypt.[113] The portrayal of the Assyrian kings holding the lotus, as well as that of the wingless genie from Khorsabad, is probably intended to emulate the use of the flower by the Egyptians as depicted in their art. In this regard, one may mention that the lotus-and-bud sprig that the Khorsabad genie holds in his lowered hand is quite similar to the arrangement of the lotus and bud plants held over the arm of an Egyptian official in a fowl hunting scene in the marshes, represented in a tomb painting of the Eighteenth Dynasty.[114]

During the seventh century B.C., the lotus garland continued to be used in the decorative arts of Assyria. Already mentioned is the example shown on the wall painting from the throne room S5 at Fort Shalmaneser. A lotus-and-cone garland forms the outermost band on several carved threshold slabs dated to the reign of Sennacherib and discovered in the Southwest Palace at Nineveh. The lotus-and-bud garland is carved on the threshold slabs from Ashurbanipal's North Palace. The lotus combined with the cone to form a quatrefoil was another design that was used for the threshold slabs.[115] At

---

110 Ibid, pl. 59, fig. 24. The assertion that the depictions of genies with 'drooping flower' (lotus) are related to 'the royal ghosts' or that a 'whole series of figures holding a drooping lotus flower represent dead kings', requires further documentation; see van Loon 1986, pp. 248–251.
111 Barnett 1976, pls. LXIV, LXV.
112 For examples of the lotus flower in Egyptian art, see Smith 1958, pls. 74 A, 129 A, 151, 162 B, 163 A. For a brief discussion, see Murray 1964, p. 83.
113 Tiglath-pileser III's campaign to the West reached as far as the border of Egypt, after which the king appointed a 'gatekeeper'; see Tadmor 1994, pp. 137–121 (summary inscription 4). Later Assyrian kings campaigned against Egypt. Esarhaddon and Ashurbanipal went into Egypt, the former king as far as the city of Memphis, and the latter as far as Thebes. See Smith 1958, p. 241.
114 See: Edwards 1964, pp. 14–15, fig. 6; Murray 1964, pl. XIX.
115 For the lotus in garlands and quatrefoils carved on the threshold slabs, see Albenda 1978, pp. 6–8, pls. 2–3, 5, 8, 9–26.

Dur-Katlimmu, in northern Syria, a silhouette version of the lotus-and-bud garland occurs in the black on white wall painting (fig. 4d).

Symmetrical grouping

The combination of two figures confronting a central motif occurs in Neo-Assyrian wall painting as early as the end of the ninth century B.C., during the reign of Adad-nirari III. This application of bilateral symmetry, the image of left and right, is one of the methods of the geometric concept of surface ornamentation. The iconographic scheme of duplicated images – mirror imagery – was known early on in the Near East, as it occurred sporadically in the arts of the third and second millennia B.C.[116] Over time the selection of subject matter varied. In the ornamental wall paintings of the Neo-Assyrian period, the figural subjects chosen for bilateral symmetry are restricted to two categories: (1) animals – goat and bull – and (2) winged genies, all confronting a geometric shape. As a decorative motif, the symmetrical grouping is generally centered in the overall design and most often treated as the prominent feature in the wall painting. However, aside from their decorative application, the figural subjects may have cultic or symbolic meaning.

Animal group

Goat

In Assyrian wall painting the earliest known occurrence of an animal confronting a central object can be traced back to the example discovered at Kar-Tukulti-Ninurta. As reconstructed in the thirteenth century B.C. painting, two goats depicted in mirror image stand on their hind legs and are positioned on either side of a tree, identifiable as a date palm (pl. 28). Low spreading branches ending in a cluster of fronds support the goats, which are poised with the raised far foreleg bent and their heads turned back. The posture of the goats imparts the notion of a momentary pause immediately before touching the tree. Another spreading branch with fronds at the end extends behind each goat there. Overall, the symmetrical composition suggests an abbreviated landscape that surrounds the paired goats that frame the central motif of the date palm. No other painted example of a similar type of composition is known in the Middle Assyrian period. Moreover, the heraldic grouping of goats and tree contrasts with the descriptive arrangement of

---

[116] On this subject, see Albenda 1998, pp. 11–14.

similar subjects carved on an ivory pyxis discovered in a tomb at Ashur.[117] Designed as a frieze, two walking goats are placed on either side of a tree and nibble at plants extending from its base. The scene alternates with a date palm. The inclusion of birds resting on the branches and circles representing the sun add to the natural setting, and is thought to have some cultic or religious meaning. Decorated cylinder seal impressions of the Middle Assyrian period are also illustrated with goats as well as deer in a variety of action poses. These examples demonstrate an interest in the depictions of these animals.[118] Moreover, one seal design datable to the reign of Tukulti-Ninurta I shows a variant of the heraldic group composition of a wild goat on either side of a palm tree. In this case, the two goats leap downward to touch the ground, the far foreleg bent forward and the near one bent on the ground line. A comparison between the painted version at Kar-Tukulti-Ninurta and the seal design shows that the formulation of a heraldic composition with goats and tree was already established by the thirteenth century, although details could vary.

The representation of two goats flanking a tree or plant in mirror image is unknown in the ninth century B.C. wall paintings of Assyria. The motif does appear in the reign of Ashurnasirpal II, on the decorated robe of an official depicted on the wall reliefs in the Northwest Palace.[119] It is also of interest to observe that the motif occurs on ivories carved in the Assyrian style.[120] These examples show the goat with its head turned forward. It lowers its body by bending the near foreleg to touch the ground, while the far foreleg is extended forward for balance. The striding gait of the hind legs elevates the hindquarters. The general impression is that of an animal kneeling down to the level of either a palmette or flowering plant set before it. The Assyrian king Shalmaneser III seems to have favored the symmetrical composition of a goat kneeling on one foreleg and confronting a plant. The composition occurs in the outermost register of a large glazed brick panel with rounded top, originally set up above the portal of a doorway at Fort Shalmaneser and dated to the reign of that king.[121] Along the sides the register shows an alternating repeat of a kneeling goat and palmette, and the uppermost section is topped by two goats flanking a palmette. Although the Kar-Tukulti-Ninurta painting and the decorated glazed panel are centuries apart, the latter example is an indicator of the sustained use of the goat-and-tree motif from the thirteenth century on, in the royal art of Assyria.

---

[117] Moortgat 1969, p. 115, pl. 242, fig. 84.
[118] Mayer-Opficius 1986, p. 163, fig. 9. For examples of the downward moving goat, see Moortgat 1940, p. 138, no. 586; Moortgat 1969, pl. J 6–8.
[119] Layard 1849b, pl. 43, 2.
[120] Mallowan and Davies 1970, nos. 135, 138–141, 161–168.
[121] Mallowan 1966, p. 454, fig. 373.

The kneeling goat motif re-appears in the eighth century wall painting from room 25 at Til Barsip (pls. 9, 10). Its pose recalls the ninth century examples shown in the embroidered textile, on the carved ivories, and on the glazed brick panel of Shalmaneser III. However, the two goats confront a large square with incurved sides instead of a plant. The combined use of a square with an animal confirms a date after the reign of Shalmaneser III. The two framing bands of rosettes also indicate that the Til Barsip wall painting is of a later date. An early comparative parallel for the rosette bands occurs on the threshold slab of Tiglath-pileser III, illustrated in plate 37, where two bands of rosettes alternate with a lotus-and-bud garland in continuous repeat pattern. It is therefore probable that the Til Barsip wall painting was produced as late as the reign of that king.

One important feature of the goat in the Til Barsip wall painting deserves comment. The near and far horns of the goat are represented respectively curving back and front. In other renderings of the goat, the visible horn is shown curving back. The two versions of representing the horn of the goat should not be considered an artistic modification only. Instead, the two versions probably indicate that two different species of wild goat (genus *Capra*) are illustrated. One species of wild goat is the Asiatic ibex (genus *ibex*), with its two large horns curving back. An exceptionally fine extant example of the ibex in Assyrian art is the one held in the arm of a wingless genie carved on a wall relief from the palace at Khorsabad.[122] Another species of wild goat is the west Caucasian ibex or Tur (*Capra caucasica*), with its two large horns curving outward and back. This ibex is probably the one represented in the Til Barsip wall painting. An exceptionally fine extant example of the Tur in Assyrian art is of the one held in the arm of a two-winged genie carved on a wall relief from the Northwest Palace of Ashurnasirpal II at Nimrud.[123] A sketch of the head of a similar goat also survives on a painted brick (see pl. 2). As early as the glyptic art of the Middle Assyrian period, wild goats are represented either with a visible horn curved back, or with one horn curved back, the other front. Thus both species of wild goat were known and depicted, during that time. If the identifications of the goats made here are correct, the ability of Assyrian artists to distinguish the known species of wild goat through the rendering of their horns is thus demonstrated.

Bull

The sketches of the fragmentary wall paintings discovered in the suite of rooms forming part of the palace of Adad-nirari III at Nimrud include two

---

[122] Albenda 1986, pl. 59, fig. 24.
[123] Curtis and Reade 1995, pl. 8.

drawings of a bull. One bull is complete and the other one is missing its head (pls. 3, 5). In the latter drawing, however, the still visible horns indicate that the bovine is a winged bull. Both representations of the bulls show them turning to the viewer's right. The pose of both bull-types is similar: the bull strides forward, while at the same time the far foreleg bends under to touch the ground. The generally passive posture of both animals is indicated by the treatment of the tail, which extends down between the hind legs. This last feature is a non-Assyrian method of representing the tail of an animal, such as a bull or a lion. In Assyrian style art the tail invariably extends behind the hind legs. In contrast, the depiction of the tail between the hind legs is typical of lion sculptures of the Neo-Hittite period.[124] Thus the renderings of the two-bull types reveal foreign influence as a consequence of direct contact between Assyria and northern Syria, during the ninth century B.C.[125] It is not clear from the original sketches how the bovine fitted into the overall design, although a circle is lightly drawn behind the figure of the wingless bull. It may be that either there was an alternate repeat of the bull and circle, or that two bulls confronted the circle in a symmetrical arrangement.

Several rooms in Adad-nirari III's palace in the outer town, a short distance from Nimrud, were also adorned with painted wall decorations that included the bull among the various motifs. The British excavation report provides a description of the wall painting in room 9 of the exposed building. As noted in a previous chapter, the published report states that the central panel that extended across one wall consists of a design of bulls, head turned back, on either side of a circle. The bodies of the bulls are red, and outlined in black. The central panel is completed with a large square with incurved sides. The description of the turned-back head of the bull is noteworthy. Such depictions of the bull in other art forms are infrequent, but an early version of a similar representation appears as costume decoration, during the reign of Ashurnasirpal II.[126] Of later date, several decorated objects show a bull with a turned-back head. They include a small ivory discovered in the outer town residence of Adad-nirari III, and cylinder seals from Ashur.[127] Because the rendering of the bull with a turned-back head is uncommon and of relatively short duration in the arts of Assyria, the decorated objects are probably datable to the reign of Adad-nirari III.

The appearance of the bull in Assyrian ornamental wall painting is met with again, in residence K at Khorsabad. The bovine occupies the central of

---

[124] Stone reliefs of lions and bulls are known from various Neo-Hittite sites; see Akurgal 1962, pls. 108, 113 (Carchemish), 126, 132 (Zincirli), 136 (Göllüdag); Akurgal 1968, figs. 70–72 (Zincirli), 74–75 (Tell Ain-Dara), 88–89 (Tell Halaf), pl. 16 a, b (Sakçegözu).
[125] The western campaigns of the ninth century B.C. Assyrian kings are recorded in the royal inscriptions; see Grayson 1976, nos.470–475, 584, 676.
[126] Layard 1849b, pls. 8, 46,3.
[127] See: Mallowan and Davies 1970, no. 124; Moortgat 1940, nos. 641–642.

three large registers that are separated from one another by narrow decorated and plain bands. As reconstructed, two bulls in mirror image confront and touch a large square with incurved sides and this grouping, followed by an incurve-sided square, is repeated across the register (pls. 32, 33). The bovine animal extends its fore and hind legs respectively forward and back, tilts its head to the chest and raises its tail over the back. Altogether, the image of the bull stresses dynamic strength held in check by the firmness of the stance and by the contact of the visible horn with the square. The decorations on the body of the bull include broad white areas that extend across the back, on the belly, and on the chest, as well as surrounding the end of the tail. Comparison with the huge human-headed bulls originally set up in the doorways of the royal palace at Khorsabad, makes it evident that the white areas on the painted bovines represent body curls.[128] It is obvious, then, that the bulls in the wall painting are intended to have a divine significance, since body curls do not occur in Assyrian representations of domesticated bovines.

An earlier parallel for the painted bulls is that of the paired doorway bulls discovered at the North Syrian site of Arslan Tash. The cuneiform inscription on one stone animal includes the name of Tiglath-pileser III, so this information provides a date for their production.[129] The renderings of the stone bulls at Arslan Tash show them assuming a passive stance. Another depiction of a bull in Assyrian art deserves mention. It is contemporary with the wall painting in residence K, and appears within the vast maritime scene carved on a series of wall relief from the palace at Khorsabad.[130] This bull is unusual for its leaping pose and for its small, flaring wing extending outward. The head turns slightly downward and the curved contour lines of the bull's body accentuate its active movement. The obvious differences in detail between this winged bull and of the ones depicted on the wall painting in residence K are offset by the divine nature of the bovine animal, as expressed in the respective arts, as well as by its portrayal, which emphasizes the characteristic physical strength of the bull.

Another design composed of confronting bulls on either side of a square with incurved sides occurs in the ornamental wall painting from room 21 at Til Barsip (pl. 17). Similar to the stance adopted by the bulls from residence K at Khorsabad, each bull turns its head to the chest as if ready to charge forward. At the same time the extended front and back feet rest firmly upon the ground line. The particular way in which the rendering of the paired bulls in the wall painting at Til Barsip express their dynamic power, closely

---

[128] Albenda 1986, p. 51, figs. 1–5.
[129] Thureau-Dangin *et al* 1931, pp. 60–64, pls. IV 1,2, V 1. For further discussion, see Albenda 1988, pp. 25–26.
[130] Albenda 1983, pp. 25–26, pls. 3, 7, 9.

parallels that shown on the Khorsabad bulls. The wall paintings from both sites, then, must have been produced in the late eighth century B.C., during the reign of Sargon II. Another contemporary rendering of the bull in a similar but more passive posture, occurs in the wall painting from passage 24/28 at Til Barsip (pl. 14). The inclusion of a winged bird-headed genie (bird-*apkallu*) standing at the near side of the animal, while at the same time leading it forward, reinforces the concept of a religious or cultic significance behind their combined imagery.

The decorative design of confronting bulls on either side of a geometric shape was also applied on a glazed vessel discovered at Ashur.[131] A patterned circle substitutes for the incurved square; however, the dynamic pose given to the two bulls reflects that of the wall painting versions. It is remarkable to find the same decorative motif, in this case applied with pigments on the vessel, originating from three different Assyrian sites (Khorsabad, Til Barsip, Ashur). Presumably artisans assigned to different workshops produced the paintings, which must be of contemporary date. As decoration, the subject matter probably had some popularity among ranked Assyrian personnel. However, one must not overlook an outstanding variant of the symmetrical design with bulls that introduces a symbolic meaning. Among the relief decorations on the bronze bands that encircled the wooden column found outside the temple of Shamash at Khorsabad, is a scene depicting the Assyrian king grasping a bull by the horn in both his right and left hands.[132] The two bulls confront the king. Their heads are turned down by the pull of the horn, while at the same time they stride with the near and far feet positioned forward and back, according to the Assyrian method. Both bulls are drawn large in comparison to the figure of the royal person. The curls on their bodies define the divine aspect of the two bulls, which are otherwise rendered realistically. Except for the substitution of the king in place of the geometric shapes, the symmetrical composition on the bronze band is similar that on the painted versions. One may conclude from the bronze example that beyond the confines of the royal residence and of its nearby temples, the image of the Assyrian king was restrictive. Thus either a square with incurved sides or a circle was substituted in the painted versions, reasonably a decorative adaptation of the official or heraldic composition developed for use by the royal workshop of Sargon II.[133]

A composite bull type represented in the large central field of the painted frieze discovered in room 47 at Til Barsip is the winged human-headed bull

---

[131] Andrae 1940, p. 39, pls. 15–16.
[132] Reproduced in Guralnick 2000, fig. 10.
[133] Albenda 1986, pp. 101–102, pls. 14, 16.

(pl. 19). Cavro's copy of the wall painting shows only a fragmentary portion of the hybrid animal. Readily visible are portions of the feathered headdress surmounted by a disk, and the occasional outlines of the wing, body, and feet. The winged human-headed bull turns to the viewer's left. It remains unclear whether the head turns in the same direction or is frontal. The last feature of the head occurs among several of the many huge bull reliefs that were set up in doorways at Khorsabad. However, the few indicators of the hair and beard on the painted version suggest that the head is rendered in side view. In this regard, one may compare the winged human-headed bull in room 47 with the more completely painted example in passage 24/25 (pl. 15).

The French excavators describe the principal motif repeated on the ornamental wall painting in room 47 as consisting of two winged human-headed bulls that face each other, two by two. Accepting this brief description of the arrangement of the bulls, without an intervening circle or square between each paired animal, one must visualize the first and second bulls face to face, the second and third bulls back to back, and so on. It is most unusual to find in Assyrian art winged human-headed bulls positioned back to back. There is one known occasion where this image does occur, namely on the stone reliefs that lined the northeast wall of Façade N at Khorsabad.[134] Paired monumental winged bulls, their bearded human heads turned frontally, line the walls framing the central entrance. One need only reconstruct the four human-headed bulls adjacent to one another, to gain an idea of how the bulls in the painted frieze of Room 47 may have been displayed originally.

Thus three types of bovine animals occur as decorative motifs among the Assyrian wall paintings: bull with or without curls on the body, winged bull, and winged human-headed bull. The ninth–early eighth century B.C. painted examples represent bulls with and without wings, and the later eighth century painted versions represent bulls with curls and winged human-headed bulls. Following is a brief summary of the previously discussed symbolic significance of the bull expressed both in text and art. In ritual texts the bull or bison is identified as *kusarikku*, and from the Early Dynastic period on, it was sometimes represented with a human face.[135] In mythological texts the animal has been described as the 'bull of heaven' and was the emblem of the Akkadian god Utu, later replaced by Ninurta. The bull was also the symbolic emblem of the god Adad. An image of the deity standing upon a leaping bull and gripping thunderbolts in both hands is carved on an eighth century B.C. stele discovered at Arslan Tash.[136] The winged human-headed bull of

---

[134] Ibid, pl. 35.
[135] For discussion of the *kusarikku* ('bison') in text and art, see Wiggermann 1992, pp. 174–177.
[136] Thureau-Dangin *et al* 1931, pl. II, 1.

the Neo-Assyrian period is identified with the *lamassu/šēdu*, a protective creature. Huge stone figures of the composite animal, carved in high relief, were set up on either side of entranceways of royal residences, and functioned as guardians of the gates.[137]

Lion

An animal not represented in the ornamental wall paintings of Assyria is the lion. It was the animal *par excellence* as the target of the royal hunt represented in narrative scenes found on wall reliefs in the palaces at Nimrud and Nineveh and in the narrative wall paintings at Til Barsip. At the latter site, the lion is mentioned as probably appearing in the principal register of the ornamental frieze that decorated room 24 of the royal residence. In one section of the frieze, the excavators could distinguish the front paws of a lion, and in another the hooves of a bull.[138] They suggested that perhaps groups of lions and of bulls alternated. Presumably each group was composed of the same animal on either side of a square with incurved sides; however, just the geometric shape was drawn in the published version of the frieze (pl. 18: right). Another bilateral arrangement of the animals is possible. It could be that a paired lion and bull confront the geometric shape. This suggested arrangement is unusual, but the combination of a bull and lion is known in several other works of artistic production.

An early example comes from a partially excavated structure, known as the Central Building, discovered on the high mound at Nimrud. On the two projecting walls of the main entrance were colossal stone reliefs, three to a wall. Still preserved on one wall was the lower part of a bull carved on one block and of a lion on the other, both animals facing outwards. Between them was a narrow space where the third slab was placed originally.[139] Fragments of similar animal reliefs were found on the second projecting wall. The wall decoration of the façade of the Central Building, thought to be a temple,

---

137 Monumental winged human-headed bulls (*lamassu*) are known in the reigns of several Assyrian kings, from the ninth to seventh centuries B.C. A selection of the excavated examples include: (1) Ashurnasirpal II: Paley and Sobolewski 1992, figs. 5–7, 8–10; (2) Shalmaneser III: Sobolewski 1977, fig. 5; (3) Tiglath-pileser III: Barnett and Falkner 1962, pl. CVII; (4) Sargon II: Loud 1936, figs.46, 56, 57; Albenda 1986, pls. 57–58, figs.1–6; Chevalier and Lavédrine 1994, figs.2, 10–13; (5) Sennacherib: Barnett *et al* 1998, pls. 20, 24, 25; (6) Esarhaddon: Barnett and Falkner 1962, pls. CVIII, CXII–CXIII, 'Nineveh,' *Iraq* 49,1987, pp. 242–243, pl. LXVII c. It is interesting to note that winged human-headed bulls or winged animals of any kind do not occur in the monumental art of Ashurbanipal.
138 Thureau-Dangin and Dunand 1936, pp. 57–58.
139 Meuszyński 1976, pp. 39–40, pls. 9 b, 10 a, b; Reade 1968, p. 69, remarks that in their original condition the two animals were probably human-headed and winged. A fragment of a winged lion (human-headed?) from entrance to room BB in the Northwest Palace is preserved in one of Layard's drawing; see Reade 1985, p. 209, pl. XXXVIII. Mention may be made of actual lions that were set up at the entrance to the temple of Ninurta at Nimrud. See Strommenger 1964, pls. 200–201.

was planned to show two huge bulls facing the entrance, two huge lions facing outwards at the ends, and between each paired bull and lion may have been a carved human or mythical figure.[140] Several of the reliefs have cuneiform inscriptions cut into the surface, confirming a date to the reign of Ashurnasirpal II.

The wall paintings at Arin-berd, located in an area west of Lake Sevan in eastern Anatolia, are assigned to the reigns of two Urartian kings, during the years 764 and 735 B.C. In technique and color scheme the Urartian wall paintings generally follow Assyrian prototypes. The discovery of painted plaster in a large hall in the palace at Arin-berd shows a combination of repeated series of motifs arranged in superimposed registers. The broad central panel or register is decorated with concave-sided squares flanked by kneeling bulls and striding lions. The reconstructed wall painting shows the lion and bull facing outwards.[141] Interestingly, the depiction of the kneeling bull and motifs on the ornamental bands find parallels with the Assyrian wall paintings of earlier date, discovered in Adad-nirari III's palace at Nimrud.

Of later date, there is a similar version of the paired lion and bull that appears in one register of a fragmented repoussé hammered bronze, excavated together with many small remains of bronze reliefs near the stadium of the Sanctuary of Zeus at Olympia. The decorations on the separately made bronzes show both the Greek Orientalizing style and Near Eastern workmanship. The final reuse of the fragments was for the embellishment of korai figures. One preserved fragment from the Near Eastern group shows a bull and a lion confronting a tree.[142] The bull turns its head down to touch the plant with its visible horn. Its tail extends down between the hind legs, a stylistic detail that indicates a Neo-Hittite or North Syrian origin. The lion confronts the bull on the opposite side of the tree; however, only the head and paws are still intact. The date of production proposed for the imported Near Eastern bronzes is late eighth or seventh century B.C.

---

[140] A similar heraldic grouping of a hybrid lion and bull on either side of a central figure is hypothesized for the decoration on the outer façade of the throne room of Ashurnasirpal II at Nimrud. See Paley and Sobolewski 1992, pp. 12, 17–20, pl. 3.

[141] Azarpay 1968, pp. 19–20, fig. 4.

[142] See: Seidl 1999, pp. 276, 279–280, Abb. 3; Guralnick 2000, pp. 13–14, fig. 1. The latter author suggests that the original purpose of the Near Eastern bronze fragments was to decorate the wooden columns of important buildings. No exact parallels for an antithetical bull and lion on either side of a tree are presently known in the art of Assyria. However, the face-to-face confrontation between a bull and lion occurs in seal designs of the second millennium B.C.; see Moortgat 1969, pl. K 3; Schaeffer-Forrer 1983, pp. 14–15, seal R.S. 3411. In the first millennium B.C., the animals are represented in violent combat on carved ivories (cf. Herrmann 1989, p. 93, pl. XVIII b).

Figural Group

Among the many small fragmentary sections of wall paintings originating from residence K at Khorsabad, one example includes the outline drawing of a bearded, two-winged genie facing left (pl. 31). His horned headdress affirms his divine nature. The genie bends his far right leg, with the near left leg resting firmly on the ground. This particular pose may be described as half-kneeling, as distinguished from that of human figures kneeling with both feet on the ground. The near left arm is raised, and an object – not drawn – may have been held in the lowered right hand. In the complete reconstruction of the wall painting to which the fragment may have belonged, the two-winged genie confronts an elaborately patterned circle in mirror image (pls. 32, 33). Therefore two side views of the half-kneeling genies are depicted. Another patterned circle serves to separate the symmetrical group, which is then repeated in sequential order across two of the many registers and bands of the ornamental wall painting. The renderings of the two genies are not entirely a reflection of one another, however. The respective right and left arms of both genies are raised while the left ones are lowered, a method of representation that was standardized when a human/divine figure was otherwise depicted in mirror image.

In religious and ritual texts two- and four-winged genies are identified with the *apkallu*, anthropomorphic gods whose presence, according to one description, 'continuously protects the inhabitants against evil influences.'[143] Winged genies with horned headdress occur in ninth and eighth centuries relief art of Assyria. Moreover, half-kneeling two-winged genies are represented among one group of wall reliefs from a single room in the Northwest Palace Ashurnasipal II at Nimrud. All the slabs that lined the walls of room I were carved with two registers of figural motifs, separated by the standard royal inscription. The upper register depicts the half-kneeling genies flanking a stylized tree and the lower register, with the exception of one slab (see below), portrays bird-headed genies flanking the same type of tree.[144]

A variant of the half-kneeling genie type is the winged beardless genie that appears in the painted ornamental friezes from rooms 25, 27 and 46 (pls. 11, 12, 13) at Til Barsip. In addition to the absence of the beard, several details distinguish this genie type. Those include the broad band of the headdress with disk or floral attachments that are still visible on several genies, the ankle bracelets, and the floral plants held by the genies, as shown in one frieze. These genies must be female (female-*apkallu*).

---

[143] Wiggermann 1992, pp. 96–97. The protective *apkallu* mentioned in the ritual texts take on different forms; see Ibid, p. 213 with page references.
[144] Room I had over 40 slabs with the same carved decoration. A reconstruction of the reliefs is given in Paley and Sobolewski 1987, pp. 3–8, pl. 1, Plan 3.

It has been concluded previously that the ornamental paintings at Til Barsip are attributable to the reigns of different Assyrian kings. The painted frieze in room 46 was produced during the reign of Sargon II, and those from rooms 25 and 27 are dated to the reign of Sennacherib.[145] The inclusion of female genies is unusual in the visual arts of Assyria. It has been suggested that there was a favorable change in the attitude of later Assyrian kings towards women of the royal household, as evidenced primarily in the arts.[146] This change of outlook may be one basis for the use of female-*apkallu* as an art form in the Til Barsip wall paintings. On the other hand, representations of two- and four-winged female-*apkallu* do occur on the wall reliefs in rooms I and L from the Northwest Palace of Ashurnasipal II. One study that deals with the representation of the female genie, in particular the ninth century B.C. examples concludes that this genie-type has an association with the goddess Ishtar.[147] However, unlike the war-like aspect generally associated with that goddess, the female-*apkallu* genies represented in the ornamental friezes at Til Barsip reflect a divine feminine quality to their image.

---

[145] An inscription of Sennacherib states that he 'set up in their doors female protective genies in alabaster and ivory, each carrying a red flower in their folded hands.' See CAD (I-J), p. 88.
[146] Reade 1987, pp. 140 ff., provides evidence in Assyrian art to show that the status of women in the royal court was better in the seventh century B.C.
[147] Albenda 1996, pp. 74–75.

CHAPTER 5. CONCLUDING COMMENTARY

Painted decoration was an important aspect of the visual arts, during the Neo-Assyrian period. It was applied to glazed bricks, clay attachments, and ceramic vessels. Wall painting in particular had an important function, which was to create a colorful and meaningful visual impact to the rooms and façades of royal residences, and of buildings belonging to important officials. There is some evidence also that Assyrian temples were decorated with wall paintings. However, the number of excavated examples of wall paintings is too limited. Therefore it is difficult to trace the kinds of designs that were applied to the temple walls, and to determine whether the designs parallel those found in the royal residences or follow a different format. Another goal for this investigation was to identify which were the motifs chosen to decorate the walls of temples. The reconstruction of a large bitumen relief of a composite bird with outstretched wings above a painted band of alternating circle and square with incurved sides, discovered in the Assyrian temple at Tell al Rimah (ancient Karana-Zamahe), at least indicates that some subjects, in addition to those found in the residences, were chosen.

Interest in painted ornamentation independent from narrative subject matter seems to have begun in the Middle Assyrian period. Based upon modern reconstructions, the thirteenth century B.C. wall paintings discovered at Kar-Tukulti-Ninurta display the skillful arrangements of ornamental motifs as to what seems to have been elaborate compositions. The artistic ability to create intricate compositions using decorative motifs may have its origin in earlier painted decoration, such as those discovered in the governor's palace at Nuzi, which are dated to the fifteenth century B.C. The selection of ornamental motifs, and their arrangements within the overall compositions in the earlier wall paintings of the second millennium B.C., is entirely different than in the later ones. While the earlier paintings from Nuzi consist of motifs in an organized but dense arrangement, the Assyrian paintings from Kar-Tukulti-Ninurta impart more spacious but compartmented compositions. In spite of a gap of several centuries, there was some continuity of the ornamental style into the early phases of Neo-Assyrian wall painting. In particular, among the motifs and designs that persist into the later period are the rosette, floral garland, and the three-part symmetrical grouping. The limited color palette of red, blue, black-and-white used in the Kar-Tukulti-Ninurta paintings is also characteristic of the later ornamental versions.

There seems to have been a second millennium B.C. tradition to utilize compartmented designs for wall paintings; however, this method of laying out the compositions was abandoned by the ninth century B.C. Experimentation, seeking to combine friezes or registers showing different motifs into a unified design that extended across one or more walls, occurred during the early phases of the Neo-Assyrian period. Evidence from the reign of Ashurnasirpal II discloses the use of mirror imagery for the outer registers that surround a central one. In the reign of Adad-nirari III, the wall paintings from the 'upper chambers' in the royal residence at Nimrud consist of individual registers with their differing motifs arranged one above the other. The seemingly random arrangement of the registers was offset by the relative importance given to the specific motifs within each of them. Battlements, if correctly interpreted as marking the upper limits of an outer wall, would of course occur in the top register. Animal and geometric motifs arranged either singly or in groups followed in the middle registers, and garlands and linear patterns (chevrons, zigzags) appeared in the lowermost registers. At Adad-Nirari III's royal residence in the outer town, the frieze on one or more painted walls in the bathroom avoided the use of repeated motifs; instead, there was a single three-part grouping of bulls confronting a roundel, framed on either side by a square with incurved sides. In this instance the focus of the subject matter moved from the more decorative aspect found in the upper chambers of the king's residence to greater interest in the symbolic intent behind the three-part grouping combined with the geometric shapes. Because the painted decorations in the bathroom were discovered *in situ*, one can conclude that ornamental wall paintings were set high on the walls, generally at the level of or slightly above the height of a human figure. Such positioning of the wall paintings on the walls of royal residences continued as late as the seventh century B.C., as for example at Arslan Tash.

Some seventy years later, evidence for painted decoration in the bathroom of a royal residence comes from the palace of Sargon II at Khorsabad. Stone slabs carved with figural processions lined the lower part of the walls. Fragments of painted plaster discovered on the floor of the same chamber provide confirmation that, above the carved stones, the upper part of the walls and ceiling were covered with repeats of ornamental motifs that were limited to circles, rosettes and hexagons. The various motifs were highlighted with flat hues of red, blue, black and white. The statement of the eleventh century B.C. Assyrian king Tiglath-pileser I, quoted in a previous chapter, describing the decoration on the walls of the rebuilt shrine of the gods as 'the brilliance of rising stars', is brought to mind when imagining the entire upper part of the chamber completely decorated with the polychrome geometric patterns. Another notable aspect of the royal bathroom with its two types of wall decoration is the separation between narrative and ornamental subject matter. This separation, when narrative subjects appear in the lower part of a wall and ornamental wall paintings are restricted to the upper part of the same wall, was standardized by the period of Sargon II, since the wall paintings with their two types of subject matter follow the same formula at Til Barsip and Fort Shalmaneser.

At Til Barsip the organization of the ornamental wall paintings placed above the painted narrative murals relied upon the principle of mirror imagery on the vertical and horizontal axis. At first, one may surmise that this method of decoration is a revival of that used in the painted decorations of the ninth century B.C. during the reign of the king, Ashurnasirpal II. However, all of the wall paintings at Til Barsip show a developed application of symmetry; thus one may want to consider whether some other factor may have been influential in designing the ornamental paintings. One common feature of the wall paintings is the use of decorated borders separated by narrow bands, above and below the central field in which the prominent motifs occur. The closest parallel for this kind of overall arrangement can be found in carpet designs dating to the post Neo-Assyrian period, with the Pazyryk carpet as an early example. Eighth century B.C. administrative texts from Nimrud mention several categories of textile workers in the service of the king; among them is the *kāmidu*, identified as the carpet maker.[1] His craft required the use of a warp-weighted loom or vertical loom, or possibly of a ground loom. Cecchini points out that the textile industry in Syria during the Iron Age is characterized by the warp-weighted loom, and that excavated objects related to weaving may indicate a technical innovation by the end of the eighth century B.C.[2] It is noted, however, that there is insufficient documentation to relate that innovation in weaving to the introduction of new fibers, such as cotton or wild silk. On the other hand the two-beam vertical loom, described as 'the tapestry loom', a type known in ancient Egypt, could be used for multicolored tapestries.[3] A painted version of an Assyrian multicolored cloth, probably utilizing both the plain and tapestry weaves such as those found in woven kilims,[4] is shown folded over the king's throne in room 47 at Til Barsip. The woven textile has a patterned border surrounding the central field filled with checks. Similarly, border bands also frame the central field of the ornamental wall paintings at the same site. Admittedly, the wall paintings are more elaborate in their choice of decorative motifs and overall arrangements, but nonetheless they may indicate that similar subjects and designs used in contemporary carpets and textiles, as well as in stone threshold slabs, were interchangeable.

The seventh century B.C. black-and-white style of wall painting emphasized the use of decorated border bands, one above the other. Generally, the motifs are reduced to plain or patterned circles, combined with horizontal stripes in a number of variant ways. Floral garlands are rare, and based on

---

[1] Wilson 1972, pp. 69–70.
[2] Cecchini 2000, pp. 214, 225.
[3] Geijer 1979, pp. 23–24.
[4] The term 'kilim' is commonly used to describe tapestry woven artifacts produced by tribal pastoralists; see Davies 1993, p. 31. For discussion of the tapestry weave, see: ibid, pp. 32–33; Geijer 1979, pp. 46–48.

current available data, they occur only at Dur-Katlimmu. Real and hybrid animals, such as the goat, bull, and human-headed bull, are unknown. The running ostrich, which is represented at Dur-Katlimmu, is the only example of a recognizable creature used for wall decoration. Evidently, the private residences excavated at north Syrian sites avoided figural imagery that had symbolic meaning; instead, non-figural linear and circular motifs were applied as pure decoration. The obvious contrast from the traditional royal style of Assyrian wall painting leads one to conclude that non-Assyrian influences, either cultural or religious, led to the transformation of ornamental wall painting in territories beyond the Assyria heartland.

A general overview of the motifs selected for the ornamental wall paintings in the Assyrian royal residences suggests that their use continued over a long period of time. However, while this observation may be correct in general, specific motifs were favored at different times. For instance some designs on wall paintings are used only during the reign of one king. A prime example is the guilloche, which was commonly found in the various arts of the second millennium B.C. But after the reign of Ashurnasirpal II the guilloche was no longer a feature of ornamental wall painting, although the motif continued to appear as decoration in other forms of art, in particular carved ivories. In contrast, the rosette was a standard motif in nearly all of the Assyrian wall paintings that have been documented in the excavated reports. Yet, not all rosettes were alike. The simple rosette consisted of eight or more petals arranged around a central boss or circle, and its pattern of repeats may have been purely decorative, as for example in the wall paintings at Khorsabad and Til Barsip. On occasion, a large circle or roundel encloses the rosette. The importance given to the ringed rosettes, and to their variants in the wall paintings dated to the reign of Adad-nirari III, seems to indicate that more than a purely decorative significance was attributed to them. In later periods, the ringed rosette was replaced by roundels decorated variously with combinations of concentric bands, floral garlands, bar motifs, and plain circles.

In Assyrian wall painting, the floral garland was a favorite ornamental motif early on, as demonstrated by its occurrence in the wall paintings at Kar-Tukulti-Ninurta. It is the only motif in Assyrian wall painting that by its very use connects individual plant elements into a continuous pattern. However, the floral garland was not a static feature of ornamentation. In the course of the production of Assyrian wall painting the floral garland design was altered time and again, in the selection of the particular elements that formed the garland. In the period of Ashurnasirpal II, the garland consisted of three plants: cone, lily, palmette. The garlands depicted in the wall paintings of Adad-nirari III were entirely different. One type was composed of the eyestone-like plant, possibly an early version of the pomegranate, and another was shown with closed red flowers. Much later, in the period of Sargon II, appeared the developed version of the pomegranate garland and the innovative lotus-and-palmette garland. In the Til Barsip wall paintings the lotus-and-bud garland replaced the lotus-and-palmette garland. The palmette garland was also found among the same group of wall paintings, and one is reminded of the early use of this plant in the garland type of the ninth century B.C.

The three-part grouping of motifs in which a subject in mirror image confronts the central one, was a characteristic feature of Assyrian ornamental wall paintings early on, as indicated by its occurrence at Kar-Tukulti-Ninurta. While the decorative aspect of the symmetrically aligned group is apparent, more interestingly is the choice of elements that make up the unified design. Invariably either an animal or winged genie frames the central motif, which is either floral or geometric. The early use of the goat was replaced by the bull, with or without wings or human-headed. The introduction of the winged genie, male at Khorsabad and female at Til Barsip, confirms the symbolic aspect that must be associated with the three-part groupings depicted in the various wall paintings. The intended meaning of each design is best understood by how one interprets the individual motifs. In certain circumstances the palmette tree as well as the single palmette have been identified as the plant attribute of the goddess Ishtar. Apart from their depictions as real animals, the wild goats take on symbolic significance related to the divine power of wildlife. A tradition in Meopotamian myths associates the goddess Ninhursaga with wildlife, and more specifically with the wild animals native to the foothills and stony desert.[5] By the mid-second millennium B.C., the goddess of wildlife, was assimilated to characterize an aspect of Ishtar. Thus the wild goats flanking the date palm in the wall painting at Kar-Tukulti-Ninurta, and flanking the palmette as in an embroidery decoration on the garments of officials carved on the stone reliefs from the Northwest Palace at Nimrud, become meaningful as symbolic references to a particular aspect of the goddess. Moreover, the submissive and half-kneeling poses of the goats in those designs amplify the reverence that is directed to the plant sign of Ishtar.

The paired goats depicted in the ornamental wall painting from Til Barsip also kneel on one foreleg and confront a geometric motif. The square that is centered between the animals can of course be seen as a form that is purely decorative, a square softened by its slightly incurved sides. This particular type of square finds an early parallel with the glazed ceramic wall attachments discovered at various Assyrian sites, and the square was used as decoration in the wall paintings of Adad-nirari III. In the paintings of later date at Til Barsip, the square is the central motif in the three-part groupings that include the bulls and winged female genies. At Khorsabad, bulls also confront a square

---

[5] Jacobsen 1976, pp. 105–107.

with incurved sides; but elsewhere in the same wall painting winged male genies confront a decorated circle or roundel. Similarly one wall painting at Til Barsip shows winged female genies confronting a roundel, but behind each figure is a square with incurved sides. It does seem unlikely that both the square with incurved sides and the large circle are purely decorative in the context of the three-part grouping. Of course, there are instances where the two geometric motifs alternate in continuous repeat, as for example in the wall paintings from the 'upper chambers' of Adad-nirari III, the small temple at Tell al Rimah, and the throne room at Fort Shalmaneser. The circle and the square can take on various meanings according to content and context, but it is less certain what these geometric shapes signified in the Assyrian wall paintings. In other contexts the circle forms the basis for the astral signs of deities, while the square with incurved signs may be an abstract sign of the king's rule of the 'four quarters,' mentioned in the royal inscriptions.[6] Thus, taking the two shapes beyond their outer form, the circle and square in the context of the three-part grouping may represent, respectively, divine celestial and terrestrial expressions of Assyrian rule, supported by the gods who appear in the guise of wild animals – goat and bull – and protected by the winged genies. In effect, the three-part group of motifs in the wall paintings was devised as an emblematic symbol of Assyrian power. However, these particular motifs used in the wall paintings were not standardized features, but served as creative variants of the type found, for example, on the monumental wall reliefs of Sargon II.

It may be mentioned that the three-part symbol, composed of select motifs and the use of mirror imagery, occurred in Mesopotamian art sporadically, and can be traced back to the third millennium B.C. One early symbol of this type is carved on a stone plaque discovered at Tello (ancient Girsu) in southern Mesopotamia. Dynamic in its conception, the design shows the lion-headed bird with outstretched wings clutching by its talons two lions striding outward, their heads up-turned.[7] Similarly, the same lion-headed bird clutches two goats or ibexes turned outward in the design that decorates a silver vessel of approximately the same date.[8] Significant in these early examples of the emblematic group is the importance given to the central image, which establishes its superior power over the lateral images. Carrying the emblematic meaning forward through the millennia, in the wall paintings the forms of the circle and the square with incurved sides are abstract symbols that must be identified with the notion of a greater power, divine or human, as defined above.

---

[6] An early use of this phrase occurs in an inscription of Adad-nirari II (911–891 B.C.); see Grayson 1976, no. 400.
[7] Moortgat 1969, p. 42, pl. 117.
[8] Ibid, pl. 115.

Finally, regardless of how one approaches the ornamental paintings that embellished the walls and ceilings of Assyrian residences, whether they were purely decorative, imbued with symbolic meaning or a combination of both, the paintings ultimately must be appraised according to their artistic merits. Except for the relatively few existing fragments and the generally poor photographs taken of paintings still visible on the walls, one must rely on the reconstructions of the fragments and designs expanded into whole units. The modern reconstructions oftentimes appear rigid and mechanical, particularly where a motif is repeated several or more times within the same register. The Assyrian artisans must have used a device such as a template in order to produce a repetitive design across a long stretch of wall. A measuring stick would measure the equal distance between individual motifs, as well as the division of registers, while the marking of large circles and concentric ones would be made with the help of a compass. Shapes outlined in black, contrasting white and black, and the limited palette of red and blue, were invariably used in the paintings and proved effective in depicting shapes and images that were viewed from a distance, above the height of an individual. Measured distance between individual motifs, which never touched or overlapped one another, added to the clarity and symmetry of the painted designs. Upon completion of the ornamental wall paintings, the resulting visual attractiveness offset the mechanical features used to produce the decorative art works.

The degree of technical skills needed by the individual artisans to accomplish their varied tasks cannot be evaluated, due to the scarcity of existing wall painting remains. The available fragments from Til Barsip do disclose the exceptional artistic sensibility that was achieved in the use of line and color to depict familiar subjects, such as animals and humans. Master artists were responsible for the configurations of the wall paintings, and in many instances the paintings exhibit innovative interpretations for a category of Assyrian art that was limited by conventional criteria. In brief, the artisans responsible for producing the ornamental wall paintings were proficient in their craft, and the artists responsible for the designs of the paintings were for the most part successful in formulating decorations that were attractive, original, and would convey a meaning to those who viewed them.

To what extent, then, are the artistic merits of the ornamental wall paintings that were produced during the period of the Assyrian Empire? In the royal residences, wall paintings were produced to convey an aura of brightness and vitality through color, harmony, and design. The limited palette of pigments, together with the black outlining of shapes, emphasized the decorative aspects of the paintings. Balance, symmetry, and repetition imparted the notion of harmony and continuity. The selection of motifs and their arrangements were given deliberate consideration. The wall paintings were conceived as monumental decorations that, because of their large scale, were comparable to the narrative paintings and the wall reliefs. One may conclude, based upon these evaluations, and relying on the available the archaeological evidence, that ornamental wall painting must rank as an important category in the visual arts of Assyria.

BIBLIOGRAPHY

Abbreviations used in Bibliography

AAA	Annals of Anthropology and Archaeology, London
AfO	Archiv für Orientforschung, Berlin
ANES	Ancient Near Eastern Studies (formerly Abr-Nahrain), Louvain
AOS	American Oriental Series, New Haven
ARRIM	Annual Review of the Royal Inscriptions of Mesopotamia Project, Toronto
BA	Biblical Archaeologist, Boston
BaF	Baghdader Forschungen, Mainz am Rhein
BAH	Bibliothèque Archéologique et Historique, Paris
BaM	Baghdader Mitteilungen, Berlin
BAR	BAR International Series, Oxford
BASOR	Bulletin of the American Schools of Oriental Research, Boston
BCSMS	Bulletin. Canadian Society for Mesopotamian Studies, Toronto
BM	Bibliotheca Mesopotamica, Malibu
BSA	Bulletin on Sumerian Agriculture, Cambridge
JANES	Journal of the Ancient Near Eastern Society of Columbia University, New York
JCS	Journal of Cuneiform Studies, New Haven
JHB	Journal of the History of Biology, Dordrecht
KJ	Kölner Jahrbuch, Berlin
MANE	Monographs on the Ancient Near East, Malibu
N.A.B.U.	Nouvelles Assyriologiques Brèves et Utilitaires, Paris
OIP	Oriental Institute Publications, Chicago
RA	Revue de Assyriologie et d'archéologie orientale, Paris
SAA	State Archives of Assyria, Helsinki
SAAB	State Archives of Assyria Bulletin, Padova
SAAS	State Archives of Assyria Studies, Helsinki
SMS	Syro-Mesopotamian Studies, Malibu
WVDOG	Wissenschaftliche Veröffentlichungen der Deutschen Orient-Gesellschaft, Leipzig-Berlin
ZA	Zeitschrift für Assyriologie und Vorderasiatische Archäologie, Berlin

Abbate, L., 1994. 'Wall Paintings from a Neo-Assyrian Building at Til Barsib,' *Abr-Nahrain* 32, pp. 7–16.

Akurgal, E., 1962. *The Art of the Hittites*, London.

Akurgal, E., 1968. *The Art of Greece. Its Origins in the Mediterranean and the Near East*, New York.

Albenda, P., 1974. 'Grapevines in Ashurbanipal's Garden,' *BASOR* 215, pp. 5–17.

Albenda, P., 1976–1977. 'Landscape Bas-Reliefs in the *Bīt-Hilāni* of Ashurbanipal,' *BASOR* 224, pp. 49–72; 225, pp. 29–48.

Bibliography

Albenda, P., 1978. 'Assyrian Carpets in Stone,' *JANES* 10, pp. 1–34.

Albenda, P., 1983. 'A Mediterranean Seascape from Khorsabad,' *Assur* 3/3, pp. 1–34.

Albenda, P., 1986. *The Palace of Sargon, King of Assyria. Monumental Wall Reliefs at Dur-Sharrukin, from Original Drawings Made at the Time of Their Discovery in 1843–1844 by Botta and Flandin.* Editions Recherche sur les Civilisations, Synthèse 22, Paris.

Albenda, P., 1988. 'The Gateway and Portal Stone Reliefs from Arslan Tash,' *BASOR* 271, pp. 5–30.

Albenda, P., 1991. 'Decorated Assyrian Knob-Plates in the British Museum,' *Iraq* 53, pp. 43–53.

Albenda, P., 1994a. 'Wall Paintings from the Upper Chambers at Nimrud,' *Source. Notes in the History of Art*, 13/4, pp. 2–14.

Albenda, P., 1994b. 'Assyrian Sacred Trees in the Brooklyn Museum,' *Iraq* 56, pp. 123–133.

Albenda, P., 1996. 'The Beardless Winged Genies from the Northwest Palace at Nimrud,' *SAAB* X/1, pp. 67–78.

Albenda, P., 1998a. 'A Royal Eunich in the Garden,' *N.A.B.U.*, pp. 88–89, no. 98.

Albenda, P. 1998b. *Monumental Art of the Assyrian Empire. Dynamics of Composition Styles*, MANE 3.

Amiet, P., (ed.) 1979. *De Sumer a Babylone. Collections du Musée du Louvre*, Paris.

Andrae, W., 1925. *Coloured Ceramics from Ashur and Earlier Ancient Assyrian Wall Paintings*, London.

Azarpay, G., 1968. *Urartian Art and Artifacts. A Chronological Study*, Berkeley and Los Angeles.

Bachmann, W., 1927. *Felsrelief in Assyrien: Bawian, Maltai, und Gŭndŭk*. WVDOG 52.

Barber, E.J.W., 1991. *Prehistoric Textiles. The Development of Cloth in the Neolithic and Bronze Ages*, Princeton.

Barber, E.J.W., 1999. *The Mummies of Urumchi*, New York.

Barnett, R.D., 1976. *Sculptures from the North Palace of Ashurbanipal at Nineveh 668–627 B.C.*, London.

Barnett, R.D., 1978. *The Nimrud Ivories*, London.

Barnett, R.D., Bleibtreu, E. and Turner, G. 1998. *Sculptures from the Southwest Palace of Sennacherib at Nineveh*, London.

Barnett, R.D. and Falkner, M., 1962. *The Sculptures of Assur-nasir-apli (883–859 B.C.), Tiglath-Pileser III (745–727 B.C.), Esarhaddon (681–669 B.C.), from the Central and South-West Palaces at Nimrud*, London.

Barnett, R.D. and Lorenzini, A. 1975. *Assyrian Sculpture in the British Museum*, London.

Barrelet, M.-Th., 1977. 'Un inventaire de Kar-Tukulti-Ninurta: textiles décorés assyriens et autres,' RA 71, pp. 51–91.

Beyer, D., 1989. 'trois fresques assyriennes ressuscitées au Louvre,' *Le Monde de Bible* 58, pp. 57–58.

Bleibtreu, E., 1980. *Die Flora der neuassyrischen Reliefs*, Wien.

Botta, P.E., 1850. *Illustrations of Discoveries at Nimrud ... Being a Translation of M. Botta's Letters on the First Discoveries at Nineveh*, London.

Bunker, E.C., 'The Chinese Artifacts Among the Pazyryk Finds,' *Source. Notes on the History of Art*, Vol. X/4, New York, pp. 20–24.

Bunnens, G., 1992. 'Melbourne University Excavations at Tell Ahmar on the Euphrates. Short Report on the 1989–1992 Seasons,' *Akkadica* 79–80, pp. 1–13.

Bunnens, G., 1997. 'Til Barsib under Assyrian Domination: A Brief Account of the Melbourne University Excavations at Tell Ahmar,' in Parpola S. and Whiting, R.M. (eds.), *Assyria 1995*. Proceedings of the 10th Anniversary Symposium of Neo-Assyrian Text Corpus Project Helsinki, September 7–11,1995, Helsinki, pp, 17–28.

Canby, J.V., 1974. 'Decorated Garments in Ashurnasirpal's Sculpture,' *Iraq* 33, pp. 31–52.

Cecchini, S.M., 2000. 'The Textile Industry in Northern Syria During the Iron Age According to the Evidence of the Tel Afis Excavations,' in Bunnens, G. (ed.), *Essays on Syria in the Iron Age*, ANES, supplement 7, pp. 211–233.

Chesney, F.R., 1850. *The Expedition for the Survey of the Rivers Euphrates and Tigris, Carried on by Order of the British Government, In the Years 1835, 1836, 1837*, vol. I. Reprinted 1969, London.

Chevalier, N., and Lavédrine, 1994. 'Débuts de la photographie et fouilles in Assyrie: les calotypes de Gabriel Tranchand,' in Fontan, E. (ed.), *De Khorsabad à Paris. La découverte des Assyriens*, Paris, pp. 196–213.

Clayden, T., 1996. 'Kurigalzu I and the Restauration of Babylonia,' *Iraq* 58, pp. 112–117.

Cole, S.W., 1996. *Nippur in Late Assyrian Times, c.755–612 BC*, SAAS IV.

Collon, D., 1986. 'The Green Jasper Cylinder Seal Workshop,' in Kelly-Buccellati, M. (ed.), *Insight Through Images. Papers in Honor of Edith Porada*, BM 21, pp. 57–70.

Collon, D., 1987. *First Impressions. Cylinder Seals in the Ancient Near East*, London.

Collon, D., 1998. 'First Catch Your Ostrich,' *Iranica Antiqua* 33, pp. 25–42.

Collon, D., 2000. 'Syrian Glyptic and the Thera Wall Paintings,' in Sherratt, S. (ed.), *The Wall Paintings of Thera*. Proceedings of the First International Symposium, 30 August – 4 September 1997, Thera, Hellas, vol. I, Athens, pp. 283–294.

Collon, D., 2001. *Catalog of the Western Asiatic Seals in the British Museum. Seals V, Neo-Assyrian and Neo-Babylonian Periods*, London.

Coutsis, J.G., 2000. 'The Insects Depicted on the Wall Paintings of Thera: an Attempt at Identification,' in Sherratt, S. (ed.), *The Wall Paintings of Thera*. Proceedings of the First International Symposium, 30 August – 4 September 1997, Thera, Hellas, vol. II, Athens, pp. 580–584.

Crawford, V. E, Harper, P.O., and Pittman, H., 1980. *Assyrian Reliefs and Ivories in the Metropolitan Museum of Art: Palace Reliefs of Assurnasirpal II and Ivory Carvings from Nimrud*, New York.

Crowfoot, E., 1995. 'Textiles from Recent Excavation at Nimrud,' *Iraq* 57, pp. 114–118.

Curtis, J., Collon, D., and Green, A., 1993. 'British Museum Excavations at Nimrud and Balawat in 1989,' *Iraq* 55, pp. 21–30.

Curtis, J.E. and Reade, J.E. (eds.), 1995. *Art and Empire. Treasures from Assyria in the British Museum*, London.

Dalley, S., 1984. *Mari and Karana. Two Old Babylonian Cities*, London.

Dalley, S., 1991. 'Ancient Assyrian Textiles and the Origins of Carpet Design,' *Iran* 29, pp. 117–135.

Davies, P., 1993. *The Tribal Eye. Antique Kilims of Anatolia*, New York.

DeVries, K, 1980. 'Greeks and Phrygians in the Early Iron Age', in DeVries, K. (ed.), *From Athens to Gordion. The Papers of a Memorial Symposium for Rodney S. Young*, Philadelphia.

Dorow, Dr., 1820. *Die Assyrische Keilschrift Erlautert Durch Zwei Noch Nicht Bekannt Gewordene*, Wiesbaden.

Edwards, I.E., 1964. *A General Introductory Guide to the Egyptian Collections in the British Museum*, London.

Ellis, R., 1981. 'The Textile Remains,' in Young, R.S. (ed.), *The Gordion Excavations Final Reports*, vol. I, Philadelphia, pp. 301–310.

Elsner, O., 1988. 'Addendum,' *BASOR* 269, pp. 87–88.

Eph'al, I., 1984. *The Ancient Arabs. Nomads on the Borders of the Fertile Crescent, 9th–5th Centuries B.C.* Revised edition, Jerusalem.

Fales, F.M. and Postgate, J.N. 1992. *Imperial Administrative Records. Part I. Palace and Temple Administration*, SAA VII.

Finkel, I. L, and Reade, J.E., 1996. 'Assyrian Hieroglyphs,' *ZA* 86, pp. 244–268.

Fontan, E., 1992. 'Les peintures murales de Til Barsip,' *Les Dossiers de l'Archèologie* 171, p. 83.

Frankfort, H., 1954. *The Art and Architecture of the Ancient Orient.* 1996 Rev. paperback edition, London.

Freestone, I.C., 1991. 'Technical Examination of Neo-Assyrian Glazed Wall Plaques,' *Iraq* 53, pp. 53–58.

Fuchs, A. and Parpola, S., 2001. *The Correspondence of Sargon II. Part III*, SAA XV.

Galter, H.D., 1987. 'On Beads and Curses,' *ARRIM* 5, 15–17.

Geijer, A., 1982. *A History of Textile Art. A Selective Account.* Revised edition, London.

Grayson, A.K., 1972. *Assyrian Royal Inscriptions. Vol. 1. From the Beginning to Ashur-resha-ishi I*, Wiesbaden.

Grayson, A.K., 1976. *Assyrian Royal Inscriptions. Vol. 2. From Tiglath-pileser I to Assur-nasir-apli II*, Wiesbaden.

Guralnick, E., 2000. 'Oriental and Orientalizing: Some Bronzes from Olympia' *KJ* 33, pp. 13–22.

Hall, R., 1986. *Egyptian Textiles*, London.

Harris, R., 1991. 'Inanna-Ishtar as Paradox and a Coincidence of Opposites,' *History of Religions* 30, pp. 261–278.

Heimpel, W., 1982. 'A Catalog of Near Eastern Venus Deities,' *SMS* 4/3, pp. 9–22.

Herrmann, G., 1989. 'The Nimrud Ivories, I. The Flame and Frond School,' *Iraq* 51, pp. 85–109.

Herrmann, G., 1992. *The Small Collections from Fort Shalmaneser. Fascicule V. Ivories from Nimrud (1949–1963)*, London.

Hogarth, D.G., 1914. *Carchemish. Report on the Excavations at Djerablus on Behalf of theBritish Museum. Part I. Introductory.* Reprint 1969, London.

Hunger, H., 1992. *Astrological Reports to Assyrian Kings.* SAA VIII.

Jacobsen, T., 1976. *The Treasures of Darkness. A History of Mesopotamian History*, New Haven.

Kataja, I., and Whitings, R., 1995. *Grants, Decrees and Gifts of the Neo-Assyrian Period*, SAA XII.

Katzenstein, H.J., 1973. *The History of Tyre*, Jerusalem.

Kawami, T.S., 1992. 'Archaeological Evidence for Textiles in Pre-Islamic Iran,' *Iranian Studies* 25, pp. 7–18.

Kolbe, D., 1981. *Die Reliefprogramme religiös-mythologischen Charakers in neu-assyrischen Palästen*, Frankfurt am Main-Bern.

Krikorian, A.D., 1975. 'Were the Opium Poppy and Opium Known in the Ancient Near East?' *JHB* 8, pp. 95–114.

Kühne, H., 1984, 'Tall Šēh Hamad/Dūr-katlimmu 1984,' *AfO* 31, pp. 170–177.

Kühne, H., 1989/90. 'Tall Šēh Hamad,' *AfO* 36/37, pp. 308–321.

Kühne, H., 1993. 'Vier Späbabylonische Tontafeln aus Tall Šēh Hamad, Ost-Syrien,' *SAAB* V11, pp. 75–107.

Landsberger, B., 1967. 'Uber Farben im Sumerisch-Akkadischen,' *JCS* 21, 154–166.

Layard, A.H., 1849a. *Nineveh and Its Remains*, 2 vols., New York.

Layard, A.H., 1849b. *The Monuments of Nineveh. From Drawings Made on the Spot*, London.

Layard, A.H., 1853. *A Second Series of the Monuments of Nineveh*, London.

Lerner, J. 1991. 'Some So-Called Achaemenid Objects from Pazyryk,' *Source. Notes on the History of Art*, X/4, New York, pp. 8–15.

Lipinski, E., 1991. 'The Cypriot Vassals of Esarhaddon,' in Cogan, M. and Eph'al (eds.) *AH, ASSYRIA … . Studies in Assyrian History and Ancient Near Eastern Historiography Presented to Hayim Tadmor*, Jerusalem, pp. 58–64.

Livingstone, A., 1989. *Court Poetry and Literary Miscellanea*, SAA III.

Loud, G., and Altman, B., 1938. *Khorsabad. Part II. The Citadel and the Town*. OIP 40, Chicago.

Loud, G., Frankfort, H. and Jacobsen T.,1936. *Khorsabad. Part I. Excavations in the Palace and at a City Gate*. OIP 38, Chicago.

Luckenbill, D.D., 1926–1927. *Ancient Records of Assyria and Babylonia*, 2 vols., Chicago.

Mac Ginnis, J., 2001. 'Excavations at Ziyaret Tepe, Lower Town, 2001,' in British School of Archaeology in Iraq, *Newsletter* 8, November 2001, pp. 13–14.

Mallowan, B.P., 1983. 'Magic and Ritual in the Northwest Palace Reliefs,' in Harper, P.O. and Pittman, H. (eds.), *Essays on Near Eastern Art and Archaeology in Honor of Charles Kyrle Wilkinson*, New York, pp. 33–39.

Mallowan, M.E.L., 1952. 'Excavations at Nimrud (Kalhu), 1951,' *Iraq* 14, pp. 1–23.

Mallowan, M.E.L., 1954. 'The Excavations at Nimrud, (Kalhu), 1953,' *Iraq* 16, pp. 59–163.

Mallowan, M.E.L., 1966. *Nimrud and Its Remains*, 2 vols., London.

Mallowan, M.E.L., 1978. *The Nimrud Ivories*, London.

Mallowan, M.E.L. and Davies, L.G., 1970. *Ivories in Assyrian Style. Commentary, Catalogue and Plates. Fascicule II. Ivories from Nimrud (1949–1963)*, London.

Mallowan, M.E.L. and Herrmann, G, 1974. *Furniture from SW.7 Fort Shalmaneser. Fascicule III. Ivories from Nimrud (1949–1963)*, London.

Maxwell-Hyslop, K.R., 1971. *Western Asiatic Jewellery. C. 3000–612 B.C.*, London.

Mayer-Opificius, R., 1986. 'Bemerkungen zur Mittelassyrischen Glyptik des 13. und 12. Jhdts. V. Chr.' In Buccellati, M. (ed.), *Insight through Images. Studies in Honor of Edith Porada*, BM 21, pp. 161–169.

McGovern, P.E. and Michel, R.H., 1988. 'Short Notes: Has Authentic *Tekelet* Been Identified?' *BASOR* 269, pp. 81–83.

Mellink, M.J., 1981. 'Conclusions.' In Young, R.S. (ed.), *Three Great Early Tumuli. The Gordion Excavations Final Reports*, vol. I, Philadelphia, pp. 263–272,

Meuszyński, J., 1975. 'The Throne-Room of Aššur-nasir-apli II. (Room B in the North-West Palace at Nimrud)', *ZA* 64, pp. 51–73.

Meuszyński, J., 1976. 'Neo-Assyrian Reliefs from the Central Area of Nimrud Citadel,' *Iraq* 37, pp. 37–43.

Millard, A., 1994. *The Eponyms of the Assyrian Empire, 910–612 B.C.*, SAAS II.

Miller, N.F., 2000. 'Plant Forms in Jewellery from the Royal Cemetery at Ur,' *Iraq* 62, pp. 149–155.

Mitchell, T.C., 2000. 'Camels in the Assyrian Bas-Reliefs,' *Iraq* 62, pp. 187–194.

Moorey, P.R.S., 1985. *Materials and Manufacture in Ancient Mesopotamia: The Evidence of Archaeology and Art. Metals and metalwork, glazed materials and glass*, BAR 237.

Moortgat, A., 1940. *Vorderasiatische Rollsiegel. Ein Beitrag zur Geschichte der Steinschneidekunst*, Berlin.

Moortgat, A., 1959. *Alt-Vorderasiatische Malerei*, Berlin.

Moortgat, A., 1969. *The Art of Ancient Mesopotamia. The Classical Art of the Near East*, London.

Murray, M.A., 1964. *The Splendour that was Egypt*. New and revised edition, London.

Nunn, A., 1988. *Die Wandmalerei und der Glasierte Wandschmuck im alten Orient*, Leiden.

Oates, D., 1962. 'The Excavations at Nimrud (Kalhu), 1962,' *Iraq* 25, pp. 6–37.

Oates, D., 1968. 'The Excavations at Tell al Rimah,' *Iraq* 30, pp. 115–138.

Oppenheim, A.L., 1967. 'Essay on Overland Trade in the First Millennium B.C.,' *JCS* 21, pp. 236–251.

Paley, S.M., 1976. *King of the World. Ashur-nasir-pal II (883–859 B.C.)*, Brooklyn.

Paley, S.M., and Sobolewski, R.P., 1987. *The Reconstruction of the Relief Representations and their Positions in the Northwest-Palace at Kalhu (Nimrūd) II (Rooms: I.S.T.Z., West Wing)*, BaF 10.

Paley, S.M., and Sobolewski, R.P., 1992. *The Reconstruction of the Relief Representations and their Positions in the Northwest-Palace at Kalhu (Nimrūd) III (The Principal Entrances and Courtyards)*, BaF 14.

Panagiotakopulu, E., 2000. 'Butterflies, Flowers and Aegean Iconography: A Story about Silk and Cotton,' in Sherratt, S. (ed.), *The Wall Paintings of Thera*. Proceedings of the First International Conference, 30 August – 4 September 1997, Thera, Hellas, vol. II, Athens, pp. 585–592.

Parpola, S., 1987. *The Correspondence of Sargon II. Part I*, SAA I.

Parpola, S., 1993a. 'The Assyrian Tree of Life: Tracing the Origins of Jewish Monotheism and Greek Philosophy,' *JNES* 52, pp. 161–199.

Parpola, S., 1993b. *Letters from Assyrian and Babylonian Scholars*, SAA X.

Parpola, S. and Porter, M. (eds.), 2001. *The Helsinki Atlas of the Near East in the Neo-Assyrian Period*, Finland.

Parpola, S. and Watanabe, K., 1988. *Neo-Assyrian Treaties and Loyaltiy Oaths*, SAA II.

Parrot, A., 1961. *The Arts of Assyria*. Trans. S. Gilbert and J. Emmons, New York.

Porter, B.N., 1993. 'Sacred Trees, Date Palms, and the Royal Persona of Ashurnasirpal II,' *JNES* 52, pp. 129–139.

Porter, B.N., 2000. '"For the Astonishment of All Enemies." Assyrian Propaganda and Its Audiences in the Reigns of Ashurnasirpal II and Esarhaddon,' *BCSMS* 35, pp. 9–13.

Postgate, J.N., 1992. 'Trees and Timber in the Assyrian Texts,' in Postgate, N. and Powell, M., (eds.), *Trees and Timber in Mesopotamia*, BSA VI, pp. 177–192.

Pottier, E., 1924. *Catalogue des antiquités Assyriennes*, Paris.

Pritchard, J.B., 1969. *Ancient Near Eastern Texts Relating to the Old Testament*. 2nd ed., Princeton.

Pritchard, J.B., 1969. *The Ancient Near East in Pictures Relating to the Old Testament*. 2nd ed. with Supplement, Princeton.

Reade, J.E., 1963. 'A Glazed Brick Panel from Nimrud,' *Iraq* 25, pp. 38–47.

Reade, J.E., 1968. 'The Palace of Tiglath-Pileser III,' *Iraq* 30, pp. 69–73.

Reade, J.E., 1979. 'Assyrian Architectural Decoration: Techniques and Subject-matter,' *BaM* 10, pp. 17–58.

Reade, J.E., 1983. *Assyrian Sculpture*, London.

Reade, J.E., 1985. 'Texts and Sculptures from the North-West Palace, Nimrud,' *Iraq* 47, pp. 203–214.

Reade, J.E., 1987. 'Was Sennacherib a Feminist?' in Durand, J-M. (ed.), *La Femme dans le Proche-Orient Antique*. Compte Rendu de la XXXIIIe Rencontre Assyriologique Internationale (Paris, 7–10 Juillet 1986), Paris, pp. 139–145.

Reade, J.E., 1995. 'The Khorsabad Glazed Bricks and Their Symbolism,' in Caubet, A. (ed.), *Khorsabad, le palais de Sargon II, roi d'Assyrie*, Paris, pp. 227–251.

Rowton, M.B., 1967. 'The Woodlands of Ancient Western Asia,' *JNES* 26, pp. 265–274.

Russell, J.M., 1999. 'Some Painted Bricks From Nineveh. A Preliminary Report,' *Iranica Antiqua* 34, pp. 87–114.

Saltzman, M., 1988. 'Addendum', *BASOR* 269, pp. 83–84.

Schaeffer-Forrer, C.F.-A., 1983. *Corpus des cylindres-sceaux de Ras Shamra-Ugarit et d'Enkomi-Alasia*. Editions Recherche sur les Civilisations, Synthèse 13, Paris.

Seidl, U., 1999. 'Orientalische Bleche in Olympia,' *ZA* 89, pp. 269–282.

Simpson, E., 1998. 'Symbols on the Gordion Screens,' *XXXIV. International Assyriology Congress*. XXXIV ème Rencontre Assyriologique Internationale (6–10/VII/1987-Istanbul), pp. 630–639.

Simpson, E., and Spirydowicz, K., 1999. *Gordion. Wooden Furniture*, Ankara.

Smith, W.S., 1965. *The Art and Architecture of Ancient Egypt*. Reprinted with corrections, London.

Sobolewski, R., 1977. 'Die Ausgrabungen in Kalhu (Nimrud) 1974–1976,' *AfO* 25, pp. 230–237.

Sobolewski, R., 1982. 'The Polish Work at Nimrud: Ten Years of Excavation and Study,' *ZA* 71, pp. 248–273.

Sollberger, 1987. 'A Bead for Sennacherib,' in Rochberg-Halton, F. (ed.), *Language, Literature, and History. Philological and Historical Studies Presented to Erica Reiner*, AOS 67, pp. 379–381

Tadmor, H., 1994. *The Inscriptions of Tiglathpileser III King of Assyria*, Jerusalem.

Thompson, and Hutchinson, 1931. 'The Site of the Palace of Ashurnasirpal at Nineveh, Excavated in 1929–1930 on Behalf of the British Museum,' *AAA* 18, pp. 79–112.

Thureau-Dangin, F., Barrois, A., Dossin, G, and Dunand, M., 1931. *Arslan Tash*, Paris.

Thureau-Dangin, F. and Dunand, M., 1936. *Til-Barsib*, BAH 23.

Tomabechi, Y, 1983. 'Wall Paintings from Dur Kurigalzu,' *JNES* 42, pp. 123–141.

Tomabechi, Y., 1983/84. 'Wall Paintings from Til Barsip,' *AfO* 29/30, pp. 63–74.

Tomabechi, Y., 1986. 'Wall Paintings from the Northwest Palace at Nimrud,' *AfO* 33, pp. 43–54.

Turner, G., 1970. 'Tell Nebi Yūnus: The Ekal Māšarti at Nineveh,' *Iraq* 32, pp. 68–85.

Van Buren, E.D., 1939. 'The Rosette in Mesopotamian Art,' *ZA* 45, pp. 100–107.

Van Loon, M., 1986. 'The Drooping Lotus Flower,' in Buccellati, M. (ed.), *Insight Through Images. Studies in Honor of Edith Porada*, BM 21, pp. 245–252.

Wiggermann, F.A.M., 1992. *Mesopotamian Protective Spirits. The Ritual Texts*, Groningen.

Wilson, J.V.K., 1972. *The Nimrud Wine Lists. A Study of Men and Administration at the Assyrian Capital in the Eighth Century, B.C.*, London.

Winter, I.J., 1983. 'The Program of the Throneroom of Assurnasirpal II,' in P.O. Harper and H. Pittman (eds.), *Essays on Near Eastern Art and Archaeology in Honor of Charles Kyrle Wilkinson*, New York, pp. 15–31.

Winter, I.J., 1995. 'Aesthetics in Ancient Mesopotamian Art,' in Sasson, J.M. (ed.), *Civilizations of the Ancient Near East*, vol. IV, New York, pp. 2569–2580.

Woolley, C.L., 1921. *Carchemish. Report on the Excavations at Jerablus on Behalf of the British Museum. Part II. The Town Defence*s. Reprint 1969, London.

Woolley L. and Barnett, R.D., 1952. *Carchemish. Report on the Excavations at Jerablus on Behalf of the British Museum. Part III. The Excavations in the Inner Town*. Reprint 1978, London.

Young, R.S., 1965. 'Early Mosaics at Gordion,' *Expedition* 7, pp. 4–13.

Ziderman, I., 1987. 'First Identification of Authentic *Tekelet*,' *BASOR* 26, pp. 25–33.

Ziderman, I. 1988. 'Response,' *BASOR* 269, pp. 84–87.

Ziderman, I., 1990. 'Sea-Shells and Ancient Purple Dyeing,' *BA* 53, pp. 98–103.

INDICES

Index of Akkadian words

ayāru (rosette flower), 84
apkallu (genie or anthropomorphic god), 91, 123, 127, 128
argamannu (blue-purple dye), 62
bēl pāhīti (governor), 72
bibbu (planet), 96
birmu (multicolored), 56
biršu, bir (felted cloth), 57
būṣu (byssos), 57
dappastu (woven blanket or rug), 65
ēnu (eyestone or agate), 93
illūri (flower), 113
kakkabu (star), 97
kāmidu (carpet maker), 131
kippatu (circle), 92

kitû (linen), 57
kudurru (boundary stone), 96
kusarikku (bison), 124
lamassu/šēdu (protective creature), 45, 125
lurmu (ostrich), 97
musakkannu (Dalbergia sisso tree), 60
pappardilû (banded stone), 4
parūtu (alabaster stone), 4
qatattu (fine garment), 57
sikkatu (knobbed cone or plaque), 1
ṣuppu (embroidered cloth), 57
takiltu (red-purple dye), 62
ṭību (cotton or silk), 57
ṭumânu (silk or cotton), 57

Index of Proper Names

Omitted are modern personal names. Included are the names of an archaeological site (a), deity (d), palace, temple, or building (h), place or region (l), personal name (p), ruler (r). Spelling for proper names follows general English usage.

Acropolis Palace (h), 31
Adad (d), 4, 124
Adad-nirari II (r), 98
Adad-nirari III (r), 9, 14, 15, 18, 19, 37, 85, 92, 93, 113, 118, 120, 121, 126, 130, 132–134
Akrotiri (l), 61
Al Rimah (a), 21, 129, 134
Aqar-Kuf (a), 3
An (d), 4
Arin-berd (a), 126
Arvad (l), 54
Arslan Tash (a), 5, 6, 25, 31, 53, 76, 94, 95, 122, 124, 130
Ashur (a), 2, 3, 98, 102, 105, 119, 123
Ashur (d), 5
Ashurbanipal (r), 4, 73, 97, 105, 117
Ashur-bel-kala (r), 98

Ashurnasirpal II (r), 2, 4, 6, 9, 10, 66, 91, 98, 106, 109, 112, 121, 126, 130, 132
Ashur-reshi-ishi I (r), 90
Babylon (a), 60
Bel-harran-belu-usur (p), 67
Carchemish (a), 106
Central Building (h), 125
Central Palace (h), 20, 115
Centre Palace (h), 19
Cyprus (l), 105
Dur-Katlimmu (a), 5, 27, 31, 75, 76, 83, 92, 95, 97, 100, 118, 132
Elam (l), 57
Esarhaddon (r), 4, 30, 60, 73, 75, 116
Fort Shalmaneser (a), 2, 4, 14, 29–30, 31, 37, 76, 89, 93, 99, 116, 117, 134
Girsu, *see* Tello

Gordion (a), 32, 56
Governors Palace (h), 31
Guzana (l), 67
Hadatu, *see* Arslan Tash
Hananu (p), 72
Hararte (l), 60
Ishtar (d), 90, 91, 95–97, 108, 109,
    111, 133
Ivriz (l), 67
Kar Shalmaneser, *see* Til Barsip
Karana-Zamahe, *see* Al Rimah
Karduniash (l), 4
Kar-Tukulti-Ninurta (a), 3, 75, 76, 80,
    81, 84, 92, 107, 110, 119, 129,
    132, 133
Khorsabad (a), 2, 4, 5, 9, 21, 59,
    67, 85, 94, 113, 117, 120, 123,
    132
    Residence K (h), 9, 19, 24, 53, 81,
        109, 115, 121, 122, 127
    Residence L (h), 24, 71, 76
Kurigalzu I (r), 3
Lachish (a), 58, 68, 96
Laqe (l), 59
Minet-el-Beida (a), 98
Mulissu (d), 96
Nabonidus (r), 96
Nabuaplaiddin (r), 96
Narunte (d), 90
Nemet-Ishtar (l), 59
Nimrud (a), 2, 4, 5, 9, 10, 14, 19, 20,
    56, 80, 102
Nineveh (a), 4, 6, 57, 58
Ninhursaga (d), 133
Ninurta (d), 5, 124
Nippur (a), 57
North Palace (h), 59, 68, 73, 89, 111, 117
Northwest Palace (h), 4, 5, 9, 10, 12,
    13, 37, 66, 80, 85, 93, 95, 99, 101,
    107, 110, 112, 120, 128
Nuzi (a), 3, 105, 129
Olympia (a), 126
Pazyryk (a), 68, 131
Ras-Shamra (a), 98
Sargon II (r), 2, 9, 21, 53, 54, 65, 68,
    70–72, 110, 113, 116, 123, 130,
    134

Sennacherib (r), 2, 54, 55, 57, 60, 65,
    68, 72, 73, 75, 116
Shadikanni (l), 59
Shalmaneser III (r), 2, 6, 14, 33, 34,
    93, 108, 119, 120
Shalmaneser V (r), 53, 54, 57, 67, 70
Shamash (d), 95–97
Sidon (l), 53
Sin (d), 95, 97
Southwest Palace (h), 64, 117
Tel Abta (a), 67
Tell ʿAhmar, *see* Til Barsip
Tell Sheikh Hamad, *see* Dur-Katlimmu
Tello (a), 105
Tiglath-pileser I (r), 4, 5, 98, 110, 113,
    130
Tiglath-pileser III (r), 20, 34, 53, 67,
    69, 70, 109, 116, 120, 122
Til Barsip (a), 5–7, 27, 31, 33, 75, 81,
    83, 85, 88, 95, 109, 115, 116, 131,
    132, 135
    Building E (h), 27, 31
Til Barsip, royal residence (a):
    Passage 24/25: 42, 45, 47, 52, 62,
        70
    Passage 24/26: 42, 52, 62, 70
    Passage 24/28: 42, 45, 47, 52, 62,
        70
    Passage 46/44: 45, 62, 70
    Room 1: 33, 43
    Room 21: 44, 52, 53, 72
    Room 22: 33, 51, 52, 54
    Room 24: 33, 45, 47, 48, 52, 53,
        54, 63, 64, 65, 70–72, 125
    Room 25/27: 33, 34, 39, 41, 45,
        54–56, 59, 63, 70, 72, 73, 120,
        127, 128
    Room 26: 36, 52, 72
    Room 46: 34, 40, 41, 45, 52, 55,
        56, 70, 72, 127, 128
    Room 47: 33, 41, 50, 52, 53, 65,
        68, 70–73
Tukulti-Ninurta I (r), 3, 76, 84, 91,
    119
Tukulti-Ninurta II (r), 98
Tyre (l), 53, 54, 58
Upper chambers (h), 14, 130

Indices

Uruk (a), 105
Urzanu (r), 99
Utu (d), 124

Warpalawas (p), 67
Zincirli (a), 73

Subject Index

Apple tree, 59
Battlement, 15, 18, 80, 82
Black-and-white style, 27, 32, 131
Bronze band, 123, 126
Bull, 2, 15, 20, 25, 44, 45, 47, 52, 53,
    58, 62, 120, 124, 133, 134
Chevron, 3, 82, 130
Circle, 14, 15, 20–31, 39, 52, 81, 92,
    113, 123, 130, 134
Cone, 12, 107
Cotton, 56, 57, 59
Dyes, 61
Eyestone, 93
Fig tree, 58
Floral sprig, 112
Garden, 4, 29
Garland:
    cone-and-palmette-and-tulip, 11,
        132
    floral, 18, 28, 38, 80, 132
    lotus-and-bud, 24, 30, 40, 44, 45,
        52, 54, 115–117
    lotus-and-palmette, 87, 109, 133
    palmette, 47, 108
    pomegranate, 47, 51, 52, 113, 114,
        133
    pomegranate-and-cone, 107, 114
    poppy-and-cone, 114
Genie:
    winged bird-headed, 3, 45, 62, 123
    winged female, 39, 40, 55, 83, 91,
        127, 128
    winged male, 24, 83, 108, 110,
        127, 133
    wingless male, 45, 62
Glazed brick, 1, 2, 4, 11, 13, 18, 24,
    109, 119
Glazed vessel, 123
Goat, 2, 36, 37, 52, 80, 99, 110, 116,
    118, 133, 134
Gold, 57
Grapevine, 58

Guilloche, 3, 6, 12, 80, 82, 101, 132
Hexagon, 6, 13, 14, 21–23, 81, 130
Ivory, carved, 37, 47, 100, 104, 110,
    119, 121
Kilim, 131
Lapis lazuli, 4
Lion, 6, 47, 51, 106, 121, 125, 126
Lion-headed bird, 134
Lily, 59, 107, 111
Lotus, 43, 77, 114, 116, 117
Mandrake, 59
Merlon, *see* battlement
Moth, 60
Mosaic, pebble, 31, 32
Mulberry tree, 60
Naval battle, 44
Obsidian, 4
Ostrich, 29, 97
Palmette, 23, 48, 107, 109, 110, 133
Poppy, 114
Ray flower, 89
Rosette, 2, 6, 13, 14, 15, 22, 23, 24,
    28, 30, 31, 36, 38, 43, 51, 52, 77,
    84, 91, 130, 132
Roundel, *see* circle
Sea battle, 54
Silk, 60–61
Square, cushion-shaped, 20, 21, 25, 36,
    39, 40, 44, 45, 47, 52, 133
Star, 91, 92, 97
Star flower, 77
Stylized tree, 20, 23, 110
Textile pattern, 34, 39, 41, 56, 63–69
Threshold slab, 14, 71, 89, 117
Weaving loom, 131
Wheeled throne, 63, 72
Winged bull, 15, 53, 80, 124
Winged creature, 21
Winged disk, 95
Winged human-headed bull, 45, 51,
    53, 123
Zigzag, 19, 82, 130

CUNEIFORM MONOGRAPHS

ISSN 0929–0052

Vol. 1.   Wiggerman, F.A.M. *Mesopotamian Protective Spirits.* The Ritual texts. 1992. ISBN 90 72371 52 6

Vol. 2.   Stol, M. *Epilepsy in Babylonia.* 1993. ISBN 90 72371 63 1

Vol. 3a/3b.   Wunsch, C. *Die Urkunden des Babylonischen Geschäftsmannes Iddin-Marduk.* (Zum Handel mit Naturalien im 6. Jahrhundert v. Chr.). 1993. ISBN 90 72371 64 X

Vol. 5.   Streck, M.P. *Zahl und Zeit.* Grammatik der Numeralia und des Verbalsystems im Spätbabylonischen. 1995. ISBN 90 72371 85 2

Vol. 6.   Vogelzang, M.E. & H.L.J. Vanstiphout (eds.). *Mesopotamian Poetic Language: Sumerian and Akkadian.* Proceedings of the Groningen Group for the Study of Mesopotamian Literature, Vol. 2. 1996. ISBN 90 72371 84 4

Vol. 7.   Finkel, I.L. & M.J. Geller (eds.). *Sumerian Gods and their Representations.* 1997. ISBN 90 5693 005 2

Vol. 8.   Groneberg, B.R.M. *Lob der Iàtar.* Gebet und Ritual an die altbabylonische Venusgöttin Tanatti Ištar. 1997. ISBN 90 5693 006 0

Vol. 9.   Izre'el, S. *The Amarna Scholarly Tablets.* 1997. ISBN 90 72371 83 6

Vol. 10.   Maul, S.M. *Eine Festschrift für Rykle Borger zu seinem 65. Geburtstag am 24. Mai 1994.* Tikip Santakki Mala Baàmu. 1998. ISBN 90 5693 010 9

Vol. 11.   Reiner, E. & D. Pingree. *Babylonian Planetary Omens: Part Three.* 1998. ISBN 90 5693 011 7

Vol. 12.   Wallenfels, R. *Seleucid Archival Texts in the Harvard Semitic Museum.* 1998. ISBN 90 5693 012 5

Vol. 13.   Westenholz, J.G. *Cuneiform Inscriptions in the Collection of The Bible Lands Museum Jerusalem, The Emar Tablets.* 2000. ISBN 90 5693 023 0

Vol. 14.   Stol, M. With a chapter by F.A.M. Wiggermann. *Birth in Babylonia and the Bible.* Its Mediterranean Setting. 2000. ISBN 90 72371 89 5

Vol. 15.   Tjerkstra, F.A. *Principles of the Relation between Local Adverb, Verb and Sentence Particle in Hittite.* 2000. ISBN 90 5693 028 1

Vol. 16.   Sallaberger, W. *"Wenn Du mein Bruder bist, ..."*. Interaktion und Textgestaltung in altbabylonischen Alltagsbriefen. 1999. ISBN 90 5693 029 X

Vol. 17.   Suter, C.E. *Gudea's Temple Building*. The Representation of an Early Mesopotamian Ruler in Text and Image. 2000. ISBN 90 5693 035 4

Vol. 18.   Brown, D. *Mesopotamian Planetary Astronomy-Astrology*. 2000. ISBN 90 5693 036 2

Vol. 19.   Cavigneaux, A. & F.N.H. Al-Rawi. *Gilgameà et La Mort*. Textes de Tell Haddad VI. 2000. ISBN 90 5693 024 9

Vol. 20a/20b. Wunsch, C. *Das Egibi Archiv I*. Band I. Die Felder und Garten. 2000. Band II. Bearbeitung der Urkunden Nr. 1–240. 2000. ISBN 90 5693 039 7

Vol. 21.   Hazenbos, J. *The Organization of the Anatolian Local Cults during the Thirteenth Century B.C.* An Appraisal of the Hittite Cult Inventories. 2003. ISBN 90 04 12383 0

Vol. 22.   Veldhuis, N. *Religion, Literature, and Scholarship*: The Sumerian Composition *Nanše and the Birds*. 2004. ISBN 90 04 13950 8

Vol. 23.   Beaulieu, P.-A. *The Pantheon of Uruk During the Neo-Babylonian Period*. 2003. ISBN 90 04 13024 1

Vol. 24.   Vanstiphout, H.L.J. (ed.). *Genre in Mesopotamian Literature*. 2001. ISBN 90 04 12384 9

Vol. 25.   Linssen, M.J.H. *The Cults of Uruk and Babylon*. The Temple Ritual Texts as Evidence for Hellenistic Cult Practice. 2003. ISBN 90 04 12402 0

Vol. 26.   Sharlach, T.M. *Provincial Taxation and the Ur III State*. 2003. ISBN 90 04 13581 2

Vol. 27.   Wasserman, N. *Style and Form in Old-Babylonian Literary Texts*. 2002. ISBN 90 04 12404 7

Vol. 28.   Albenda, P. *Ornamental Wall Painting in the Art of the Assyrian Empire*. 2005. ISBN 90 04 14154 5

Vol. 29.   Jakob, S. *Mittelassyrische Verwaltung und Sozialstruktur*. Untersuchungen. 2002. ISBN 90 04 12398 9

Vol. 30.   Reiner, E. & D. Pingree *Babylonian Planetery Omens. Part IV*. 2005. ISBN 90 04 14212 6